Sunset

Best Home Plans

Friendly covered front porch gives this handsome home a nostalgic link
with the past. See plan E-1811 on page 50.

Sunset Publishing Corporation ■ Menlo Park, California

SUNSET BOOKS
President and Publisher:
  Susan J. Maruyama
Director, Sales & Marketing:
  Richard A. Smeby
Director, New Business Development:
  Kenneth Winchester
Editorial Director:
  Bob Doyle
Production Director:
  Lory Day
Assistant Editor:
  Kevin Freeland
Contributing Editor:
  Don Vandervort

**SUNSET PUBLISHING
CORPORATION**
Chairman:
  Jim Nelson
**President/Chief Executive
  Officer:** Stephen J. Seabolt
Chief Financial Officer:
  James E. Mitchell
**Director, Finance & Business
  Affairs:** Lawrence J. Diamond
Publisher:
  Anthony P. Glaves
Vice President, Manufacturing:
  Lorinda Reichert
Circulation Director:
  Robert I. Gursha
Editor, Sunset Magazine:
  William R. Marken

Photographers: Mark Englund/
HomeStyles: 4, 5; Philip Harvey:
10 top, back cover; Stephen Marley:
11 top left and right; Russ Widstrand:
10 bottom; Tom Wyatt: 11 bottom.

Cover: Pictured is plan PI-87-466
on page 157. Cover design by Naganuma
Design & Direction. Photography by
Mark Englund/ HomeStyles.

♻ Printed on recycled paper

A Dream Come True

In response to the success of Sunset's first edition of *Best Home Plans,* we present this new, updated edition, a collection of plans for more than 200 of the latest, most popular home designs available. All of these plans have been created for families just like yours by architects and professional designers. In addition to viewing a myriad of designs, you'll learn how to plan and manage your home-building project— and how to ensure its success.

Peruse the following pages and study the floor plans to find a home that's just right for you. When you're ready to order blueprints, you can simply call or mail in your order, and you'll receive the plans within days.

Enjoy the adventure!

For more information on Sunset's *Best Home Plans*
or any other Sunset book, call (800) 634-3095.
For special sales, bulk orders, and premium sales
information, call Sunset Custom Publishing
Services at (415) 324-5577.

Classic Victorian farmhouse offers all the modern-day amenities, including a spacious great room, an island kitchen, and a luxurious master suite. See plan DW-2112 on page 165.

Contents

Cream of the Crop

Whether you intend to build a new home or you're just dreaming about the possibilities, you'll enjoy browsing through the wonderful home plans presented here. This new edition of Sunset's popular *Best Home Plans* book offers the cream of the crop, those plans most ordered and used by American families from the thousands of professionally designed stock home plans available. On these pages you'll find classic traditional homes, striking contemporary houses, country charmers, affordable starters, even rustic vacation homes. All are proven designs created by some of America's foremost residential architects and designers.

The two keys to success in building a home are capable project management and good design. The next few pages will walk you through some of the most important aspects of project management: you'll find an overview of the building process, directions for selecting the right plan and getting the most from it, and methods for working with a builder and other professionals.

The balance of this book presents professionally designed stock plans for homes in a wide range of styles and configurations. Once you find a plan that will work for you—perhaps with a few modifications made later to personalize it for your family—you can order construction blueprints for a fraction of the cost of a custom design, a savings of many thousands of dollars (see pages 12–15 for information on how to order).

Cedar siding and brick accents give this traditional home a touch of class. The main level includes a formal living room and dining room and a gourmet kitchen. Four bedrooms, including the master suite, are located upstairs. See plan A-2293-DS on page 130.

Stately home is as impressive inside as it is on the outside. The first floor contains formal living areas, a large family room with a fireplace, a den/office, and an island kitchen with a breakfast bay. Above are two bedrooms and a large master suite. See plan B-94021 on page 140.

Dramatic contemporary offers three elevation options, along with much architectural interest inside. On the first floor, the entry and a front study/bedroom boast vaulted ceilings. The master suite upstairs has large closets and a spacious bathroom. See plan R-2152 on page 145.

Two-story bay window lends elegance and distinction to this executive home. On the upper floor are three bedrooms and a deluxe master suite with sitting room. A balcony overlooks the foyer below. See plan AX-2319 on page 150.

The Art of Building

As you embark on your home-building project, think of it as a trip—clearly not a vacation but rather an interesting, adventurous, at times difficult expedition. Meticulous planning will make your journey not only far more enjoyable but also much more successful. By careful planning, you can avoid—or at least minimize—some of the pitfalls along the way.

Start with realistic expectations of the road ahead. To do this, you'll want to gain an understanding of the basic house-building process, settle on a design that will work for you and your family, and make sure your project is actually doable. By taking those initial steps, you can gain a clear idea of how much time, money, and energy you'll need to invest to make your dream come true.

The Building Process

Your role in planning and managing a house-building project can be divided into two parts: prebuilding preparation and construction management.

■ **Prebuilding preparation.** This is where you should focus most of your attention. In the hands of a qualified contractor whose expertise you can rely on, the actual building process should go fairly smoothly. But during most of the prebuilding stage, you're generally on your own. Your job will be to launch the project and develop a talented team that can help you bring your new home to fruition.

When you work with stock plans, the prebuilding process usually goes as follows:

First, you research the general area where you want to live, selecting one or more possible home sites (unless you already own a suitable lot). Then you choose a basic house design, with the idea that it may require some modification. Finally, you analyze the site, the design, and your budget to determine if the project is actually attainable.

If you decide that it is, you purchase the land and order blue-prints. If you want to modify them, you consult an architect, designer, or contractor. Once the plans are finalized, you request bids from contractors and arrange any necessary construction financing.

After selecting a builder and signing a contract, you (or your contractor) then file the plans with the building department. When the plans are approved, often several weeks—or even months—later, you're ready to begin construction.

■ **Construction management.** Unless you intend to act as your own contractor, your role during the building process is mostly one of quality control and time management. Even so, it's important to know the sequence of events and something about construction methods so you can discuss progress with your builder and prepare for any important decisions you may need to make along the way.

Decision-making is critical. Once construction begins, the builder must usually plunge ahead, keeping his carpenters and subcontractors progressing steadily. If you haven't made a key decision—which model bathtub or sink to install, for example—it can bring construction to a frustrating and expensive halt.

Usually, you'll make such decisions before the onset of building, but, inevitably, some issue or another will arise during construction. Being knowledgeable about the building process will help you anticipate and circumvent potential logjams.

Selecting a House Plan

Searching for the right plan can be a fun, interactive family experience—one of the most exciting parts of a house-building project. Gather the family around as you peruse the home plans in this book. Study the size, location, and configuration of each room; traffic patterns both inside the house and to the outdoors; exterior style; and how you'll use the available space. Discuss the pros and cons of the various plans.

Browse through pictures of homes in magazines to stimulate ideas. Clip the photos you like so you can think about your favorite options. When you visit the homes of friends, note special features that appeal to you. Also, look carefully at the homes in your neighborhood, noting their style and how they fit the site.

Mark those plans that most closely suit your ideals. Then, to narrow down your choices, critique each plan, using the following information as a guide.

■ **Overall size and budget.** How large a house do you want? Will the house you're considering fit your family's requirements? Look at the overall square footage and room sizes. If you have a hard time visualizing room sizes, measure some of the rooms in your present home and compare.

It's often better for the house to be a little too big than a little too small, but remember that every extra square foot will cost more money to build and maintain.

■ **Number and type of rooms.** Beyond thinking about the number of bedrooms and baths you want, consider your family's life-style and how you use space. Do you want both a family room and a living room? Do you need a formal dining space? Will you require some extra rooms, or "swing spaces," that can serve multiple purposes, such as a home office–guest room combination?

■ **Room placement and traffic patterns.** What are your preferences for locations of formal living areas, master bedroom, and children's rooms? Do you prefer a kitchen that's open to family areas or one that's private and out of the way? How much do you use exterior spaces and how should they relate to the interior?

Once you make those determinations, look carefully at the floor plan of the house you're considering to see if it meets your needs and if the traffic flow will be convenient for your family.

■ Architectural style. Have you always wanted to live in a Victorian farmhouse? Now is your chance to create a house that matches your idea of "home" (taking into account, of course, styles in your neighborhood). But don't let your preference for one particular architectural style dictate your home's floor plan. If the floor plan doesn't work for your family, keep looking.

■ Site considerations. Most people choose a site before selecting a plan—or at least they've zeroed in on the basic type of land where they'll situate their house. It sounds elementary, but choose a house that will fit the site.

When figuring the "footprint" of a house, you must know about any restrictions that will affect your home's height or proximity to the property lines. Call the local building department (look under city or county listings in the phone book) and get a very clear description of any restrictions, such as setbacks, height limits, and lot coverage, that will affect what you can build on the site (see "Working with City Hall," at right).

When you visit potential sites, note trees, rock outcroppings, slopes, views, winds, sun, neighboring homes, and other factors. All will impact on how your house works on a particular site.

Once you've narrowed down the choice of sites, consult an architect or building designer (see page 8) to help you evaluate how some potential houses will work on the sites you have in mind.

Is Your Project Doable?

Before you purchase land, make sure your project is doable. Although it's too early at this stage to pinpoint costs, making a few phone calls will help you determine whether your project is realistic. You'll be able to learn if you can afford to build the house, how long it will take, and what obstacles may stand in your way.

To get a ballpark estimate of cost, multiply a house's total square footage (of livable space) by the local average cost per square foot for new construction. (To obtain local averages, call a contractor, an architect, a realtor, or the local chapter of the National Association of Home Builders.) Some contractors may even be willing to give you a preliminary bid. Once you know approximate costs, speak to your lender to explore financing.

Working with City Hall

For any building project, even a minor one, it's essential to be familiar with building codes and other restrictions that can affect your project.

■ Building codes, generally implemented by the city or county building department, set the standards for safe, lasting construction. Codes specify minimum construction techniques and materials for foundations, framing, electrical wiring, plumbing, insulation, and all other aspects of a building. Although codes are adopted and enforced locally, most regional codes conform to the standards set by the national Uniform Building Code, Standard Building Code, or Basic Building Code. In some cases, local codes set more restrictive standards than national ones.

■ Building permits are required for home-building projects nearly everywhere. If you work with a contractor, the builder's firm should handle all necessary permits.

More than one permit may be needed; for example, one will cover the foundation, another the electrical wiring, and still another the heating equipment installation. Each will probably involve a fee and require inspections by building officials before work can proceed. (Inspections benefit *you*, as they ensure that the job is being done satisfactorily.) Permit fees are generally a percentage (1 to 1.5 percent) of the project's estimated value, often calculated on square footage.

It's important to file for the necessary permits. Failure to do so can result in fines or legal action against you. You can even be forced to undo the work performed. At the very least, your negligence may come back to haunt you later when you're ready to sell your house.

■ Zoning ordinances, particular to your community, restrict setbacks (how near to property lines you may build), your house's allowable height, lot coverage factors (how much of your property you can cover with structures), and other factors that impact design and building. If your plans don't conform to zoning ordinances, you can try to obtain a variance, an exception to the rules. But this legal work can be expensive and time-consuming. Even if you prove that your project won't negatively affect your neighbors, the building department can still refuse to grant the variance.

■ Deeds and covenants attach to the lot. Deeds set out property lines and easements; covenants may establish architectural standards in a neighborhood. Since both can seriously impact your project, make sure you have complete information on any deeds or covenants before you turn over a spadeful of soil.

It's a good idea to discuss your project with several contractors (see page 8). They may be aware of problems in your area that could limit your options—bedrock that makes digging basements difficult, for example. These conversations are actually the first step in developing a list of contractors from which you'll choose the one who will build your home.

Recruiting Your Home Team

A home-building project will inter-ject you and your family into the building business, an area that may be unfamiliar territory. Among the people you'll be working with are architects, designers, landscapers, contractors, and subcontractors.

Design Help

A qualified architect or designer can help you modify and personalize your home plan, taking into account your family's needs and budget and the house's style. In fact, you may want to consider consulting such a person while you're selecting a plan to help you articulate your needs.

Design professionals are capable of handling any or all aspects of the design process. For example, they can review your house plans, suggest options, and then provide rough sketches of the options on tracing paper. Many architects will even secure needed permits and negotiate with contractors or subcontractors, as well as oversee the quality of the work.

Of course, you don't necessarily need an architect or designer to implement minor changes in a plan; although most contractors aren't trained in design, some can help you with modifications.

An open-ended, hourly-fee arrangement that you work out with your architect or designer allows for flexibility, but it often turns out to be more costly than working on a flat-fee basis. On a flat fee, you agree to pay a specific amount of money for a certain amount of work.

To find architects and designers, contact such trade associations as the American Institute of Architects (AIA), American Institute of Building Designers (AIBD), American Society of Landscape Architects (ASLA), and American Society of Interior Designers (ASID). Although many professionals choose not to belong to trade associations, those who do have met the standards of their respective associations. For phone numbers of local branches, check the Yellow Pages.

■ **Architects** are licensed by the state and have degrees. They're trained in all facets of building design and construction. Although some can handle interior design and structural engineering, others hire specialists for those tasks.

■ **Building designers** are generally unlicensed but may be accredited by the American Institute of Building Designers. Their backgrounds are varied: some may be unlicensed architects in apprenticeship; others are interior designers or contractors with design skills.

■ **Draftspersons** offer an economical route to making simple changes on your drawings. Like building designers, these people may be unlicensed architect apprentices, engineers, or members of related trades. Most are accomplished at drawing up plans.

■ **Interior designers,** as their job title suggests, design interiors. They work with you to choose room finishes, furnishings, appliances, and decorative elements. Part of their expertise is in arranging furnishings to create a workable space plan. Some interior designers are employed by architectural firms; others work independently. Financial arrangements vary, depending on the designer's preference.

Related professionals are kitchen and bathroom designers, who concentrate on fixtures, cabinetry, appliances, materials, and space planning for the kitchen and bath.

■ **Landscape architects, designers, and contractors** design outdoor areas. Landscape architects are state-licensed to practice landscape design. A landscape designer usually has a landscape architect's education and training but does not have a state license. Licensed landscape contractors specialize in garden construction, though some also have design skills and experience.

■ **Soils specialists and structural engineers** may be needed for projects where unstable soils or uncommon wind loads or seismic forces must be taken into account. Any structural changes to a house require the expertise of a structural engineer to verify that the house won't fall down.

Services of these specialists can be expensive, but they're imperative in certain conditions to ensure a safe, sturdy structure. Your building department will probably let you know if their services are required.

General Contractors

To build your house, hire a licensed general contractor. Most states require a contractor to be licensed and insured for worker's compensation in order to contract a building project and hire other subcontractors. State licensing ensures that contractors have met minimum training standards and have a specified level of experience. Licensing does not guarantee, however, that they're good at what they do.

When contractors hire subcontractors, they're responsible for overseeing the quality of work and materials of the subcontractors and for paying them.

■ **Finding a contractor.** How do you find a good contractor? Start by getting referrals from people you know who have built or remodeled their home. Nothing beats a personal recommendation. The best contractors are usually busily moving from one satisfied client to another prospect, advertised only by word of mouth.

You can also ask local real estate brokers and lenders or even your building inspector for names of qualified builders. Experienced lumber dealers are another good source of names.

In the Yellow Pages, look under "Contractors–Building, General"; or call the local chapter of the National Association of Home Builders.

■ **Choosing a contractor.** Once you have a list of names of prospective builders, call several of them. On the telephone, ask first whether they handle your type of job and can work within your schedule. If they can, arrange a meeting with each one and ask them to be prepared with references of former clients and photos of previous jobs. Better still, meet them at one of their current work sites so you can get a glimpse of the quality of their work and how organized and thorough they are.

Take your plan to the meeting and discuss it enough to request a rough estimate (some builders will comply, while others will be reluctant to offer a ballpark estimate, preferring to give you a hard bid based on complete drawings). Don't hesitate to probe for advice or suggestions that might make building your house less expensive.

Be especially aware of each contractor's personality and how well you communicate. Good chemistry between you and your builder is a key ingredient for success.

Narrow down the candidates to three or four. Ask each for a firm bid, based on the exact same set of plans and specifications. For the bids to be accurate, your plans need to be complete and the specifications as precise as possible, call-

ing out particular appliances, fixtures, floorings, roofing material, and so forth. (Some of these are specified in a stock-plan set; others are not.)

Call the contractors' references and ask about the quality of their work, their relationship with their clients, their promptness, and their readiness to follow up on problems. Visit former clients to check the contractor's work firsthand.

Be sure your final candidates are licensed, bonded, and insured for worker's compensation, public liability, and property damage. Also, try to determine how financially solvent they are (you can call their bank and credit references). Avoid contractors who are operating hand-to-mouth.

Don't automatically hire the contractor with the lowest bid if you don't think you'll get along well or if you have any doubts about the quality of the person's work. Instead, look for both the most reasonable bid and the contractor with the best credentials, references, terms, and compatibility with your family.

A word about bonds: You can request a performance bond that guarantees that your job will be finished by your contractor. If the job isn't completed, the bonding company will cover the cost of hiring another contractor to finish it. Bonds cost from 2 to 6 percent of the value of the project.

Your Building Contract

A building contract (see below) binds and protects both you and your contractor. It isn't just a legal document. It's also a list of the expectations of both parties. The best way to minimize the possibility of misunderstandings and costly changes later on is to write down every possible detail. Whether the contract is a standard form or one composed by you, have an attorney look it over before both you and the contractor sign it.

The contract should clearly specify all the work that needs to be done, including particular materials and work descriptions, the time schedule, and method of payment. It should be keyed to the working drawings.

A Sample Building Contract

Project and participants. Give a general description of the project, its address, and the names and addresses of both you and the builder.

Construction materials. Identify all construction materials by brand name, quality markings (species, grades, etc.), and model numbers where applicable. Avoid the clause "or equal," which allows the builder to substitute other materials for your choices. For materials you can't specify now, set down a budget figure.

Time schedule. Include both start and completion dates and specify that work will be "continuous." Although a contractor cannot be responsible for delays caused by strikes and material shortages, your builder should assume responsibility for completing the project within a reasonable period of time.

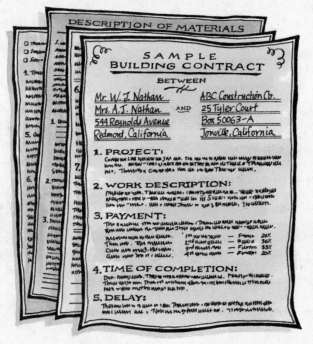

Work to be performed. State all work you expect the contractor to perform, from initial grading to finished painting.

Method and schedule of payment. Specify how and when payments are to be made. Typical agreements specify installment payments as particular phases of work are completed. Final payment is withheld until the job receives its final inspection and is cleared of all liens.

Waiver of liens. Protect yourself with a waiver of liens signed by the general contractor, the subcontractors, and all major suppliers. That way, subcontractors who are not paid for materials or services cannot place a lien on your property.

Personalizing Stock Plans

The beauty of buying stock plans for your new home is that they offer tested, well-conceived design at an affordable price. And stock plans dramatically reduce the time it takes to design a house, since the plans are ready when you are.

Because they were not created specifically for your family, stock plans may not reflect your personal taste. But it's not difficult to make revisions in stock plans that will turn your home into an expression of your family's personality. You'll surely want to add personal touches and choose your own finishes.

Ideally, the modifications you implement will be fairly minor. The more extensive the changes, the more expensive the plans. Major changes take valuable design time, and those that affect a house's structure may require a structural engineer's approval.

If you anticipate wholesale changes, such as moving a number of bearing walls or changing the roofline significantly, you may be better off selecting another plan. On the other hand, reconfiguring or changing the sizes of some rooms can probably be handled fairly easily.

Some structural changes may even be necessary to comply with local codes. Your area may have specific requirements for snow loads, energy codes, seismic or wind resistance, and so forth. Those types of modifications are likely to require the services of an architect or structural engineer.

Plan Modifications

Before you pencil in any changes, live with your plans for a while. Study them carefully—at your building site, if possible. Try to picture the finished house: how rooms will interrelate, where the sun will enter and at what angle, what the view will be from each window. Think about traffic patterns, access to rooms, room sizes, window and door locations, natural light, and kitchen and bathroom layouts.

Typical changes might involve adding windows or skylights to

bring in natural light or capture a view. Or you may want to widen a hallway or doorway for roomier access, extend a room, eliminate doors, or change window and door sizes. Perhaps you'd like to shorten a room, stealing the gained space for a large closet. Look closely at the kitchen; it's not difficult to reconfigure the layout if it makes the space more convenient for you.

Above all, take your time—this is your home and it should reflect your taste and needs. Make your changes now, during the planning stage. Once construction begins, it will take crowbars, hammers, saws, new materials, and, most significantly, time to alter the plans. Because changes are not part of your building contract, you can count on them being expensive extras once construction begins.

Specifying Finishes

One way to personalize a house without changing its structure is to substitute your favorite finishes for those specified on the plan.

Would you prefer a stuccoed exterior rather than the wood siding shown on the plan? In most cases, this is a relatively easy change. Do you like the look of a wood shingle roof rather than the composition shingles shown on the plan? This, too, is easy. Perhaps you would like to change the windows from sliders to casements, or upgrade to high-efficiency glazing. No problem. Many of those kinds of changes can be worked out with your contractor.

Inside, you may want hardwood where vinyl flooring is shown. In fact, you can—and should—choose types, colors, and styles of floorings, wall coverings, tile, plumbing fixtures, door hardware, cabinetry, appliances, lighting fixtures, and other interior details, for it's these materials that will personalize your home. For help in making selections, consult an architect or interior designer (see page 8).

Each material you select should be spelled out clearly and precisely in your building contract.

Finishing touches can transform a house built from stock plans into an expression of your family's taste and style. Clockwise, from far left: Colorful tilework and custom cabinetry enliven a bathroom (Design: Osburn Design); highly organized closet system maximizes storage space (Architect: David Jeremiah Hurley); low-level deck expands living space to outdoor areas (Landscape architects: The Runa Group, Inc.); built-ins convert the corner of a guest room into a home office (Design: Lynn Williams of The French Connection); French country cabinetry lends style and old-world charm to a kitchen (Design: Garry Bishop/Showcase Kitchens).

What the Plans Include

Complete construction blueprints are available for every house shown in this book. Clear and concise, these detailed blueprints are designed by licensed architects or members of the American Institute of Building Designers (AIBD). Each plan is designed to meet standards set down by nationally recognized building codes (the Uniform Building Code, Standard Building Code, or Basic Building Code) at the time and for the area where they were drawn.

Remember, however, that every state, county, and municipality has its own codes, zoning requirements, ordinances, and building regulations. Modifications may be necessary to comply with such local requirements as snow loads, energy codes, seismic zones, and flood areas.

Although blueprint sets vary depending on the size and complexity of the house and on the individual designer's style, each set may include the elements described below and shown at right.

■ **Exterior elevations** show the front, rear, and sides of the house, including exterior materials, details, and measurements.

■ **Foundation plans** include drawings for a full, partial, or daylight basement, crawlspace, pole, pier, or slab foundation. All necessary notations and dimensions are included. (Foundation options will vary for each plan. If the plan you choose doesn't have the type of foundation you desire, a generic conversion diagram is available.)

■ **Detailed floor plans** show the placement of interior walls and the dimensions of rooms, doors, windows, stairways, and similar elements for each level of the house.

■ **Cross sections** show details of the house as though it were cut in slices from the roof to the foundation. The cross sections give the home's construction, insulation, flooring, and roofing details.

■ **Interior elevations** show the specific details of cabinets (kitchen, bathroom, and utility room), fireplaces, built-in units, and other special interior features.

■ **Roof details** give the layout of rafters, dormers, gables, and other roof elements, including clerestory windows and skylights. These details may be shown on the elevation sheet or on a separate diagram.

■ **Schematic electrical layouts** show the suggested locations for switches, fixtures, and outlets. These details may be shown on the floor plan or on a separate diagram.

■ **General specifications** provide instructions and information regarding excavation and grading, masonry and concrete work, carpentry and woodwork, thermal and moisture protection, drywall, tile, flooring, glazing, and caulking and sealants.

Other Helpful Building Aids

In addition to the construction information on every set of plans, you can buy the following guides.

■ **Reproducible blueprints** are helpful if you'll be making changes to the stock plan you've chosen. These blueprints are original line drawings produced on erasable, reproducible paper for the purpose of modification. When alterations are complete, working copies can be made.

■ **Itemized materials list** details the quantity, type, and size of materials needed to build your home. (This list is extremely helpful in obtaining an accurate construction bid. It's not intended for use to order materials.)

■ **Mirror-reverse plans** are useful if you want to build your home in the reverse of the plan that's shown. Because the lettering and dimensions read backwards, be sure to buy at least one regular-reading set of blueprints.

■ **Description of materials** gives the type and quality of materials suggested for the home. This form may be required for obtaining FHA or VA financing.

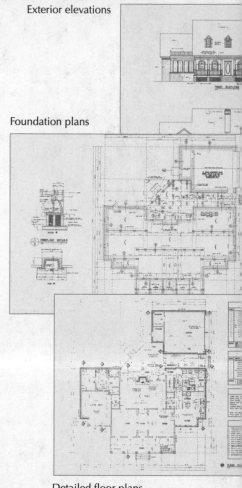

Exterior elevations

Foundation plans

Detailed floor plans

■ **How-to diagrams** for plumbing, wiring, solar heating, framing and foundation conversions show how to plumb, wire, install a solar heating system, convert plans with 2 by 4 exterior walls to 2 by 6 construction (or vice versa), and adapt a plan for a basement, crawlspace, or slab foundation. These diagrams are not specific to any one plan.

NOTE: Due to regional variations, local availability of materials, local codes, methods of installation, and individual preferences, detailed heating, plumbing, and electrical specifications are not included on plans. The duct work, venting, and other details will vary, depending on the heating and cooling system you use and the type of energy that operates it. These details and specifications are easily obtained from your builder or local supplier.

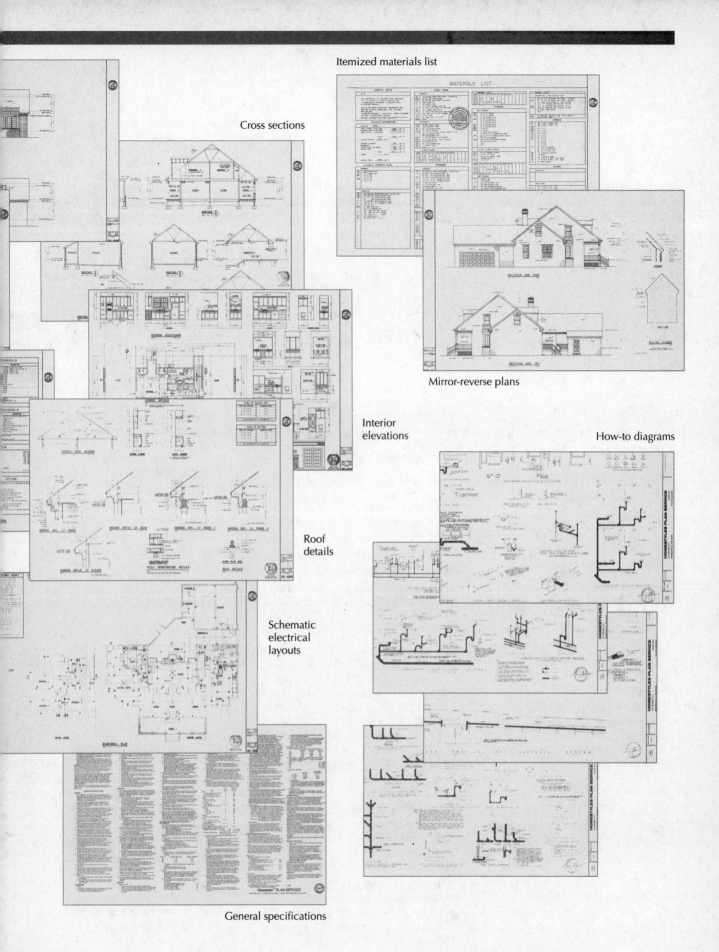

Itemized materials list

Cross sections

Mirror-reverse plans

Interior elevations

How-to diagrams

Roof details

Schematic electrical layouts

General specifications

Before You Order

Once you've chosen the one or two house plans that work best for you, you're ready to order blueprints. Before filling in the form on the facing page, note the information that follows.

How Many Blueprints Will You Need?

A single set of blueprints will allow you to study a home design in detail. You'll need more for obtaining bids and permits, as well as some to use as reference at the building site. If you'll be modifying your home plan, order a reproducible set (see page 12).

Figure you'll need at least one set each for yourself, your builder, the building department, and your lender. In addition, some subcontractors—foundation, plumber, electrician, and HVAC—may also need at least partial sets. If they do, ask them to return the sets when they're finished. The chart below can help you calculate how many sets you're likely to need.

Blueprint Checklist

____ **Owner's set(s)**

____ **Builder** usually requires at least three sets: one for legal documentation, one for inspections, and a minimum of one set for subcontractors.

____ **Building department** requires at least one set. Check with your local department before ordering.

____ **Lending institution** usually needs one set for a conventional mortgage, three sets for FHA or VA loans.

____ **TOTAL SETS NEEDED**

Blueprint Prices

The cost of having an architect design a new custom home typically runs from 5 to 15 percent of the building cost, or from $5,000 to $15,000 for a $100,000 home. A single set of blueprints for the plans in this book ranges from $295 to $505, depending on the house's size. Working with these drawings, you can save enough on design fees to add a deck, a swimming pool, or a luxurious kitchen.

Pricing is based on "total finished living space." Garages, porches, decks, and unfinished basements are not included.

Building Costs

Building costs vary widely, depending on a number of factors, includ-

Price Code (Size)	1 Set	4 Sets	7 Sets	Reproducible Set
AAA (under 500 sq. ft.)	$245	$295	$330	$430
AA (500-999 sq. ft.)	$285	$335	$370	$470
A (1,000-1,499 sq. ft.)	$325	$375	$410	$510
B (1,500-1,999 sq. ft.)	$365	$415	$450	$550
C (2,000-2,499 sq. ft.)	$405	$455	$490	$590
D (2,500-2,999 sq. ft.)	$445	$495	$530	$630
E (3,000-3,499 sq. ft.)	$485	$535	$570	$670
F (3,500-3,999 sq. ft.)	$525	$575	$610	$710
G (4,000-4,499 sq. ft.)	$565	$615	$650	$750
H (4,500-4,999 sq. ft.)	$605	$655	$690	$790
I (5,000 sq. ft. & above)	$645	$695	$730	$830

ing local material and labor costs and the finishing materials you select. For help estimating costs, see "Is Your Project Doable?" on page 7.

Foundation Options & Exterior Construction

Depending on your site and climate, your home will be built with a slab, pier, pole, crawlspace, or basement foundation. Exterior walls will be framed with either 2 by 4s or 2 by 6s, determined by structural and insulation standards in your area. Most contractors can easily adapt a home to meet the foundation and/or wall requirements for your area. Or ask for a conversion how-to diagram (see page 12).

Service & Blueprint Delivery

Service representatives are available to answer questions and assist you in placing your order. Every effort is made to process and ship orders within 48 hours.

Returns & Exchanges

Each set of blueprints is specially printed and shipped to you in response to your specific order; consequently, requests for refunds cannot be honored. However, if the prints you order cannot be used, you may exchange them for another plan from any Sunset home plan book. For an exchange, you must return all sets of plans within 30 days. A nonrefundable service charge will be assessed for all exchanges; for more information, call the toll-free number on the facing page. Note: Reproducible sets cannot be exchanged.

Compliance with Local Codes & Regulations

Because of climatic, geographic, and political variations, building codes and regulations vary from one area to another. These plans are authorized for your use expressly conditioned on your obligation and agreement to comply strictly with all local building codes, ordinances, regulations, and requirements, including permits and in-spections at time of construction.

Architectural & Engineering Seals

With increased concern about energy costs and safety, many cities and states now require that an architect or engineer review and "seal" a blueprint prior to construction. To find out whether this is a requirement in your area, contact your local building department.

License Agreement, Copy Restrictions & Copyright

When you purchase your blueprints, you are granted the right to use those documents to construct a single unit. All the plans in this publication are protected under the Federal Copyright Act, Title XVII of the United States Code and Chap-ter 37 of the Code of Federal Regu-lations. Each designer retains title and ownership of the original documents. The blueprints licensed to you cannot be used by or resold to any other person, copied, or reproduced by any means. The copying restrictions do not apply to reproducible blueprints. When you buy a reproducible set, you may modify and reproduce it for your own use.

Blueprint Order Form

Complete this order form in just three easy steps. Then mail in your order or, for faster service, call toll-free.

1. Blueprints & Accessories

BLUEPRINT CHART

Price Code	1 Set	4 Sets	7 Sets	Reproducible Set*
AAA	$245	$295	$330	$430
AA	$285	$335	$370	$470
A	$325	$375	$410	$510
B	$365	$415	$450	$550
C	$405	$455	$490	$590
D	$445	$495	$530	$630
E	$485	$535	$570	$670
F	$525	$575	$610	$710
G	$565	$615	$650	$750
H	$605	$655	$690	$790
I	$645	$695	$730	$830

*A reproducible set is produced on erasable paper for the purpose of modification. It is only available for plans with prefixes A, AG, AGH, AH, AHP, APS, AX, B, C, CC, CPS, DCL, DD, DW, E, EOF, FB, GL, GML, GSA, H, HDS, HFL, J, K, KD, KLF, L, LRD, LS, M, NW, OH, PH, PI, RD, S, SDG, THD, U, UDG, V.

Prices subject to change

Mirror-Reverse Sets: $50 surcharge. From the total number of sets you ordered above, choose the number you want to be reversed. *Note: All writing on mirror-reverse plans is backwards. Order at least one regular-reading set.*

Itemized Materials List: One set $50; each additional set $15. Details the quantity, type, and size of materials needed to build your home.

Description of Materials: Sold in a set of two for $50 (for use in obtaining FHA or VA financing).

Typical How-To Diagrams: One set $20; two sets $30; three sets $40; four sets $45. General guides on plumbing, wiring, and solar heating, plus information on how to convert from one foundation or exterior framing to another. *Note: These diagrams are not specific to any one plan.*

2. Sales Tax & Shipping

Determine your subtotal and add appropriate local state sales tax, plus shipping and handling (see chart below).

SHIPPING & HANDLING

	1–3 Sets	4–6 Sets	7 or More Sets	Reproducible Set
U.S. Regular (5–6 business days)	$17.50	$20.00	$22.50	$17.50
U.S. Express (2–3 business days)	$29.50	$32.50	$35.00	$29.50
Canada Regular (2–3 weeks)	$20.00	$22.50	$25.00	$20.00
Canada Express (5–6 business days)	$35.00	$40.00	$45.00	$35.00
Overseas/Airmail (7–10 business days)	$57.50	$67.50	$77.50	$57.50

3. Customer Information

Choose the method of payment you prefer. Include check, money order, or credit card information, complete name and address portion, and mail, fax, or call using the information at the right.

SS16

COMPLETE THIS FORM

Plan Number _____ Price Code _____

Foundation _____
(Review your plan carefully for foundation options—basement, pole, pier, crawlspace, or slab. Many plans offer several options; others offer only one.)

Number of Sets: $_____
- ☐ One Set   *(See chart at left)*
- ☐ Four Sets
- ☐ Seven Sets
- ☐ One Reproducible Set

Additional Sets _____ $_____
          ($40 each)

Mirror-Reverse Sets _____ $_____
          ($50 surcharge)

Itemized Materials List $_____
Only available for plans with prefixes AH, AHP, APS*, AX*, B*, C, CAR, CC, CDG*, CPS, DD*, DW, E, GSA, H, HFL, I*, J, K, LMB*, LRD, NW*, P, PH, R, S, THD, U, UDG, VL. *Not available on all plans. Please call before ordering.

Description of Materials $_____
Only available for plans with prefixes AHP, C, DW, H, J, K, P, PH, VL.

Typical How-To Diagrams $_____
- ☐ Plumbing   ☐ Wiring   ☐ Solar Heating   ☐ Foundation & Framing Conversion

SUBTOTAL	$_____
SALES TAX	$_____
SHIPPING & HANDLING	$_____
GRAND TOTAL	$_____

☐ Check/money order enclosed (in U.S. funds)
☐ VISA   ☐ MasterCard   ☐ AmEx   ☐ Discover

Credit Card # _____ Exp. Date _____

Signature _____

Name _____

Address _____

City _____ State ____ Country _____

Zip _____ Daytime Phone (____) _____

☐ Please check if you are a contractor.

Mail form to: Sunset/HomeStyles Plan Service
                P.O. Box 50670
                Minneapolis, MN 55405

Or fax to: (612) 338-1626

FOR FASTER SERVICE CALL 1-800-820-1283

SS16

Luxury in a Small Package

- The elegant exterior of this design sets the tone for the luxurious spaces within.
- The foyer opens to the centrally located living room, which features a 15-ft. cathedral ceiling, a two-way fireplace and access to a lovely rear terrace.
- The unusual kitchen design includes an angled snack bar that lies between the bayed breakfast den and the formal dining room. Sliding glass doors open to another terrace.
- The master suite is a dream come true, with its romantic fireplace, built-in desk and 9-ft.-high tray ceiling. The private bath includes a whirlpool tub and a dual-sink vanity.
- Another full bath serves the remaining two bedrooms, one of which boasts a cathedral ceiling and a tall arched window.

Plan AHP-9300

Bedrooms: 3	Baths: 2
Living Area:	
Main floor	1,513 sq. ft.
Total Living Area:	**1,513 sq. ft.**
Standard basement	1,360 sq. ft.
Garage	400 sq. ft.
Exterior Wall Framing:	2x4 or 2x6

Foundation Options:
Standard basement
Crawlspace
Slab
(All plans can be built with your choice of foundation and framing. A generic conversion diagram is available. See order form.)

BLUEPRINT PRICE CODE: **B**

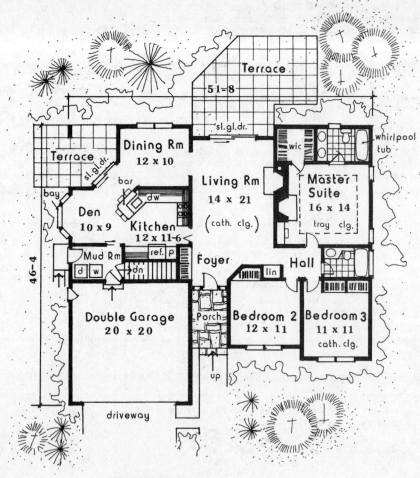

MAIN FLOOR

Plan AHP-9300

PRICES AND DETAILS ON PAGES 12-15

Extra-Special Ranch-Style

- Repeating gables, wood siding and brick adorn this ranch-style home, which offers numerous amenities in its compact interior.
- The entry leads directly into a spectacular 21-ft.-high vaulted family room, an ideal entertainment area accented by a corner fireplace and a French door to the backyard.
- A serving bar connects the family room with the efficient kitchen, which has a handy pantry, ample counter space and a sunny breakfast room.
- The luxurious master suite boasts a 10½-ft. tray ceiling, a large bank of windows and a walk-in closet. The master bath features a garden tub.
- Two more bedrooms, one with a 14½-ft. vaulted ceiling, share another full bath.
- The two-car garage provides convenient access to the kitchen and laundry area.

Plan FB-1104

Bedrooms: 3	Baths: 2
Living Area:	
Main floor	1,104 sq. ft.
Total Living Area:	**1,104 sq. ft.**
Daylight basement	1,104 sq. ft.
Garage	400 sq. ft.
Exterior Wall Framing:	2x4

Foundation Options:

Daylight basement
Crawlspace
(All plans can be built with your choice of foundation and framing. A generic conversion diagram is available. See order form.)

BLUEPRINT PRICE CODE: **A**

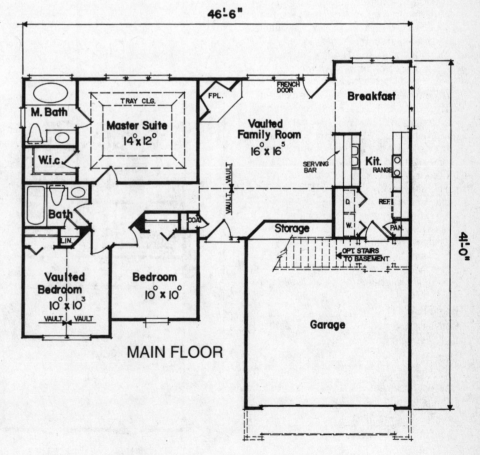

MAIN FLOOR

Eye-Catching Details

- This eye-catching home features a handsome exterior and an exciting floor plan that maximizes square footage.
- The covered porch leads into a vaulted foyer with an angled coat closet. Straight ahead, the 16½-ft.-high vaulted Great Room combines with the dining room and kitchen to create one expansive living and entertaining area.
- The Great Room offers a fireplace and access to the backyard. The galley-style kitchen has a 16½-ft.-high ceiling and is bordered by the vaulted dining room on one side and a breakfast area with a laundry closet on the other.
- The master suite boasts a 15-ft., 8-in. tray ceiling. The 13-ft.-high vaulted bath has a garden tub, a separate shower and a vanity with knee space.
- The two remaining bedrooms are located on the opposite side of the home and share a full bath. A plant shelf is an attention-getting detail found here.

Plan FB-1289

Bedrooms: 3	Baths: 2
Living Area:	
Main floor	1,289 sq. ft.
Total Living Area:	**1,289 sq. ft.**
Daylight basement	1,289 sq. ft.
Garage	430 sq. ft.
Exterior Wall Framing:	2x4

Foundation Options:

Daylight basement
Crawlspace
Slab

(All plans can be built with your choice of foundation and framing. A generic conversion diagram is available. See order form.)

BLUEPRINT PRICE CODE: A

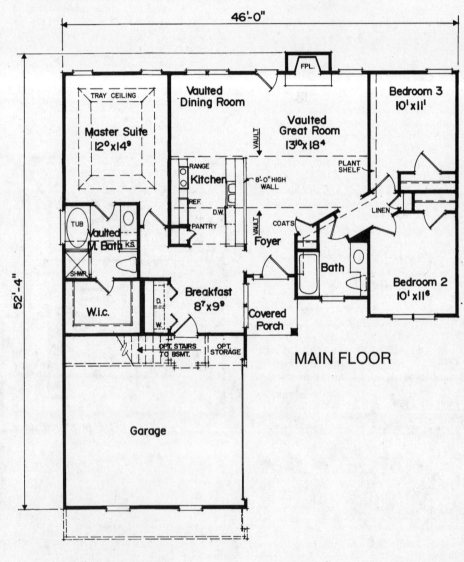

MAIN FLOOR

Plan FB-1289

High-Profile Contemporary

- This design does away with wasted space, putting the emphasis on quality rather than on size.
- The angled floor plan minimizes hall space and creates smooth traffic flow while adding architectural appeal. The roof framing is square, however, to allow for economical construction.
- The spectacular living and dining rooms share a 16-ft. cathedral ceiling and a fireplace. Both rooms have lots of glass overlooking an angled rear terrace.
- The dining room includes a glass-filled alcove and sliding patio doors topped by transom windows. Tall windows frame the living room fireplace and trace the slope of the ceiling.
- A pass-through joins the dining room to the combination kitchen and family room, which features a snack bar and a clerestory window.
- The sleeping wing provides a super master suite, which boasts a skylighted dressing area and a luxurious bath. The optional den, or third bedroom, shares a second full bath with another bedroom that offers a 14-ft. sloped ceiling.

Plan K-688-D

Bedrooms: 2+	**Baths:** 2½
Living Area:	
Main floor	1,340 sq. ft.
Total Living Area:	**1,340 sq. ft.**
Standard basement	1,235 sq. ft.
Garage	484 sq. ft.
Exterior Wall Framing:	2x4 or 2x6
Foundation Options:	
Standard basement	
Slab	

(All plans can be built with your choice of foundation and framing. A generic conversion diagram is available. See order form.)

BLUEPRINT PRICE CODE: **A**

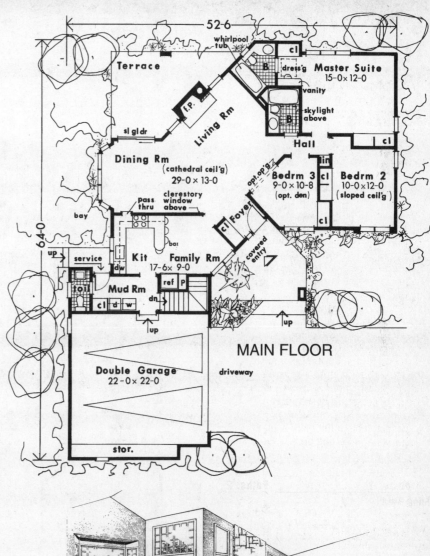

MAIN FLOOR

VIEW INTO DINING ROOM AND LIVING ROOM

All in One!

- This plan puts today's most luxurious home-design features into one attractive, economical package.
- The covered front porch and the gabled roofline, accented by an arched window and a round louver vent, give the exterior a homey yet stylish appeal.
- Just inside the front door, the ceiling rises to 11 ft., offering an impressive greeting. The spacious living room is flooded with light through a central skylight and a pair of French doors that frame the smart fireplace.
- The living room flows into the nice-sized dining room, also with an 11-ft. ceiling. The adjoining kitchen offers a handy laundry closet, lots of counter space and a sunny dinette that opens to an expansive backyard terrace.
- The bedroom wing includes a wonderful master suite with a sizable sleeping room and an adjacent dressing area with two closets. Glass blocks above the dual-sink vanity in the master bath let in light yet maintain privacy. A whirlpool tub and a separate shower complete the suite.
- The larger of the two remaining bedrooms boasts an 11-ft.-high ceiling and an arched window.

Plan HFL-1680-FL

Bedrooms: 3	Baths: 2
Living Area:	
Main floor	1,367 sq. ft.
Total Living Area:	**1,367 sq. ft.**
Standard basement	1,367 sq. ft.
Garage	431 sq. ft.
Exterior Wall Framing:	2x6

Foundation Options:

Standard basement
(All plans can be built with your choice of foundation and framing. A generic conversion diagram is available. See order form.)

BLUEPRINT PRICE CODE: A

VIEW INTO LIVING ROOM

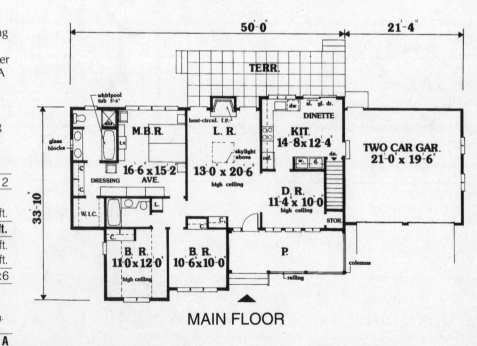

MAIN FLOOR

Plan HFL-1680-FL

PRICES AND DETAILS
ON PAGES 12-15

Charming
Traditional

- The attractive facade of this traditional home features decorative fretwork and louvers in the gables, plus eye-catching window and door treatments.
- The entry area features a commanding view of the living room, which boasts a 12½-ft. ceiling and a corner fireplace. A rear porch and patio are visible through French doors.
- The bayed dining room shares an eating bar with the U-shaped kitchen. The nearby utility room includes a pantry and laundry facilities.
- The quiet master suite includes a big walk-in closet and a private bath with a dual-sink vanity.
- On the other side of the home, double doors close off the two secondary bedrooms from the living areas. A full bath services this wing.

Plan E-1428

Bedrooms: 3	Baths: 2
Living Area:	
Main floor	1,415 sq. ft.
Total Living Area:	**1,415 sq. ft.**
Garage	484 sq. ft.
Storage	60 sq. ft.
Exterior Wall Framing:	2x6

Foundation Options:

Crawlspace

Slab

(All plans can be built with your choice of foundation and framing. A generic conversion diagram is available. See order form.)

BLUEPRINT PRICE CODE: **A**

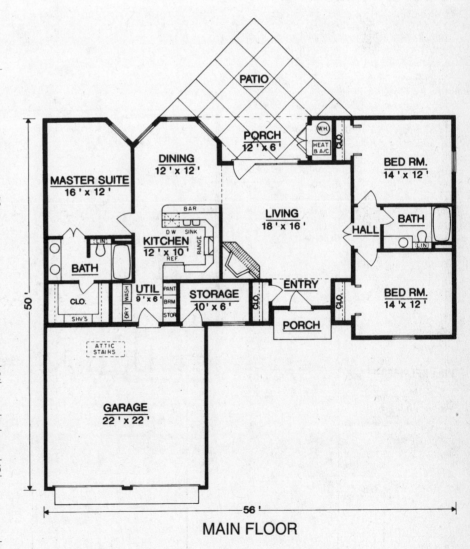

MAIN FLOOR

Wide Angles Add Style

- The comfortably-sized living areas of this gorgeous home are stylishly enhanced by wide, interesting angles.
- Past the covered front porch, the sidelighted front door brightens the living room just ahead.
- The spacious living room is warmed by a dramatic corner fireplace and opens to an angled, covered back porch.
- A stunning bayed dining room merges with the kitchen and its functional angled snack bar. Laundry facilities and access to the garage are nearby.
- The master suite is removed from the secondary bedrooms and features double doors to a deluxe private bath with an angled spa tub, a dual-sink vanity and a large walk-in closet.
- Another full bath serves the two additional bedrooms at the opposite end of the home.

Plan E-1426

Bedrooms: 3	Baths: 2

Living Area:	
Main floor	1,420 sq. ft.
Total Living Area:	**1,420 sq. ft.**
Garage and storage	540 sq. ft.
Exterior Wall Framing:	2x6

Foundation Options:
Crawlspace
Slab
(All plans can be built with your choice of foundation and framing. A generic conversion diagram is available. See order form.)

BLUEPRINT PRICE CODE: **A**

6' HIGH WOOD PRIVACY FENCE

BATH — CLO. — LINEN

MASTER SUITE 15' x 14'

PORCH 10' x 10'

DINING 12' x 10'

BED RM. 13' x 12'

BAR — SINK

BATH — HALL

LIVING 18' x 16'

KITCHEN 12' x 10'
RANGE — REF — D.W.

UTIL 8' x 6'

STOR 12' x 5'

BED RM. 13' x 12'

SLOPE — CEILING

PORCH 12' x 6'

HEAT & A/C — W.H.

ATTIC STAIRS

GARAGE 22' x 21'

56'

52'

MAIN FLOOR

Plan E-1426

PRICES AND DETAILS
ON PAGES 12-15

Distinctive Inside and Out

- A decorative columned entry, shuttered windows and a facade of stucco and stone offer a distinct look to this economical one-story home.
- The focal point of the interior is the huge, central family room. The room is enhanced by a dramatic corner fireplace, a 15-ft.-high vaulted ceiling and a neat serving bar that extends from the kitchen and includes a wet bar.
- A decorative plant shelf adorns the entrance to the adjoining breakfast room, which features a lovely bay window. The kitchen offers a pantry and a pass-through to the family room.
- The formal dining room is easy to reach from both the kitchen and the family room, and is set off with columned arches and a raised ceiling.
- The secluded master suite boasts a vaulted private bath with dual sinks, an oval garden tub, a separate toilet room and a large walk-in closet.
- Two more bedrooms share a second bath at the other end of the home.

Plan FB-5001-SAVA

Bedrooms: 3	Baths: 2
Living Area:	
Main floor	1,429 sq. ft.
Total Living Area:	**1,429 sq. ft.**
Daylight basement	1,429 sq. ft.
Garage and storage	436 sq. ft.
Exterior Wall Framing:	2x4
Foundation Options:	
Daylight basement	
Crawlspace	
Slab	

(All plans can be built with your choice of foundation and framing. A generic conversion diagram is available. See order form.)

BLUEPRINT PRICE CODE:	**A**

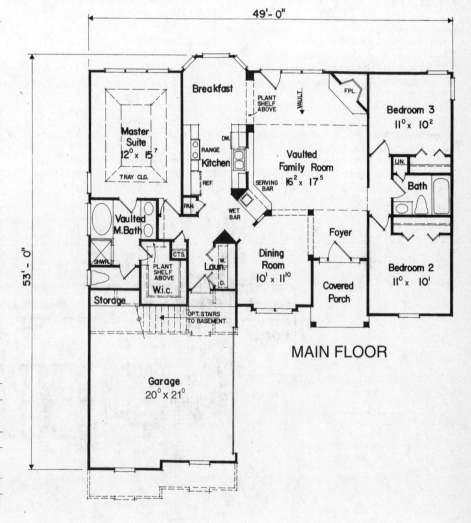

MAIN FLOOR

European Flair

- Arched window arrangements, striking stone and metal roofing above the garage give this home a European flair.
- To the left of the tiled foyer, the living room features a 10-ft. vaulted ceiling and a warm fireplace. A tall window bathes the entire room in sunlight.
- The adjacent dining room includes a pass-through to the kitchen and access to a lovely deck or screen porch.
- An inviting bayed breakfast nook is a great spot for a leisurely cup of coffee. The nook shares a 10½-ft. vaulted

ceiling with the gourmet kitchen, which includes a pantry closet.
- In the master suite, a 10-ft. vaulted ceiling creates an open feel. Two walk-in closets and a private bath with a dual-sink vanity and a separate tub and shower are added conveniences.
- A secondary bedroom nearby is serviced by a full hall bath.
- Double doors introduce a quiet den with an extra door for easy bathroom access. The den, which could also serve as a guest room or an informal gathering area, features a ceiling that jumps to 10 ft. at the window.

Plan B-94024

Bedrooms: 2+	Baths: 2
Living Area:	
Main floor	1,431 sq. ft.
Total Living Area:	**1,431 sq. ft.**
Standard basement	1,431 sq. ft.
Garage	380 sq. ft.
Exterior Wall Framing:	2x6

Foundation Options:

Standard basement
(All plans can be built with your choice of foundation and framing. A generic conversion diagram is available. See order form.)

BLUEPRINT PRICE CODE: A

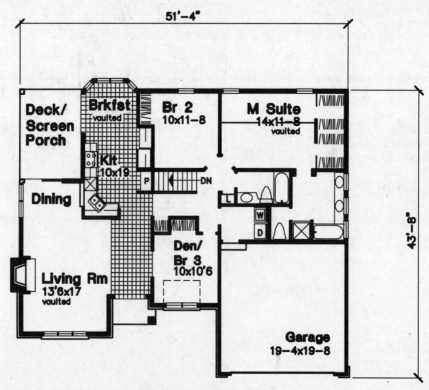

MAIN FLOOR

Plan B-94024

PRICES AND DETAILS ON PAGES 12-15

Quality Details Inside and Out

- A sparkling stucco finish, an eye-catching roofline and elegant window treatments hint at the quality features found inside this exquisite home.
- The airy entry opens to a large, central living room, which is embellished with a 10-ft. ceiling and a dramatic fireplace.
- The living room flows into a nice-sized dining area. A covered side porch expands the entertaining area.
- A functional eating bar and pantry are featured in the adjoining U-shaped kitchen. The nearby hallway to the garage neatly stores a washer, a dryer and a laundry sink.
- Secluded to the back of the home is a private master suite with a romantic sitting area and a large walk-in closet. The master bath offers dual sinks and an exciting oval tub.
- Two secondary bedrooms and another bath are located on the other side of the living room and entry.

Plan E-1435	
Bedrooms: 3	**Baths:** 2
Living Area:	
Main floor	1,442 sq. ft.
Total Living Area:	**1,442 sq. ft.**
Garage and storage	516 sq. ft.
Exterior Wall Framing:	2x4
Foundation Options:	
Crawlspace	
Slab	

(All plans can be built with your choice of foundation and framing. A generic conversion diagram is available. See order form.)

| **BLUEPRINT PRICE CODE:** | **A** |

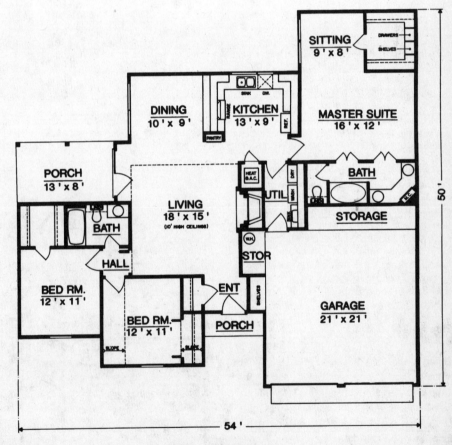

MAIN FLOOR

Victorian Form

- This beautiful home flaunts true-to-form Victorian styling in a modest one-story.
- A delightful, covered front porch and a stunning, sidelighted entry give way to the welcoming foyer.
- The foyer flows into the Great Room, which is warmed by a corner fireplace and topped by a 10-ft. stepped ceiling.
- Sliding French doors open to the backyard from both the Great Room and the adjoining formal dining room.
- On the other side of the open kitchen, a turreted breakfast room overlooks the front porch with cheery windows under an incredible 16-ft. ceiling!
- The restful master suite is graced by a charming window seat and crowned by a 10-ft. stepped ceiling. A dressing area leads to the master bath, which offers a separate tub and shower.
- To the right of the foyer, two more bedrooms share a hall bath. One bedroom features an impressive 11-ft. vaulted ceiling.
- Unless otherwise specified, all rooms have 9-ft. ceilings.

Plan AX-94319

Bedrooms: 3	Baths: 2
Living Area:	
Main floor	1,466 sq. ft.
Total Living Area:	**1,466 sq. ft.**
Standard basement	1,498 sq. ft.
Garage, storage and utility	483 sq. ft.
Exterior Wall Framing:	2x4

Foundation Options:

Standard basement
Crawlspace
Slab
(All plans can be built with your choice of foundation and framing. A generic conversion diagram is available. See order form.)

BLUEPRINT PRICE CODE: A

VIEW INTO BREAKFAST ROOM

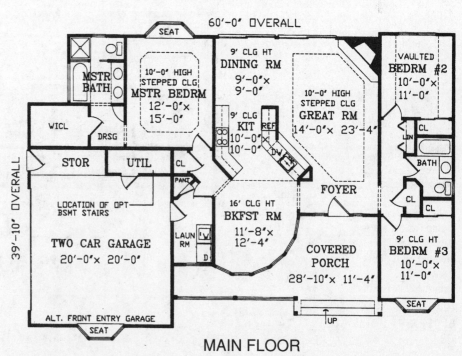

MAIN FLOOR

Plan AX-94319

PRICES AND DETAILS ON PAGES 12-15

Refined One-Story

- A symmetrical roofline and a stucco facade with corner quoins and keystone accents add a refined look to this elegant one-story.
- The eye-catching entry leads into a surprisingly spacious interior, beginning with a family room that features an 11-ft., 8-in.-high ceiling and a handsome window-flanked fireplace.
- The kitchen showcases an angled serving bar that faces the sunny breakfast room. A French door between the breakfast room and the formal dining room opens to a covered patio for more dining and entertaining space.
- The fantastic master suite features an elegant 10-ft. tray ceiling. The superb private bath boasts a 13-ft. vaulted ceiling, an overhead plant shelf, a garden tub and a walk-in closet.
- The two front-facing bedrooms share a hall bath that includes a vanity with knee space.

Plan FB-1531

Bedrooms: 3	Baths: 2
Living Area:	
Main floor	1,531 sq. ft.
Total Living Area:	**1,531 sq. ft.**
Garage	440 sq. ft.
Exterior Wall Framing:	2x4

Foundation Options:

Crawlspace

Slab

(All plans can be built with your choice of foundation and framing. A generic conversion diagram is available. See order form.)

BLUEPRINT PRICE CODE: B

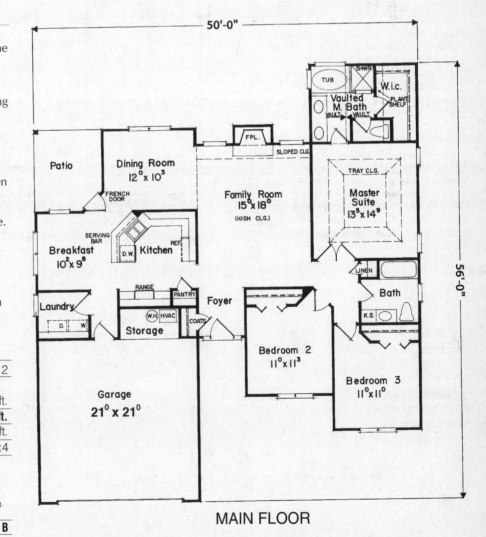

MAIN FLOOR

One-Story with Impact

- Striking gables, a brick facade and an elegant sidelighted entry give this one-story plenty of impact.
- The impressive interior spaces begin with an 11-ft., 8-in. raised ceiling in the foyer. To the left of the foyer, decorative columns and a large picture window grace the dining room.
- The wonderful living spaces center around a huge family room, which features a 14-ft.-high vaulted ceiling and another pair of columns that separate it from the hall. A stunning fireplace is framed by a window and a beautiful French door.
- The open kitchen and breakfast area features a built-in desk, a pantry closet and a pass-through above the sink.
- An elegant 10-ft. tray ceiling is featured in the master suite, which also boasts a 13-ft. vaulted bath with a garden spa tub, a separate shower, a big walk-in closet and an attractive plant shelf.

Plan FB-1553

Bedrooms: 3	Baths: 2
Living Area:	
Main floor	1,553 sq. ft.
Total Living Area:	**1,553 sq. ft.**
Daylight basement	1,553 sq. ft.
Garage	410 sq. ft.
Exterior Wall Framing:	2x4

Foundation Options:

Daylight basement

Crawlspace

Slab

(All plans can be built with your choice of foundation and framing. A generic conversion diagram is available. See order form.)

BLUEPRINT PRICE CODE: B

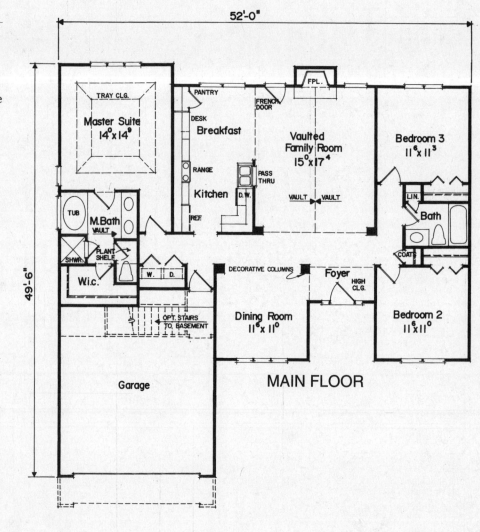

MAIN FLOOR

Plan FB-1553

Elegant Touch

- A stunning exterior of brick, siding and copper flashing adds an elegant touch to this feature-filled one-story home.
- The recessed sidelighted entry opens directly into the bright and airy family room, which boasts a 12-ft. ceiling and a striking window-flanked fireplace.
- The adjacent formal dining room features a 9-ft. tray ceiling and includes a French door to a backyard patio.
- Designed with the gourmet in mind, the spacious kitchen offers a pantry, an angled eating bar and a sunny breakfast area. A French door accesses a covered back porch.
- Enhanced by a 14-ft. vaulted ceiling and decorative plant shelves, the master suite unfolds to a sitting area and a roomy walk-in closet. The vaulted master bath showcases a garden tub, a separate shower and a functional dual-sink vanity with knee space.
- On the opposite side of the home, two additional bedrooms are serviced by a second full bath.
- A laundry room is conveniently located between the entry and the garage.

Plan APS-1516

Bedrooms: 3	Baths: 2
Living Area:	
Main floor	1,593 sq. ft.
Total Living Area:	**1,593 sq. ft.**
Garage	482 sq. ft.
Exterior Wall Framing:	2x4

Foundation Options:
Slab
(All plans can be built with your choice of foundation and framing. A generic conversion diagram is available. See order form.)

BLUEPRINT PRICE CODE:	B

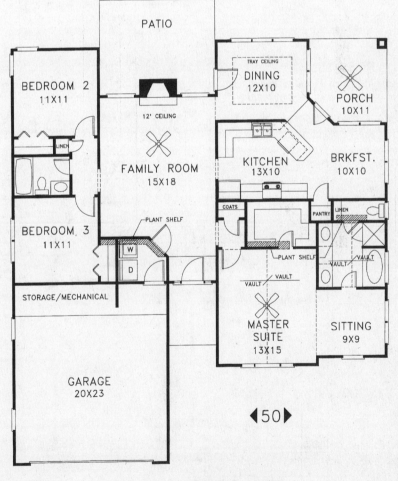

MAIN FLOOR

Friendly Country Charm

- An inviting front porch welcomes you to this friendly one-story home.
- The porch opens to a spacious central living room with a warm fireplace and functional built-in storage shelves.
- The bay window of the adjoining dining room allows a view of the backyard.

The dining area also enjoys an eating bar provided by the adjacent walk-through kitchen.
- The nice-sized kitchen also has a windowed sink and easy access to the laundry room and carport.
- Three bedrooms and two baths occupy the sleeping wing. The oversized master bedroom features a lovely boxed-out window, two walk-in closets and a private bath. The secondary bedrooms share the second full bath.

Plan J-8692	
Bedrooms: 3	**Baths:** 2
Living Area:	
Main floor	1,633 sq. ft.
Total Living Area:	**1,633 sq. ft.**
Standard basement	1,633 sq. ft.
Carport	380 sq. ft.
Exterior Wall Framing:	2x4

Foundation Options:
Standard basement
Crawlspace
Slab
(All plans can be built with your choice of foundation and framing. A generic conversion diagram is available. See order form.)

BLUEPRINT PRICE CODE: B

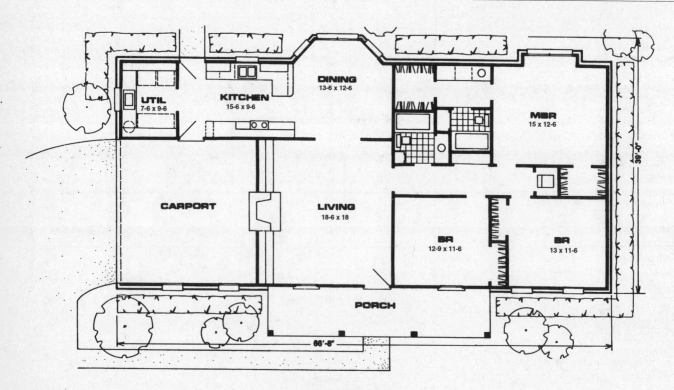

MAIN FLOOR

Plan J-8692

Distinctive and Elegant

- A distinctive look is captured in the exterior of this elegant one-story. Half-round transoms grace the three glass doors that open to the columned, covered front porch.

- The spacious living room at the center of the homer commands attention, with its 15-ft. ceiling and inviting fireplace. A glass door flanked by windows opens to a skylighted porch, which is also accessible from the secondary bedroom at the back of the home.

- The unique dining room overlooks the two backyard porches and boasts an elegant octagonal design, shaped by columns and cased openings.

- A 14-ft. sloped, skylighted ceiling adds drama to the gourmet kitchen, which also showcases an angled cooktop bar and a windowed sink. Laundry facilities and storage space are nearby.

- The luxurious master suite is secluded at the rear of the home, with private access to the porch. The sumptuous master bath features an oval spa tub, a separate shower, dual vanities and a huge walk-in closet.

Plan E-1628

Bedrooms: 3	Baths: 2
Living Area:	
Main floor	1,655 sq. ft.
Total Living Area:	**1,655 sq. ft.**
Garage and storage	549 sq. ft.
Exterior Wall Framing:	2x6

Foundation Options:

Crawlspace
Slab
(All plans can be built with your choice of foundation and framing. A generic conversion diagram is available. See order form.)

BLUEPRINT PRICE CODE: B

MAIN FLOOR

Fine Dining

- This fine stucco home showcases a huge round-top window arrangement, which augments the central dining room with its 14½-ft. ceiling.
- A cute covered porch opens to the bright foyer, where a 13-ft.-high ceiling extends past a decorative column to the airy Great Room.
- The sunny dining room merges with the Great Room, which features a warm fireplace, a kitchen pass-through and a French door to the backyard.
- The kitchen boasts a pantry closet, a nice serving bar and an angled sink. The vaulted breakfast nook with an optional bay hosts casual meals.
- The secluded master suite has a tray ceiling and a vaulted bath with a dual-sink vanity, a large garden tub and a separate shower. Across the home, two secondary bedrooms share another full bath.

Plan FB-5351-GENE

Bedrooms: 3	**Baths:** 2

Living Area:	
Main floor	1,670 sq. ft.
Total Living Area:	**1,670 sq. ft.**
Daylight basement	1,670 sq. ft.
Garage	400 sq. ft.
Exterior Wall Framing:	2x4

Foundation Options:
Daylight basement
Crawlspace
(All plans can be built with your choice of foundation and framing. A generic conversion diagram is available. See order form.)

BLUEPRINT PRICE CODE:	B

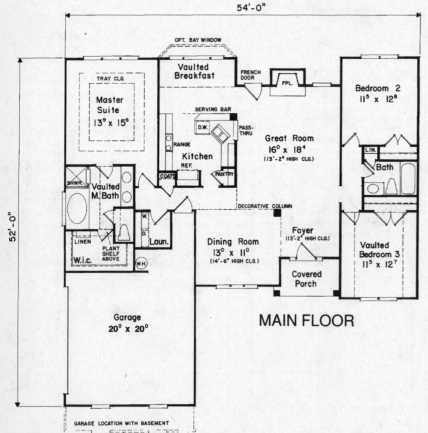

MAIN FLOOR

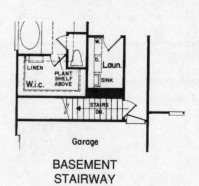

BASEMENT STAIRWAY LOCATION

TO ORDER THIS BLUEPRINT, CALL TOLL-FREE 1-800-820-1283

Plan FB-5351-GENE

PRICES AND DETAILS ON PAGES 12-15

Captivating Showpiece

- This design is sure to be the showpiece of the neighborhood, with its captivating blend of traditional and contemporary features.
- The angled front porch creates an eye-catching look. Inside, the foyer, the dining room and the Great Room are expanded by 9-ft., 4-in. tray ceilings and separated by columns.
- The dining room features a spectacular arched window, while the spacious Great Room hosts a fireplace framed by windows overlooking the rear terrace.
- The glass-filled breakfast room is given added impact by a 9-ft., 4-in. tray ceiling. The adjoining kitchen offers an expansive island counter with an eating bar and a cooktop.
- A wonderful TV room or home office views out to the front porch.
- The master suite is highlighted by a 9-ft., 10-in. tray ceiling and a sunny sitting area with a large picture window topped by an arched transom.

Plan AX-92322

Bedrooms: 3+	Baths: 2
Living Area:	
Main floor	1,699 sq. ft.
Total Living Area:	**1,699 sq. ft.**
Standard basement	1,740 sq. ft.
Garage	480 sq. ft.
Exterior Wall Framing:	2x4

Foundation Options:

Standard basement

Crawlspace

Slab

(All plans can be built with your choice of foundation and framing. A generic conversion diagram is available. See order form.)

BLUEPRINT PRICE CODE: B

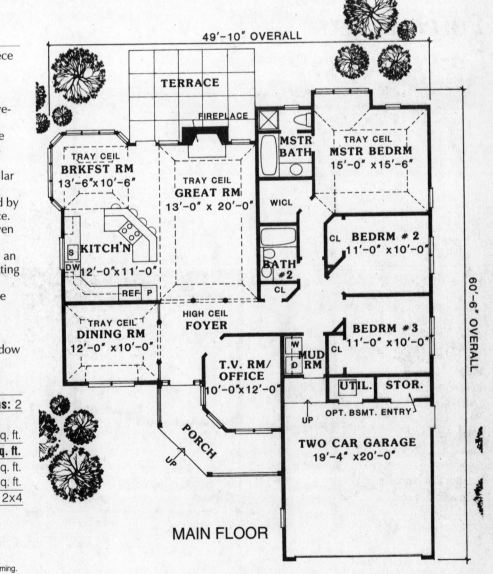

MAIN FLOOR

Porch Offers Three Entries

- Showy window treatments, stately columns and three sets of French doors give this Plantation-style home an inviting exterior.
- High 12-ft. ceilings in the living room, dining room and kitchen add volume to the economically-sized home.
- A corner fireplace and a view to the back porch are found in the living room. The porch is accessed from a door in the dining room.
- The adjoining kitchen features an angled snack bar that easily serves the dining room and the casual eating area.
- The secluded master suite offers a cathedral ceiling, a walk-in closet and a luxurious private bath with a spa tub and a separate shower.
- Across the home, two additional bedrooms share a second full bath.

Plan E-1602

Bedrooms: 3	Baths: 2
Living Area:	
Main floor	1,672 sq. ft.
Total Living Area:	**1,672 sq. ft.**
Standard basement	1,672 sq. ft.
Garage	484 sq. ft.
Exterior Wall Framing:	2x6

Foundation Options:

Standard basement
Crawlspace
Slab

(All plans can be built with your choice of foundation and framing. A generic conversion diagram is available. See order form.)

BLUEPRINT PRICE CODE:	B

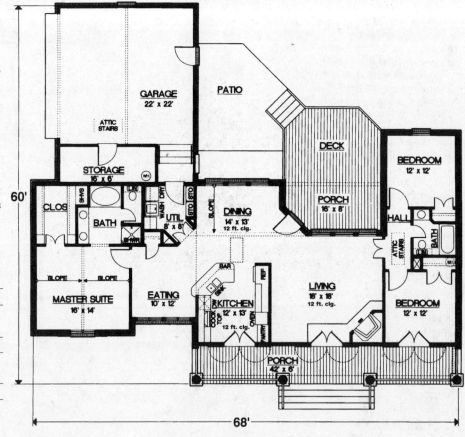

MAIN FLOOR

Plan E-1602
PRICES AND DETAILS ON PAGES 12-15

Smashing Master Suite!

- Corniced gables accented with arched louvers and a covered front porch with striking columns take this one-story design beyond the ordinary.
- The vaulted ceiling in the foyer rises to join the 19-ft. vaulted ceiling in the family room. A central fireplace heats the casual areas and is framed by a window and a French door.
- An angled serving bar/snack counter connects the family room to the sunny dining room and kitchen. The adjoining breakfast room has easy access to the garage, the optional basement and the laundry room with a plant shelf.
- The master suite is simply smashing, with a 10-ft. tray ceiling and private access to the backyard. The master bath has an 11½-ft. vaulted ceiling and all the amenities, while the 13-ft.-high vaulted sitting area offers an optional fireplace.

Plan FB-1671

Bedrooms: 3	Baths: 2
Living Area:	
Main floor	1,671 sq. ft.
Total Living Area:	**1,671 sq. ft.**
Daylight basement	1,671 sq. ft.
Garage	240 sq. ft.
Exterior Wall Framing:	2x4

Foundation Options:

Daylight basement

Crawlspace

(All plans can be built with your choice of foundation and framing. A generic conversion diagram is available. See order form.)

BLUEPRINT PRICE CODE:	B

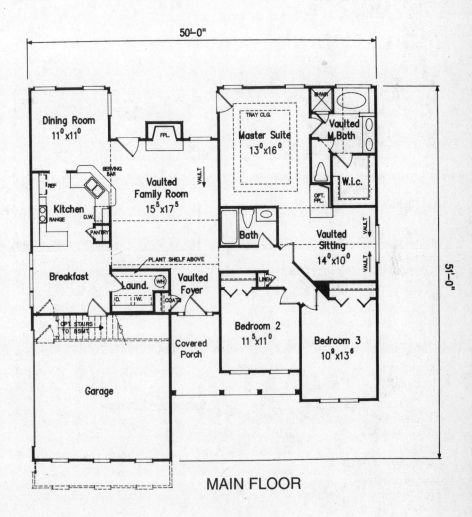

MAIN FLOOR

Dramatic Dining Room

- The highlight of this lovely one-story design is its dramatic dining room, which boasts a 14-ft.-high ceiling and a soaring window wall.
- The airy foyer ushers guests through a 14-ft.-high arched opening and into the 18-ft. vaulted Great Room, which is warmed by an inviting fireplace.
- The kitchen features a large pantry, a serving bar and a handy pass-through to the Great Room. The bright breakfast area offers a convenient laundry closet and outdoor access.
- The two secondary bedrooms share a compartmentalized bath.
- The removed master suite features a 14-ft. tray ceiling, overhead plant shelves and an adjoining 13½-ft. vaulted sitting room. An exciting garden tub is found in the luxurious master bath.

Plan FB-5008-ALLE

Bedrooms: 3	Baths: 2
Living Area:	
Main floor	1,715 sq. ft.
Total Living Area:	**1,715 sq. ft.**
Daylight basement	1,715 sq. ft.
Garage	400 sq. ft.
Exterior Wall Framing:	2x4

Foundation Options:
Daylight basement
Crawlspace
Slab
(All plans can be built with your choice of foundation and framing. A generic conversion diagram is available. See order form.)

BLUEPRINT PRICE CODE:	B

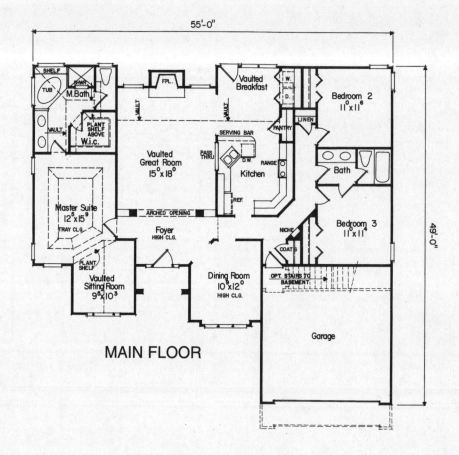

MAIN FLOOR

TO ORDER THIS BLUEPRINT, CALL TOLL-FREE 1-800-820-1283

Plan FB-5008-ALLE

PRICES AND DETAILS ON PAGES 12-15

Breathtaking Open Space

- Soaring ceilings and an open floor plan add breathtaking volume to this charming country-style home.
- The inviting covered-porch entrance opens into the spacious living room, which boasts a spectacular 21-ft.-high cathedral ceiling. Two overhead dormers fill the area with natural light, while a fireplace adds warmth.
- Also under the cathedral ceiling, the kitchen and bayed breakfast room share an eating bar. Skylights brighten the convenient laundry room and the computer room, which provides access to a covered rear porch.
- The secluded master bedroom offers private access to another covered porch. The skylighted master bath has a walk-in closet and a 10-ft. sloped ceiling above a whirlpool tub.
- Optional upper-floor areas provide future expansion space for the needs of a growing family.

Plan J-9302

Bedrooms: 3	Baths: 2
Living Area:	
Main floor	1,745 sq. ft.
Total Living Area:	**1,745 sq. ft.**
Upper floor (future area)	500 sq. ft.
Future area above garage	241 sq. ft.
Standard basement	1,745 sq. ft.
Garage and storage	559 sq. ft.
Exterior Wall Framing:	2x4

Foundation Options:

Standard basement
Crawlspace
Slab

(All plans can be built with your choice of foundation and framing. A generic conversion diagram is available. See order form.)

BLUEPRINT PRICE CODE: B

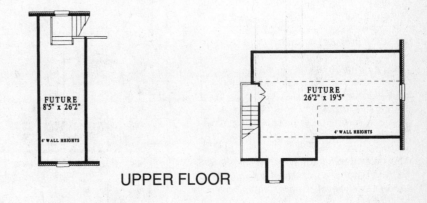

UPPER FLOOR

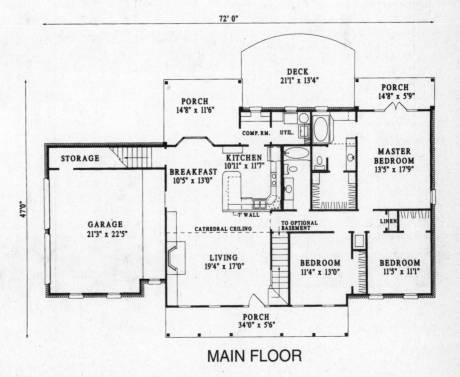

MAIN FLOOR

Enticing Interior

- Filled with elegant features, this modern country home's exciting floor plan is as impressive as it is innovative.
- Past the inviting columned porch, the entrance gallery flows into the spacious living room/dining room area.
- Boasting a 14-ft.-high sloped ceiling, the living room is enhanced by a semi-circular window bay and includes a handsome fireplace. The adjoining dining room offers sliding glass doors to a backyard terrace.
- The skylighted kitchen features an eating bar that serves the sunny bayed dinette. A convenient half-bath and a laundry/mudroom are nearby.
- Brightened by a bay window, the luxurious master bedroom shows off his-and-hers walk-in closets. The master bath showcases a whirlpool garden tub under a glass sunroof.
- Two additional bedrooms share a skylighted hallway bath.

Plan K-685-DA

Bedrooms: 3	Baths: 2½
Living Area:	
Main floor	1,760 sq. ft.
Total Living Area:	**1,760 sq. ft.**
Standard basement	1,700 sq. ft.
Garage	482 sq. ft.
Exterior Wall Framing:	2x4 or 2x6

Foundation Options:

Standard basement
Slab
(All plans can be built with your choice of foundation and framing. A generic conversion diagram is available. See order form.)

BLUEPRINT PRICE CODE:	B

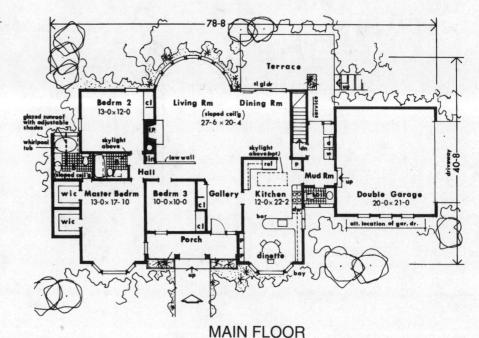

MAIN FLOOR

VIEW INTO LIVING AND DINING ROOMS

Plan K-685-DA

PRICES AND DETAILS ON PAGES 12-15

Country Charm, Cottage Look

- An interesting combination of stone and stucco gives a charming cottage look to this attactive country home.
- Off the inviting sidelighted entry, the formal dining room is defined by striking columns.
- The dining room expands into the living room, which boasts a fireplace and built-in shelves. A French door provides access to a cute backyard patio.
- The galley-style kitchen unfolds to a sunny morning room.
- All of the living areas are expanded by 10-ft. ceilings.
- The master bedroom features a 10-ft. ceiling and a nice bayed sitting area. The luxurious master bath boasts an exciting garden tub and a glass-block shower, as well as a big walk-in closet and a dressing area with two sinks.
- Across the home, two additional bedrooms with walk-in closets and private dressing areas share a tidy compartmentalized bath.

Plan DD-1790

Bedrooms: 3	Baths: 2½
Living Area:	
Main floor	1,790 sq. ft.
Total Living Area:	**1,790 sq. ft.**
Standard basement	1,790 sq. ft.
Garage	438 sq. ft.
Exterior Wall Framing:	2x4

Foundation Options:

Standard basement

Crawlspace

Slab

(All plans can be built with your choice of foundation and framing. A generic conversion diagram is available. See order form.)

BLUEPRINT PRICE CODE: **B**

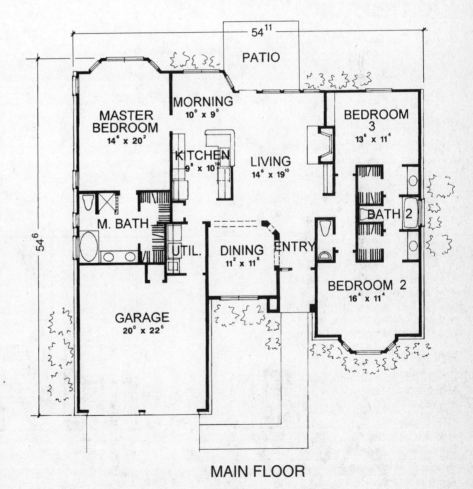

MAIN FLOOR

Gracious Demeanor

- Elegant windows and a covered porch adorn the facade of this country-style home, giving it a gracious demeanor.
- Directly ahead of the ornate foyer, the skylighted living room boasts a cozy fireplace flanked by shelves and cabinets. An impressive 12-ft., 5-in. vaulted ceiling rises overhead, while oversized windows provide great backyard views.
- The adjoining dining room is topped by an elaborate 10-ft. vaulted ceiling and offers a door to a skylighted porch. The porch unfolds to a large patio and accesses the huge garage.
- Behind double doors, the master bedroom presents a 12-ft., 5-in. vaulted ceiling. The master bath flaunts a garden tub and a private toilet.
- At the front of the home, two good-sized bedrooms share a full bath near the laundry room. The den or study may be used as an extra bedroom.

Plan J-9421

Bedrooms: 3+	Baths: 2
Living Area:	
Main floor	1,792 sq. ft.
Total Living Area:	**1,792 sq. ft.**
Standard basement	1,792 sq. ft.
Garage and storage	597 sq. ft.
Exterior Wall Framing:	2x4

Foundation Options:

Standard basement
Crawlspace
Slab

(All plans can be built with your choice of foundation and framing. A generic conversion diagram is available. See order form.)

BLUEPRINT PRICE CODE:	**B**

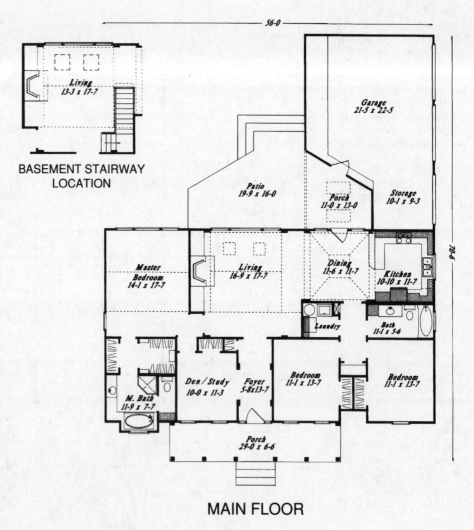

BASEMENT STAIRWAY LOCATION

MAIN FLOOR

TO ORDER THIS BLUEPRINT, CALL TOLL-FREE 1-800-820-1283

Plan J-9421

PRICES AND DETAILS ON PAGES 12-15

Stunning Style

- The stunning detailing of this three-bedroom stucco home includes a stately roofline, round louvers and a sidelighted entry door topped with a half-round transom.
- The open floor plan begins at the foyer, where a decorative column is all that separates the dining room from the living room. Lovely French doors and windows overlook the backyard, while a 13½-ft. ceiling creates a dramatic effect for this spacious area.

- A sunny breakfast room and a great kitchen with a huge serving bar adjoin a 14½-ft.-high vaulted family room.
- A laundry/mudroom lies near the garage, which is supplemented by a handy storage or shop area.
- The opulent master suite has an 11-ft. tray ceiling, a rear window wall and a French door to the outdoors. The master bath includes a spa tub, a separate shower, a spacious walk-in closet and a dual-sink vanity with a sit-down makeup area. Another full bath serves the two remaining bedrooms.

Plan FB-1802

Bedrooms: 3	Baths: 2
Living Area:	
Main floor	1,802 sq. ft.
Total Living Area:	**1,802 sq. ft.**
Garage and storage	492 sq. ft.
Exterior Wall Framing:	2x4

Foundation Options:
Crawlspace
Slab
(All plans can be built with your choice of foundation and framing. A generic conversion diagram is available. See order form.)

BLUEPRINT PRICE CODE: **B**

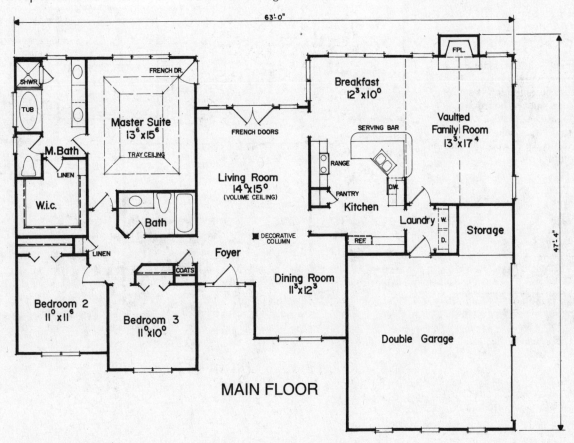

MAIN FLOOR

Dormered Delight

- Twin dormers add exterior character to this traditionally appealing one-story plan.
- The dormers add interior excitement as well, allowing sunlight to stream into the entry, living and formal dining rooms from their vaulted ceilings.
- The rear-facing informal living area includes kitchen, breakfast bay and family room with fireplace.
- The master suite, which is set apart from the secondary bedrooms, for privacy, features a lavish master bath with a large walk-in closet, double vanity, and separate shower and tub under glass.

Plan DD-1818

Bedrooms: 3	Baths: 2

Space:

Total living area:	1,807 sq. ft.
Garage:	380 sq. ft.
Storage area:	25 sq. ft.

Exterior Wall Framing:	2x4

Ceiling Heights:

Main floor:	8, 10'

Foundation options:
Crawlspace.
Slab.
(Foundation & framing conversion diagram available — see order form.)

Blueprint Price Code:	B

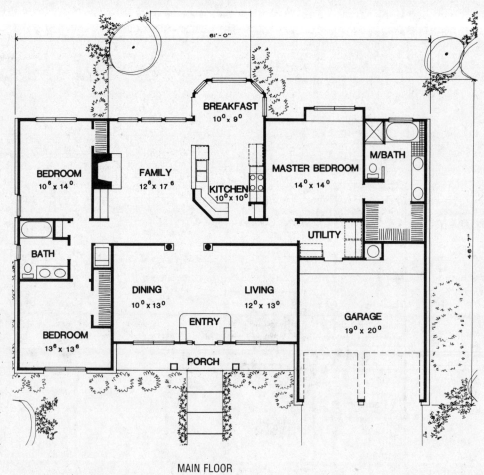

MAIN FLOOR

TO ORDER THIS BLUEPRINT, CALL TOLL-FREE 1-800-820-1283

Plan DD-1818

PRICES AND DETAILS ON PAGES 12-15

Delightful Great Room

- An expansive Great Room with a 10-ft. vaulted ceiling, a warm corner fireplace and an angled wet bar highlights this tastefully appointed home.
- On the exterior, decorative plants thrive in the lush wraparound planter that leads to the sheltered entry. The foyer is brightened by a sidelight and a skylight.
- To the left, the kitchen offers an island cooktop with lots room for food preparation and serving. The bayed breakfast nook is enhanced by bright windows and a 12½-ft. vaulted ceiling.
- Formal dining is hosted in the space adjoining the Great Room. Graced by a lovely bay window, the room also offers French doors to a covered patio.
- In the sleeping wing of the home, the master bedroom features a sitting area and a walk-in closet. The private master bath boasts a relaxing Jacuzzi tub.
- Two secondary bedrooms share a full bath nearby. Laundry facilities are also convenient.

Plan S-52394

Bedrooms: 3	Baths: 2
Living Area:	
Main floor	1,841 sq. ft.
Total Living Area:	**1,841 sq. ft.**
Standard basement	1,789 sq. ft.
Garage	432 sq. ft.
Exterior Wall Framing:	2x6

Foundation Options:

Standard basement
Crawlspace
Slab

(All plans can be built with your choice of foundation and framing. A generic conversion diagram is available. See order form.)

BLUEPRINT PRICE CODE:	B

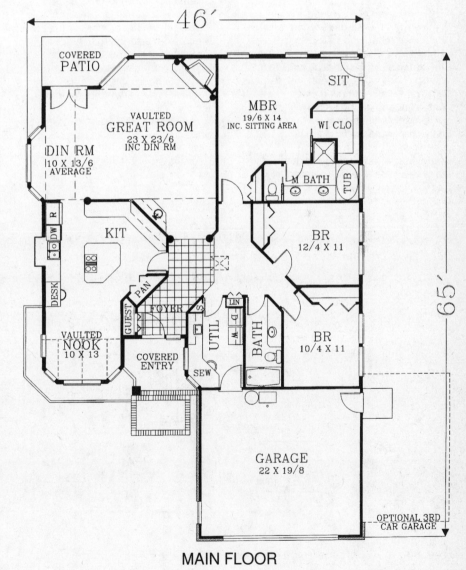

MAIN FLOOR

Open Invitation

- The wide front porch of this friendly country farmhouse presents an open invitation to all who visit.
- Highlighted by a round-topped transom, the home's entrance opens directly into the spacious living room, which features a warm fireplace flanked by windows.
- The adjoining dining area is enhanced by a lovely bay window and is easily serviced by the updated kitchen's angled snack bar.
- A bright sun room off the kitchen provides a great space for informal meals or relaxation. Access to a covered backyard porch is nearby.
- The good-sized master bedroom is secluded from the other sleeping areas. The lavish master bath includes a garden tub, a separate shower, a dual-sink vanity and a walk-in closet.
- Two more bedrooms share a second full bath. A laundry/utility room is nearby.
- An additional 1,007 sq. ft. of living space can be made available by finishing the upper floor.
- All ceilings are 9 ft. high for added spaciousness.

Plan J-91078	
Bedrooms: 3	**Baths:** 2
Living Area:	
Main floor	1,846 sq. ft.
Total Living Area:	**1,846 sq. ft.**
Future upper floor	1,007 sq. ft.
Standard basement	1,846 sq. ft.
Garage	484 sq. ft.
Exterior Wall Framing:	2x6

Foundation Options:
Standard basement
Crawlspace
Slab
(All plans can be built with your choice of foundation and framing. A generic conversion diagram is available. See order form.)

BLUEPRINT PRICE CODE:	B

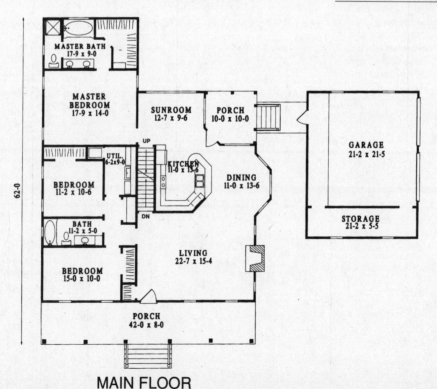

MAIN FLOOR

Plan J-91078

Impressive Master Suite

- This attractive one-story home features an impressive master suite located apart from the secondary bedrooms.
- A lovely front porch opens to the entry, which flows to the formal dining room, the rear-oriented living room and the secondary bedroom wing.
- The living room boasts a large corner fireplace, a ceiling that slopes to 11 ft. and access to a backyard patio.
- A U-shaped kitchen services the dining room and its own eating area. It also boasts a built-in desk, a handy pantry closet and access to the nearby laundry room and carport.
- The wide master bedroom hosts a lavish master bath with a spa tub, a separate shower and his-and-hers dressing areas.
- Across the home, the two secondary bedrooms share another full bath.

Plan E-1818

Bedrooms: 3	Baths: 2
Living Area:	
Main floor	1,868 sq. ft.
Total Living Area:	**1,868 sq. ft.**
Carport	484 sq. ft.
Storage	132 sq. ft.
Exterior Wall Framing:	2x6

Foundation Options:

Crawlspace
Slab
(All plans can be built with your choice of foundation and framing. A generic conversion diagram is available. See order form.)

BLUEPRINT PRICE CODE: **B**

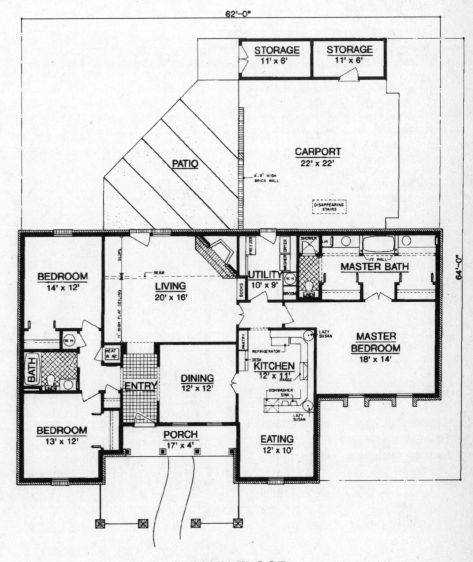

MAIN FLOOR

Attainable Luxury

- This traditional ranch home offers a large, central living room with a 12-ft. ceiling, a corner fireplace and an adjoining patio.
- The U-shaped kitchen easily services both the formal dining room and the bayed eating area.
- The luxurious master suite features a large bath with separate vanities and dressing areas.
- Two secondary bedrooms share a second full bath.
- A covered carport boasts a decorative brick wall, attic space above and two additional storage areas.

Plan E-1812

Bedrooms: 3	Baths: 2
Living Area:	
Main floor	1,860 sq. ft.
Total Living Area:	**1,860 sq. ft.**
Carport	484 sq. ft.
Storage	132 sq. ft.
Exterior Wall Framing:	2x6

Foundation Options:

Crawlspace

Slab

(All plans can be built with your choice of foundation and framing. A generic conversion diagram is available. See order form.)

BLUEPRINT PRICE CODE:	B

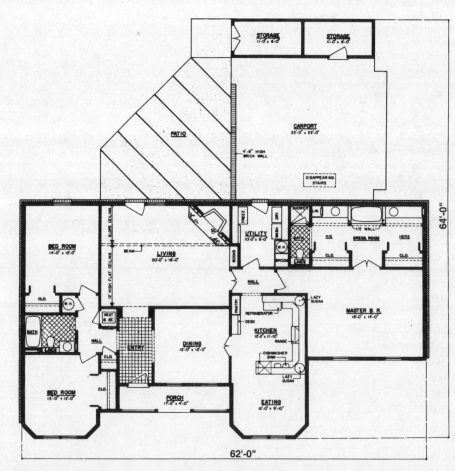

MAIN FLOOR

Plan E-1812

PRICES AND DETAILS ON PAGES 12-15

Classic Ranch

- With decorative brick quoins, a columned porch and stylish dormers, the exterior of this classic one-story provides an interesting blend of Early American and European design.
- Flowing from the foyer, the bay-windowed dining room is enhanced by an 11½-ft.-high stepped ceiling.
- The spacious Great Room, separated from the dining room by a columned arch, features a stepped ceiling, a built-in media center and a striking fireplace. Lovely French doors lead to a big backyard patio.
- The breakfast room, which shares an eating bar with the kitchen, boasts a ceiling that slopes to 12 feet. French doors access a covered rear porch.
- The master bedroom has a 10-ft. tray ceiling, a sunny bay window and a roomy walk-in closet. The master bath features a whirlpool tub in a bayed nook and a separate shower.
- The front-facing bedroom is enhanced by a 10-ft.-high vaulted area over an arched transom window.

Plan AX-93304

Bedrooms: 3	Baths: 2
Living Area:	
Main floor	1,860 sq. ft.
Total Living Area:	**1,860 sq. ft.**
Standard basement	1,860 sq. ft.
Garage/utility/storage	434 sq. ft.
Exterior Wall Framing:	2x4

Foundation Options:

Standard basement
Crawlspace
Slab

(All plans can be built with your choice of foundation and framing. A generic conversion diagram is available. See order form.)

BLUEPRINT PRICE CODE: **B**

VIEW INTO GREAT ROOM

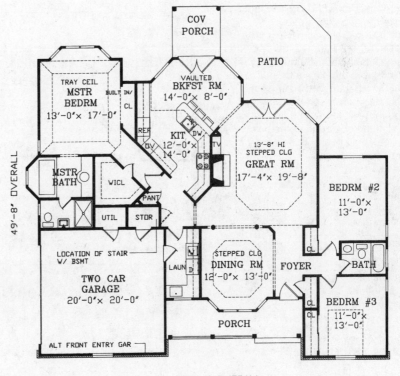

MAIN FLOOR

Showy One-Story

- Dramatic windows embellish the exterior of this showy one-story home.
- Inside, the entry provides a sweeping view of the living room, where sliding glass doors open to the backyard patio and flank a dramatic fireplace.
- Skylights accent the living room's 12-ft. sloped ceiling, while arched openings define the formal dining room.
- Double doors lead from the dining room to the kitchen and informal eating area. The kitchen features a built-in work desk and a pantry. An oversized utility room adjoins the kitchen and accesses the two-car garage.
- A 10-ft. tray ceiling adorns the master suite. The private bath is accented with a skylight above the fabulous fan-shaped marble tub. His-and-hers vanities, a separate shower and a huge walk-in closet are also featured.
- Two more bedrooms and a full bath are located at the other end of the home.
- The front-facing bedroom boasts a 12-ft. sloped ceiling.

Plan E-1830

Bedrooms: 3	Baths: 2
Living Area:	
Main floor	1,868 sq. ft.
Total Living Area:	**1,868 sq. ft.**
Garage and storage	616 sq. ft.
Exterior Wall Framing:	2x6

Foundation Options:

Crawlspace

Slab

(All plans can be built with your choice of foundation and framing. A generic conversion diagram is available. See order form.)

BLUEPRINT PRICE CODE: B

MAIN FLOOR

Plan E-1830

Extra Sparkle

- A lovely front porch with a cameo front door, decorative posts, bay windows and dormers give this country-style home extra sparkle.
- The Great Room is at the center of the floor plan, where it merges with the dining room and the screened porch. The Great Room features a 10-ft. tray ceiling, a fireplace, a built-in wet bar and a wall of windows to the patio.
- The eat-in kitchen has a half-wall that keeps it open to the Great Room and hallway. The dining room offers a half-wall facing the foyer and a bay window overlooking the front porch.
- The delectable master suite is isolated from the other bedrooms and includes a charming bay window, a 10-ft. tray ceiling and a luxurious private bath.
- The two smaller bedrooms are off the main foyer and separated by a full bath.
- A mudroom with a washer and dryer is accessible from the two-car garage.

Plan AX-91312

Bedrooms: 3	Baths: 2
Space:	
Main floor	1,595 sq. ft.
Total Living Area	**1,595 sq. ft.**
Screened Porch	178 sq. ft.
Basement	1,595 sq. ft.
Garage, Storage and Utility	508 sq. ft.
Exterior Wall Framing	2x4

Foundation Options:

Daylight basement

Standard basement

Slab

(All plans can be built with your choice of foundation and framing. A generic conversion diagram is available. See order form.)

Blueprint Price Code	B

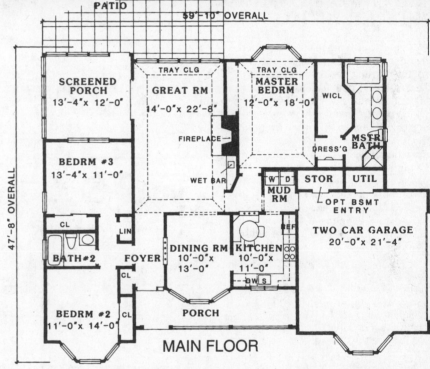

MAIN FLOOR

VIEW INTO GREAT ROOM

Masterful Master Suite

- This gorgeous home features front and rear covered porches and a master suite so luxurious it deserves its own wing.
- The expansive entry welcomes visitors into a spacious, skylighted living room, which boasts a handsome fireplace. The adjacent formal dining room overlooks the front porch.
- Designed for efficiency, the kitchen features an angled snack bar, a bayed eating area and views of the porch. An all-purpose utility room is conveniently located off the kitchen.
- The kitchen, eating area, living room and dining room are all heightened by 12-ft. ceilings.
- The sumptuous and secluded master suite features a tub and a separate shower, a double-sink vanity, a walk-in closet with built-in shelves and a compartmentalized toilet.
- The two secondary bedrooms share a hall bath at the other end of the home. The rear bedroom offers porch access.
- The garage features built-in storage and access to unfinished attic space.

Plan E-1811

Bedrooms: 3	Baths: 2

Living Area:	
Main floor	1,800 sq. ft.
Total Living Area:	**1,800 sq. ft.**
Garage and storage	634 sq. ft.
Exterior Wall Framing:	2x6

Foundation Options:

Crawlspace
Slab
(All plans can be built with your choice of foundation and framing. A generic conversion diagram is available. See order form.)

BLUEPRINT PRICE CODE:	B

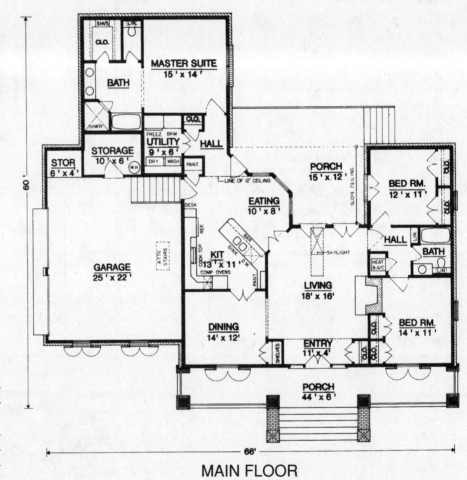

MAIN FLOOR

Plan E-1811

PRICES AND DETAILS ON PAGES 12-15

Tradition Updated

- The nostalgic exterior of this home gives way to dramatic cathedral ceilings and illuminating skylights inside.
- The covered front porch welcomes guests into the stone-tiled foyer, which flows into the living spaces.
- The living and dining rooms merge, forming a spacious, front-oriented entertaining area.

- A large three-sided fireplace situated between the living room and the family room may be enjoyed in both areas.
- The skylighted family room is also brightened by sliding glass doors that access a rear patio.
- The sunny island kitchen offers a nice breakfast nook and easy access to the laundry room and the garage.
- The master suite boasts a walk-in closet and a skylighted bath with a dual-sink vanity, a soaking tub and a separate shower. Two additional bedrooms share another full bath.

Plan AX-90303-A	
Bedrooms: 3	**Baths:** 2
Living Area:	
Main floor	1,615 sq. ft.
Total Living Area:	**1,615 sq. ft.**
Basement	1,615 sq. ft.
Garage	412 sq. ft.
Exterior Wall Framing:	2x4

Foundation Options:
Daylight basement
Standard basement
Crawlspace
Slab
(All plans can be built with your choice of foundation and framing. A generic conversion diagram is available. See order form.)

BLUEPRINT PRICE CODE:	B

72'-4" OVERALL

32'-4" OVERALL

PATIO

SL GL DR

SKYLITE

CL W D

LAUN RM

CATH CEIL
BRKFST RM
8'-6"x 11'-4"

CATH CEIL
KITCHEN
9'-6"x 13'-4"

DW S

CATH CEIL
FAMILY RM
15'-0"x 13'-4"

MSTR BATH

MSTR BEDRM
15'-0"x 13'-4"

UTIL RM

SKYLITE

SKYLITE

BATH #2

WICL

REF

FIREPLACE

TWO CAR GARAGE
20'-0"x 20'-0"

CATH CEIL
DINING RM
10'-2"x 12'-4"

CATH CEIL
LIVING RM
12'-6"x 13'-4"

LIN

CL

CL

FOYER

CL

BEDRM #3
10'-0"x 9'-8"

BEDRM #2
11'-4"x 11'-0"

PORCH

UP

MAIN FLOOR

Planned to Perfection

- This attractive and stylish home offers an interior design that is planned to perfection.
- The covered entry and vaulted foyer create an impressive welcome.
- The vaulted Great Room features a corner fireplace, a wet bar and lots of windows. The adjoining dining room offers a bay window and access to a covered patio.
- The gourmet kitchen includes an island cooktop, a garden window above the sink and a built-in desk. The attached nook is surrounded by windows that overlook a delightful planter.
- The master suite boasts a tray ceiling that rises to 9½ ft. and a peaceful reading area that accesses a private patio. The superb master bath features a garden tub and a separate shower.
- Two secondary bedrooms share a compartmentalized bath.

Plan S-4789

Bedrooms: 3	Baths: 2

Living Area:	
Main floor	1,665 sq. ft.
Total Living Area:	**1,665 sq. ft.**
Standard basement	1,665 sq. ft.
Garage	400 sq. ft.
Exterior Wall Framing:	2x6

Foundation Options:

Standard basement
Crawlspace
Slab

(All plans can be built with your choice of foundation and framing. A generic conversion diagram is available. See order form.)

BLUEPRINT PRICE CODE:	**B**

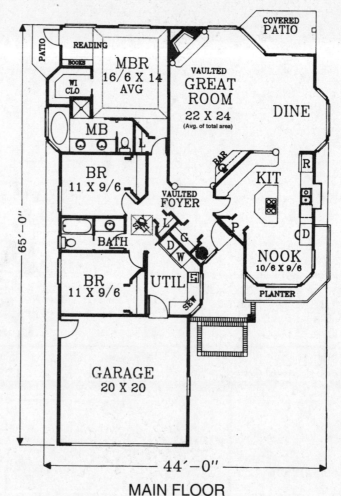

MAIN FLOOR

BASEMENT STAIRWAY LOCATION

Plan S-4789

PRICES AND DETAILS ON PAGES 12-15

Rustic Welcome

- This rustic design boasts an appealing exterior with a covered front porch that offers guests a friendly welcome.
- Inside, the centrally located Great Room features an 11-ft., 8-in. cathedral ceiling with exposed wood beams. A massive fireplace separates the living area from the large dining room, which offers access to a nice backyard patio.
- The galley-style kitchen flows between the formal dining room and the bayed

breakfast room, which offers a handy pantry and access to laundry facilities.
- The master suite features a walk-in closet and a compartmentalized bath.
- Across the Great Room, two additional bedrooms have extra closet space and share a second full bath.
- The side-entry garage gives the front of the home an extra-appealing and uncluttered look.
- The optional daylight basement offers expanded living space. The stairway (not shown) would be located along the wall between the dining room and the back bedroom.

Plan C-8460

Bedrooms: 3	Baths: 2
Living Area:	
Main floor	1,670 sq. ft.
Total Living Area:	**1,670 sq. ft.**
Daylight basement	1,600 sq. ft.
Garage	427 sq. ft.
Exterior Wall Framing:	2x4

Foundation Options:
Daylight basement
Crawlspace
Slab
(All plans can be built with your choice of foundation and framing. A generic conversion diagram is available. See order form.)

BLUEPRINT PRICE CODE: B

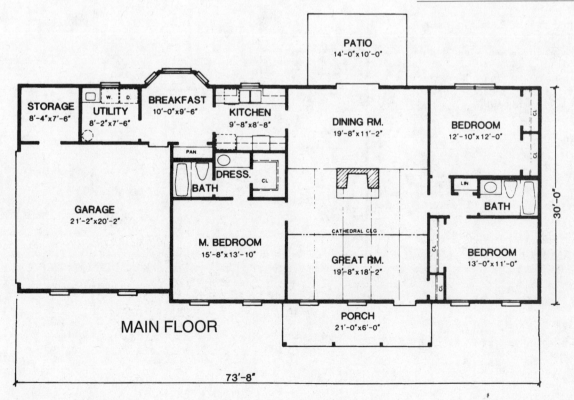

MAIN FLOOR

Designed for Livability

- As you enter this excitingly spacious traditional home, you see through the extensive windows to the backyard.
- This four-bedroom home was designed for the livability of the maturing family with the separation of the master suite.
- The formal dining room expands spatially to the living room while being set off by a decorative column and plant shelves.
- The bay that creates the morning room and the sitting area for the master suite also adds excitement to this plan, both inside and out.
- The master bath offers an exciting oval tub under glass and a separate shower, as well as a spacious walk-in closet and a dressing area.

Plan DD-1696

Bedrooms: 4	Baths: 2
Living Area:	
Main floor	1,748 sq. ft.
Total Living Area:	**1,748 sq. ft.**
Standard basement	1,748 sq. ft.
Garage	393 sq. ft.
Exterior Wall Framing:	2x4

Foundation Options:

Standard basement

Crawlspace

Slab

(All plans can be built with your choice of foundation and framing. A generic conversion diagram is available. See order form.)

BLUEPRINT PRICE CODE:	**B**

MAIN FLOOR

Plan DD-1696

PRICES AND DETAILS ON PAGES 12-15

Free-Flowing Floor Plan

- A fluid floor plan with open indoor/outdoor living spaces characterizes this exciting luxury home.
- The stylish columned porch opens to a spacious living room and dining room expanse that overlooks the outdoor spaces. The breathtaking view also includes a dramatic corner fireplace.
- The dining area opens to a bright kitchen with an angled eating bar. The overall spaciousness of the living areas is increased with high 12-ft. ceilings.
- A sunny, informal eating area adjoins the kitchen, and an angled set of doors opens to a convenient main-floor laundry room near the garage entrance.
- The vaulted master bedroom has a walk-in closet and a sumptuous bath with an oval tub.
- A separate wing houses two additional bedrooms and another full bath.
- Attic space is accessible from stairs in the garage and in the bedroom wing.

REAR VIEW

Plan E-1710

Bedrooms: 3	Baths: 2
Living Area:	
Main floor	1,792 sq. ft.
Total Living Area:	**1,792 sq. ft.**
Standard basement	1,792 sq. ft.
Garage	484 sq. ft.
Storage	96 sq. ft.
Exterior Wall Framing:	2x6

Foundation Options:

Standard basement
Crawlspace
Slab

(All plans can be built with your choice of foundation and framing. A generic conversion diagram is available. See order form.)

BLUEPRINT PRICE CODE: **B**

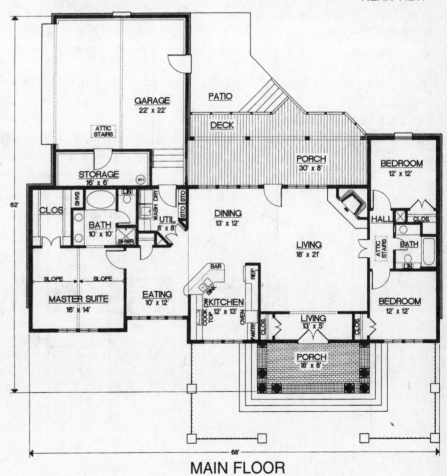

MAIN FLOOR

Fresh Air

- With its nostalgic look and country style, this lovely home brings a breath of fresh air into any neighborhood.
- Past the inviting wraparound porch, the foyer is brightened by an arched transom window above the front door.
- The adjoining formal dining room is defined by decorative columns and features a 9-ft., 4-in. stepped ceiling.
- The bright and airy kitchen includes a pantry, a windowed sink and a sunny breakfast area with porch access.
- Enhanced by an 11-ft stepped ceiling, the spacious Great Room is warmed by a fireplace flanked by sliding glass doors to a covered back porch.
- The lush master bedroom boasts an 11-ft. tray ceiling and a bayed sitting area. The master bath showcases a circular spa tub with a glass-block wall.
- The two remaining bedrooms are serviced by a second bath and a nearby laundry room. The protruding bedroom has a 12-ft. vaulted ceiling.
- Additional living space can be made available by finishing the upper floor.

Plan AX-93308

Bedrooms: 3+	Baths: 2
Living Area:	
Main floor	1,793 sq. ft.
Total Living Area:	**1,793 sq. ft.**
Standard basement	1,793 sq. ft.
Unfinished upper floor	779 sq. ft.
Garage and utility	471 sq. ft.
Exterior Wall Framing:	2x4

Foundation Options:

Standard basement
Crawlspace
Slab

(All plans can be built with your choice of foundation and framing. A generic conversion diagram is available. See order form.)

BLUEPRINT PRICE CODE:	**B**

VIEW INTO GREAT ROOM

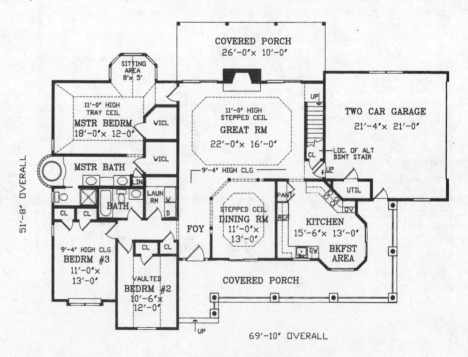

MAIN FLOOR

Plan AX-93308

PRICES AND DETAILS ON PAGES 12-15

Cozy Covered Porches

- Twin dormers give this raised one-story design the appearance of a two-story. Two covered porches and a deck supplement the main living areas with plenty of outdoor entertaining space.
- The large central living room features a dramatic fireplace, a 12-ft. ceiling with a skylight and access to both porch areas.
- Double doors open to a bayed eating area, which overlooks the adjoining deck and includes a sloped ceiling that rises to 12 ft. in the kitchen. An angled snack bar and a pantry are also featured.
- The elegant master suite is tucked to one side of the home and also overlooks the backyard and deck. Laundry facilities and garage access are nearby.
- Across the home, two additional bedrooms share another full bath.

Plan E-1826

Bedrooms: 3	Baths: 2
Living Area:	
Main floor	1,800 sq. ft.
Total Living Area:	**1,800 sq. ft.**
Garage	550 sq. ft.
Storage	84 sq. ft.
Exterior Wall Framing:	2x6

Foundation Options:

Crawlspace

Slab

(All plans can be built with your choice of foundation and framing. A generic conversion diagram is available. See order form.)

BLUEPRINT PRICE CODE:	B

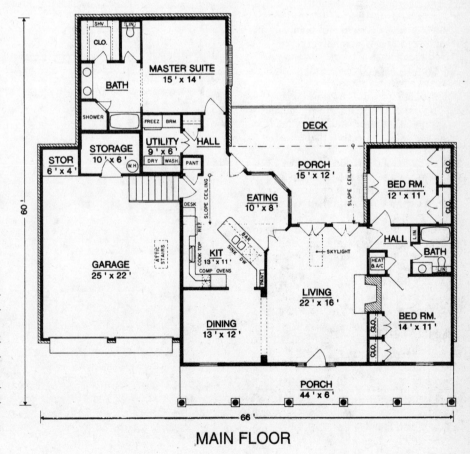

MAIN FLOOR

Photo by Mark Englund/HomeStyles

Elaborate Entry

- This home's important-looking covered entry greets guests with heavy, banded support columns, sunburst transom windows and dual sidelights.
- Once inside the home, the 15-ft.-high foyer is flanked by the formal living and dining rooms, which have 10½-ft. vaulted ceilings. Straight ahead and beyond five decorative columns lies the spacious family room.
- Surrounded by 8-ft.-high walls, the family room features a 13-ft. vaulted ceiling, a fireplace and sliding doors to a covered patio. A neat plant shelf above the fireplace adds style.
- The bright and airy kitchen has a 13-ft. ceiling and serves the family room and the breakfast area, which is enhanced by a corner window and a French door.
- The master suite enjoys a 13-ft. vaulted ceiling and features French-door patio access, a large walk-in closet and a private bath with a corner platform tub and a separate shower.
- Across the home, three secondary bedrooms share a hall bath, which boasts private access to the patio.

Plan HDS-90-806

Bedrooms: 4	Baths: 2

Living Area:

Main floor	2,041 sq. ft.
Total Living Area:	**2,041 sq. ft.**
Garage	452 sq. ft.

Exterior Wall Framing:

2x4 or 8-in. concrete block

Foundation Options:

Slab
(All plans can be built with your choice of foundation and framing. A generic conversion diagram is available. See order form.)

BLUEPRINT PRICE CODE: C

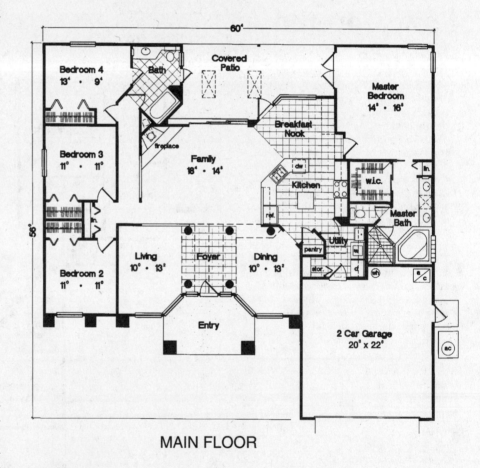

MAIN FLOOR

NOTE:
The above photographed home may have been modified by the homeowner. Please refer to floor plan and/or drawn elevation shown for actual blueprint details.

Modern Charmer

- This attractive plan combines country-style charm with a modern floor plan.
- The central foyer ushers guests past a study and on into the huge living room, which is highlighted by an 11-ft. ceiling, a corner fireplace and access to a big, covered backyard porch.
- An angled snack bar joins the living room to the bayed nook and the efficient kitchen. The formal dining room is easily reached from the kitchen and the foyer. A utility room and a half-bath are just off the garage entrance.
- The master suite, isolated for privacy, boasts a magnificent bath with a garden tub, a separate shower, double vanities and two walk-in closets.
- Two more bedrooms are located on the opposite side of the home and are separated by a hall bath.
- Ceilings in all rooms are at least 9 ft. high for added spaciousness.

REAR VIEW

Plan VL-2069

Bedrooms: 3	Baths: 2½
Living Area:	
Main floor	2,069 sq. ft.
Total Living Area:	**2,069 sq. ft.**
Garage	460 sq. ft.
Exterior Wall Framing:	2x4

Foundation Options:

Crawlspace

Slab

(All plans can be built with your choice of foundation and framing. A generic conversion diagram is available. See order form.)

BLUEPRINT PRICE CODE: C

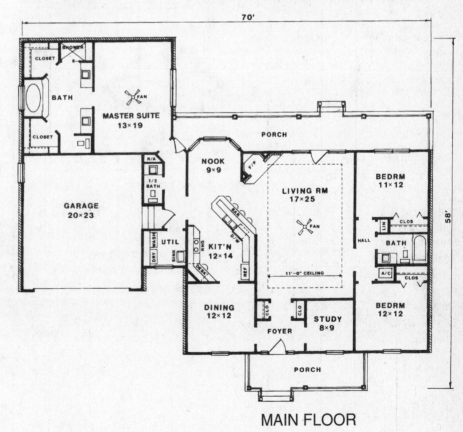

MAIN FLOOR

Spacious Country-Style

- This distinctive country-style home is highlighted by a wide front porch and multi-paned windows with shutters.
- Inside, the dining room is off the foyer and open to the living room, but is defined by elegant columns and beams above.
- The central living room boasts a 12-ft. cathedral ceiling, a fireplace and French doors to the rear patio.
- The delightful kitchen/nook area is spacious and well planned for both work and play.
- A handy utility room and a half-bath are on either side of a short hallway leading to the carport, which includes a large storage area.
- The master suite offers his-and-hers walk-in closets and an incredible bath that incorporates a plant shelf above the raised spa tub.
- The two remaining bedrooms share a hall bath that is compartmentalized to allow more than one user at a time.

Plan J-86140

Bedrooms: 3	Baths: 2½
Living Area:	
Main floor	2,177 sq. ft.
Total Living Area:	**2,177 sq. ft.**
Standard basement	2,177 sq. ft.
Carport	440 sq. ft.
Storage	120 sq. ft.
Exterior Wall Framing:	2x4

Foundation Options:
Standard basement
Crawlspace
Slab
(All plans can be built with your choice of foundation and framing. A generic conversion diagram is available. See order form.)

BLUEPRINT PRICE CODE: C

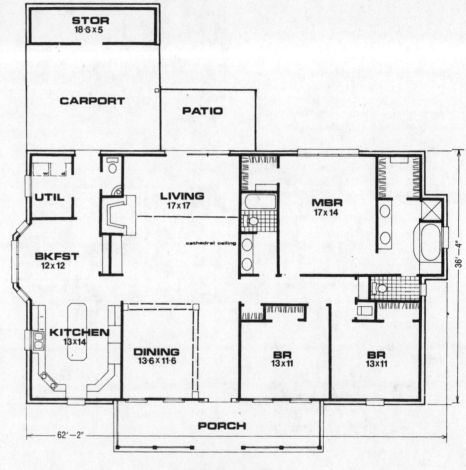

MAIN FLOOR

Photo by Mark Englund/HomeStyles

Alluring Arches

- Massive columns, high, dramatic arches and expansive glass attract passersby to this alluring one-story home.
- Inside, 12-ft. coffered ceilings are found in the foyer, dining room and living room. A bank of windows in the living room provides a sweeping view of the covered backyard patio, creating a bright, open effect that is carried throughout the home.
- The informal, family activity areas are oriented to the back of the home as well. Spectacular window walls in the breakfast room and family room offer tremendous views. The family room's inviting corner fireplace is positioned to be enjoyed from the breakfast area and the spacious island kitchen.
- Separated from the secondary bedrooms, the superb master suite is entered through double doors and features a sitting room and a garden bath. Another full bath is across the hall from the den, which would also make a great guest room or nursery.

Plan HDS-99-179

Bedrooms: 3+	Baths: 3
Living Area:	
Main floor	2,660 sq. ft.
Total Living Area:	**2,660 sq. ft.**
Garage	527 sq. ft.
Exterior Wall Framing:	2x4

Foundation Options:

Slab

(All plans can be built with your choice of foundation and framing. A generic conversion diagram is available. See order form.)

BLUEPRINT PRICE CODE:	D

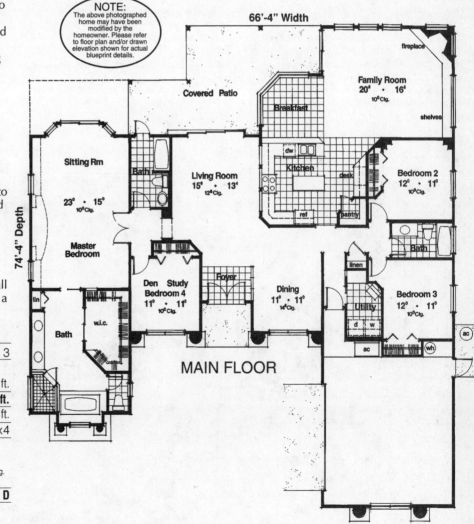

NOTE: The above photographed home may have been modified by the homeowner. Please refer to floor plan and/or drawn elevation shown for actual blueprint details.

66'-4" Width

74'-4" Depth

Covered Patio

Sitting Rm
23⁰ · 15⁰
10⁰Clg.

Master Bedroom

Bath

w.i.c.

Bath

Bath

Living Room
15⁸ · 13⁴
12⁸Clg.

Den Study
Bedroom 4
11⁰ · 11⁰
10⁰Clg.

Foyer

Dining
11⁰ · 11⁰
14⁴Clg.

Breakfast

Kitchen

dw

ref

pantry

desk

Family Room
20⁸ · 16⁸
10⁰Clg.

fireplace

shelves

Bedroom 2
12⁰ · 11⁰
10⁰Clg.

Bath

linen

Utility

d w

ac

Bedroom 3
12⁰ · 11⁰
10⁰Clg.

ac

wh

MAIN FLOOR

Photo by Mark Englund/HomeStyles

Extraordinary Estate Living

- Extraordinary estate living is at its best in this palatial beauty.
- The double-doored entry opens to a large central living room that overlooks a covered patio with a vaulted ceiling. Volume 14-ft. ceilings are found in the living room, in the formal dining room and in the den or study, which may serve as a fourth bedroom.
- The gourmet chef will enjoy the spacious kitchen, which flaunts a

cooktop island, a walk-in pantry and a peninsula snack counter shared with the breakfast room and family room.
- This trio of informal living spaces also shares a panorama of glass and a corner fireplace centered between TV and media niches.
- Isolated at the opposite end of the home is the spacious master suite, which offers private patio access. Dual walk-in closets define the entrance to the adjoining master bath, complete with a garden Jacuzzi and separate dressing areas.
- The hall bath also opens to the outdoors for use as a pool bath.

Plan HDS-99-177	
Bedrooms: 3+	**Baths:** 3
Living Area:	
Main floor	2,597 sq. ft.
Total Living Area:	**2,597 sq. ft.**
Garage	761 sq. ft.
Exterior Wall Framing:	2x4

Foundation Options:

Slab
(All plans can be built with your choice of foundation and framing. A generic conversion diagram is available. See order form.)

BLUEPRINT PRICE CODE: D

NOTE:
The above photographed home may have been modified by the homeowner. Please refer to floor plan and/or drawn elevation shown for actual blueprint details.

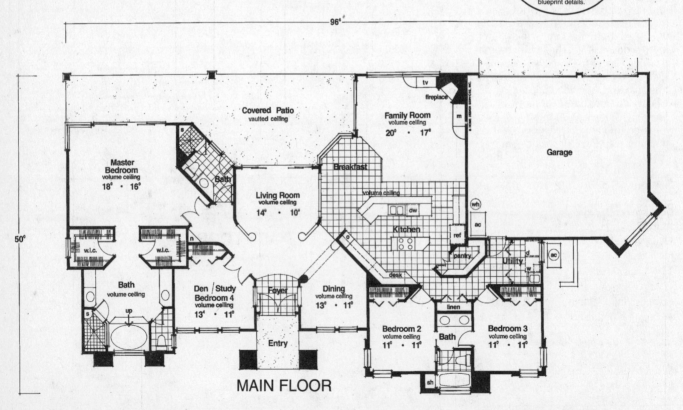

MAIN FLOOR

TO ORDER THIS BLUEPRINT, CALL TOLL-FREE 1-800-820-1283

Plan HDS-99-177

PRICES AND DETAILS ON PAGES 12-15

Versatile
Sun Room

- This cozy country-style home offers an inviting front porch and an interior just as welcoming.
- The spacious living room features a warming fireplace and windows that overlook the porch.
- The living room opens to a dining area, where French doors access a covered porch and a sunny patio.
- The island kitchen has a sink view, plenty of counter space, and a handy pass-through to the adjoining sun room. The bright sun room is large enough to serve as a formal dining room, a family room or a hobby room.
- The private master suite is secluded to the rear. A garden spa tub, dual walk-in closets and separate dressing areas are nice features found in the master bath.

Plan J-90014

Bedrooms: 3	Baths: 2½
Living Area:	
Main floor	2,190 sq. ft.
Total Living Area:	**2,190 sq. ft.**
Standard basement	2,190 sq. ft.
Garage	465 sq. ft.
Storage	34 sq. ft.
Exterior Wall Framing:	2x6

Foundation Options:

Standard basement
Crawlspace
Slab

(All plans can be built with your choice of foundation and framing. A generic conversion diagram is available. See order form.)

BLUEPRINT PRICE CODE:	C

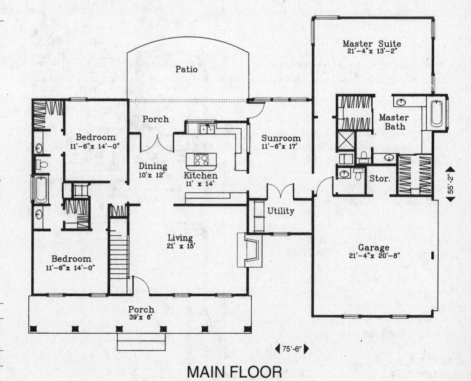

MAIN FLOOR

Spectacular Design

- The spectacular brick facade of this home conceals a stylish floor plan. Endless transoms crown the windows that wrap around the rear of the home, flooding the interior with natural light.

- The foyer opens to a huge Grand Room with a 14-ft. ceiling. French doors access a delightful covered porch.

- A three-sided fireplace warms the three casual rooms, which share a high 12-ft. ceiling. The Gathering Room is surrounded by tall windows; the Good Morning Room features porch access; and the island kitchen offers a double oven, a pantry and a snack bar.

- Guests will dine in style in the formal dining room, with its 13-ft. tray ceiling and trio of tall, arched windows.

- Curl up with a good book in the quiet library, which has an airy 10-ft. ceiling.

- A 12-ft. ceiling enhances the fantastic master suite, which is wrapped in windows. The superb master bath boasts a step-up garden tub, a separate shower, two vanities, a makeup table and a bidet.

- Two sleeping suites on the other side of the home have 10-ft. ceilings and share a unique bath with private vanities.

Plan EOF-8

Bedrooms: 3+	Baths: 3½
Living Area:	
Main floor	3,392 sq. ft.
Total Living Area:	**3,392 sq. ft.**
Garage	871 sq. ft.
Exterior Wall Framing:	2x6

Foundation Options:

Slab
(All plans can be built with your choice of foundation and framing. A generic conversion diagram is available. See order form.)

BLUEPRINT PRICE CODE: E

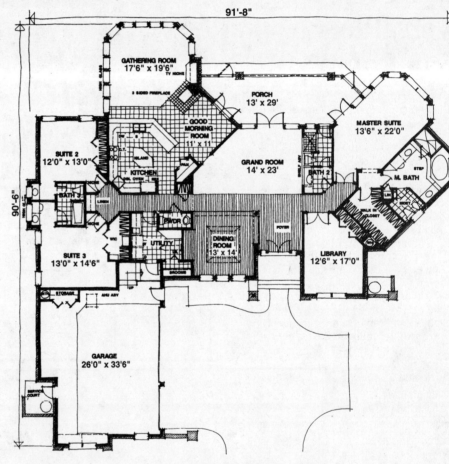

MAIN FLOOR

TO ORDER THIS BLUEPRINT,
CALL TOLL-FREE 1-800-820-1283

Plan EOF-8

PRICES AND DETAILS
ON PAGES 12-15

Upscale Charm

- Country charm and the very latest in conveniences mark this upscale home. To add extra appeal, all of the living areas are housed on one floor, yet may be expanded to the upper floor later.
- Set off from the foyer, the dining room is embraced by elegant columns. Arched windows in the dining room and in the bedroom across the hall echo the delicate detailing of the covered front porch.
- Straight ahead, the family room flaunts a wall of French doors overlooking a covered back porch and a large deck.
- A curved island snack bar smoothly connects the gourmet kitchen to the sunny breakfast area, which features a dramatic 13-ft. vaulted ceiling brightened by skylights. All other rooms have 9-ft. ceilings. A nearby computer room and a laundry/utility room with a recycling center are other amenities.
- The master bedroom's private bath includes a dual-sink vanity and a floor-to-ceiling storage unit with a built-in chest of drawers. Other extras include a step-up spa tub and a separate shower.

Plan J-92100

Bedrooms: 3+	Baths: 2
Living Area:	
Main floor	1,877 sq. ft.
Total Living Area:	**1,877 sq. ft.**
Upper floor (future areas)	1,500 sq. ft.
Standard basement	1,877 sq. ft.
Garage and storage	551 sq. ft.
Exterior Wall Framing:	2x4
Foundation Options:	

Standard basement
Crawlspace
Slab
(All plans can be built with your choice of foundation and framing. A generic conversion diagram is available. See order form.)

BLUEPRINT PRICE CODE:	B

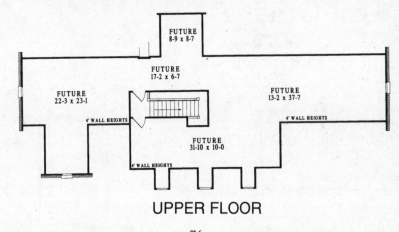

UPPER FLOOR

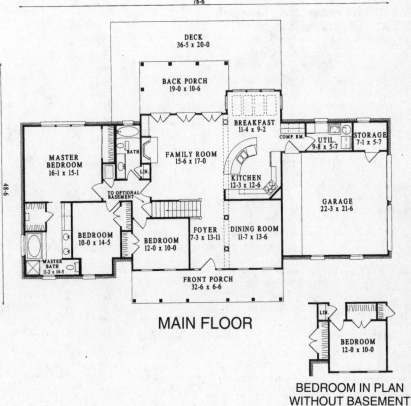

MAIN FLOOR

BEDROOM IN PLAN
WITHOUT BASEMENT

A Real Original

- This home's round window, elegant entry and transom windows create an eye-catching, original look.
- Inside, high ceilings and tremendous views let the eyes wander. The foyer provides an exciting look at an expansive deck and inviting spa through the living room's tall windows. The windows frame a handsome fireplace, while a 10-ft. ceiling adds volume and interest.
- To the right of the foyer is a cozy den or home office with its own fireplace, 10-ft. ceiling and dramatic windows.
- The spacious kitchen/breakfast area features an oversized snack bar island and opens to a large screen porch. Within easy reach are the laundry room and the entrance to the garage.
- The bright formal dining room overlooks the deck and boasts a ceiling that vaults up to 10 feet.
- The secluded master suite looks out to the deck as well, with access through a patio door. The private bath features a dynamite corner spa tub, a separate shower and a large walk-in closet.
- A second bedroom and bath complete the main floor.

Plan B-90065

Bedrooms: 2+	Baths: 2
Living Area:	
Main floor	1,889 sq. ft.
Total Living Area:	**1,889 sq. ft.**
Screen porch	136 sq. ft.
Standard basement	1,889 sq. ft.
Garage	406 sq. ft.
Exterior Wall Framing:	2x6

Foundation Options:

Standard basement
(All plans can be built with your choice of foundation and framing. A generic conversion diagram is available. See order form.)

BLUEPRINT PRICE CODE: B

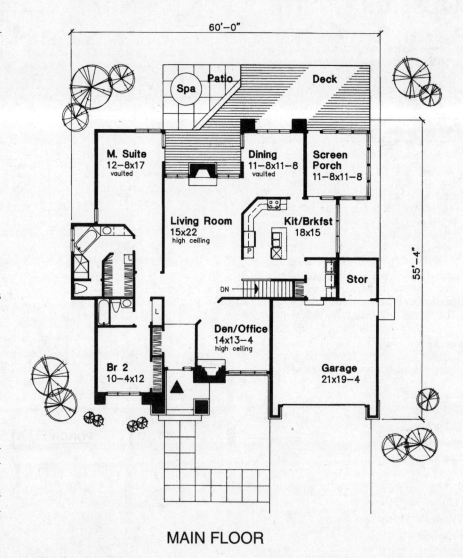

MAIN FLOOR

TO ORDER THIS BLUEPRINT, CALL TOLL-FREE 1-800-820-1283

Plan B-90065

PRICES AND DETAILS ON PAGES 12-15

Garden Home with a View

- This clever design proves that privacy doesn't have to be compromised even in high-density urban neighborhoods. From within, views are oriented to a beautiful, lush entry courtyard and a covered rear porch.
- The exterior appearance is sheltered, but warm and welcoming.
- The innovative interior design centers on a unique kitchen, which directs traffic away from the working areas while still serving the entire home.
- The sunken family room features a 14-ft. vaulted ceiling and a warm fireplace.
- The master suite is highlighted by a sumptuous master bath with an oversized shower and a whirlpool tub, plus a large walk-in closet.
- The formal living room is designed and placed in such a way that it can become a third bedroom, a den, or an office or study room, depending on family needs and lifestyles.

Plan E-1824

Bedrooms: 2+	Baths: 2
Living Area:	
Main floor	1,891 sq. ft.
Total Living Area:	**1,891 sq. ft.**
Garage	506 sq. ft.
Storage	60 sq. ft.
Exterior Wall Framing:	2x4

Foundation Options:
Crawlspace
Slab
(All plans can be built with your choice of foundation and framing. A generic conversion diagram is available. See order form.)

BLUEPRINT PRICE CODE: B

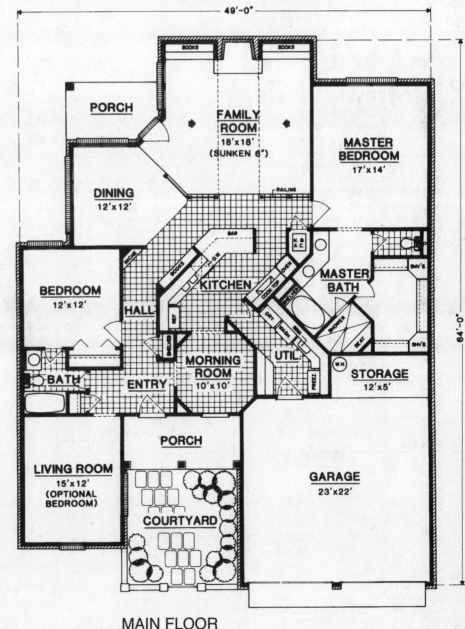

MAIN FLOOR

Town-and-Country Classic

- A railed front porch, a charming cupola and stylish shutters add town and country flair to this classic one-story.
- The welcoming entry flows into the vaulted family room, which boasts a 14-ft. vaulted ceiling with exposed beams, a handsome fireplace and a French door to a backyard patio.

- The living room and the formal dining room are separated by a half-wall with decorative wooden spindles. The adjoining kitchen features wraparound counter space. The eating nook has a laundry closet and garage access.
- The master bedroom enjoys a private bath with a separate dressing and a roomy walk-in closet.
- Two additional bedrooms are serviced by a compartmentalized hallway bath.
- The two-car garage includes a separate storage area at the back.

Plan E-1815

Bedrooms: 3	**Baths:** 2

Living Area:	
Main floor	1,898 sq. ft.
Total Living Area:	**1,898 sq. ft.**
Garage and storage	513 sq. ft.
Exterior Wall Framing:	2x4

Foundation Options:
Crawlspace
Slab
(All plans can be built with your choice of foundation and framing. A generic conversion diagram is available. See order form.)

BLUEPRINT PRICE CODE:	**B**

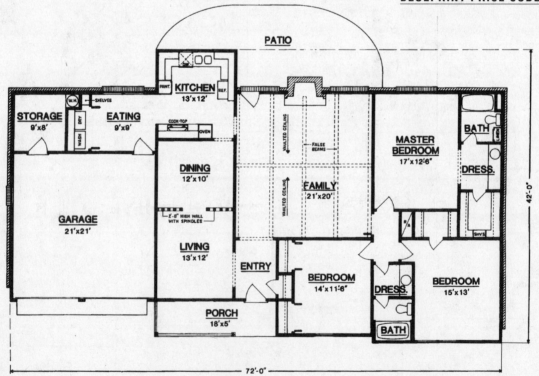

MAIN FLOOR

Plan E-1815

Magnificent Great Room

- A magnificent Great Room anchors this gorgeous Mediterranean-style home.
- From the foyer, an arched entrance introduces the den, study or extra bedroom. If desired, the closet could be modified to house a wet bar.
- The formal dining room offers an excellent space for special meals.
- Straight ahead, the massive Great Room boasts a handsome fireplace. Pocket sliding glass doors open to a covered patio with skylights.
- Secluded from the rest of the home and beyond two arched entryways, the master bedroom has its own patio access. Highlights in the master bath include a walk-in closet, a raised whirlpool tub and a separate shower beneath a 14½-ft. vaulted ceiling.
- Natural light floods the breakfast nook and the adjoining kitchen, which sports a serving counter. Handy laundry facilities are just a few steps away.
- Two more good-sized bedrooms share a full bath and easy patio access.

Plan HDS-99-196	
Bedrooms: 3+	**Baths:** 2
Living Area:	
Main floor	1,901 sq. ft.
Total Living Area:	**1,901 sq. ft.**
Garage	484 sq. ft.
Exterior Wall Framing:	8-in. concrete block
Foundation Options:	

Slab
(All plans can be built with your choice of foundation and framing. A generic conversion diagram is available. See order form.)

BLUEPRINT PRICE CODE:	B

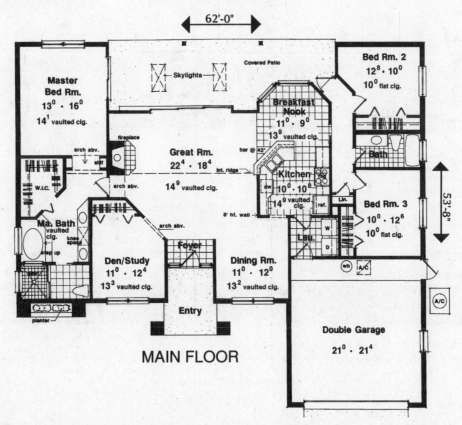

MAIN FLOOR

Family Home, Formal Accents

- Captivating roof angles and European detailing highlight the exterior of this graceful home.
- The generous foyer is flanked by the spacious living and dining rooms, both with tall, ornate windows.
- Beyond the foyer lies an expansive family room, highlighted by a dramatic fireplace and sliding glass doors that open to a sunny patio.
- The kitchen makes use of an L-shaped counter and a central island to maximaze efficiency. The adjacent breakfast room offers casual dining. A nearby utility room features a washer and dryer and a door to the backyard.
- The large master suite boasts two closets and a private bath with a dual-sink vanity and a step-up tub.
- Across the hall, two additional bedrooms share a second full bath.

Plan C-8103

Bedrooms: 3	Baths: 2

Living Area:

Main floor	1,940 sq. ft.
Total Living Area:	**1,940 sq. ft.**
Daylight basement	1,870 sq. ft.
Garage	400 sq. ft.

Exterior Wall Framing:	2x4

Foundation Options:

Daylight basement
Crawlspace
Slab

(All plans can be built with your choice of foundation and framing. A generic conversion diagram is available. See order form.)

BLUEPRINT PRICE CODE:	B

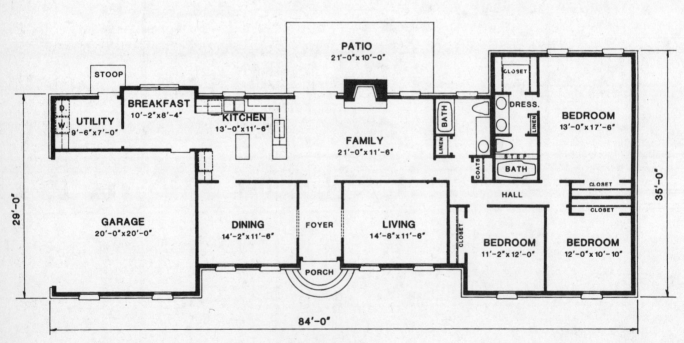

MAIN FLOOR

TO ORDER THIS BLUEPRINT, CALL TOLL-FREE 1-800-820-1283

Plan C-8103

PRICES AND DETAILS ON PAGES 12-15

Updated Tudor

- Updated Tudor styling gives this home an extra-appealing exterior. Inside, the bright and open living spaces are embellished with a host of wonderfully contemporary details.

- An inviting brick arch frames the front door, which opens directly into the living room. Here, a 14-ft. sloped ceiling, a fireplace and a view to the covered rear porch provide an impressive welcome.

- The octagonal dining area is absolutely stunning—the perfect complement for the skylighted kitchen, which boasts an angled cooktop/snack bar and a 12-ft. sloped ceiling. Double doors in the kitchen lead to a roomy utility area and the cleverly disguised side-entry garage.

- No details were left out in the sumptuous master suite, which features access to a private porch with a 14-ft. sloped ceiling and skylights. The luxurious bath offers a platform tub, a sit-down shower, his-and-hers vanities and lots of storage and closet space.

- Two more bedrooms are situated at the opposite side of the home and share a hall bath. One bedroom features a window seat, while the other has direct access to the central covered porch.

Plan E-1912

Bedrooms: 3	Baths: 2
Living Area:	
Main floor	1,946 sq. ft.
Total Living Area:	**1,946 sq. ft.**
Garage and storage	562 sq. ft.
Exterior Wall Framing:	2x6

Foundation Options:

Crawlspace

Slab

(All plans can be built with your choice of foundation and framing. A generic conversion diagram is available. See order form.)

BLUEPRINT PRICE CODE: C

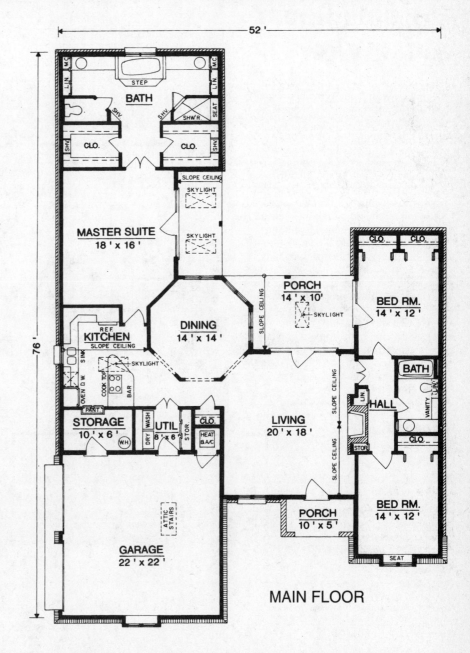

MAIN FLOOR

Morning Room with a View

- This modern-looking ranch is stylishly decorated with a pair of arched-window dormers, handsome brick trim and a covered front porch.
- Inside, the dining room is set off by columns, as it merges with the entry.
- The main living areas are oriented to the rear, where a huge central family room offers a patio view and a fireplace that may also be enjoyed from the bayed morning room and adjoining kitchen.
- The walk-through kitchen features a pantry, a snack bar to the family room and easy service to the formal dining room across the hall.
- The secluded master suite boasts a wide window seat and a private bath with a walk-in closet, a corner garden tub and a separate shower.
- Across the home, the three secondary bedrooms share another full bath. The fourth bedroom may double as a study.
- High 10-ft. ceilings are found throughout the home, except in the secondary bedrooms.

Plan DD-1962

Bedrooms: 3+	Baths: 2
Living Area:	
Main floor	1,962 sq. ft.
Total Living Area:	**1,962 sq. ft.**
Standard basement	1,962 sq. ft.
Garage	386 sq. ft.
Exterior Wall Framing:	2x4

Foundation Options:

Standard basement

Crawlspace

Slab

(All plans can be built with your choice of foundation and framing. A generic conversion diagram is available. See order form.)

BLUEPRINT PRICE CODE: B

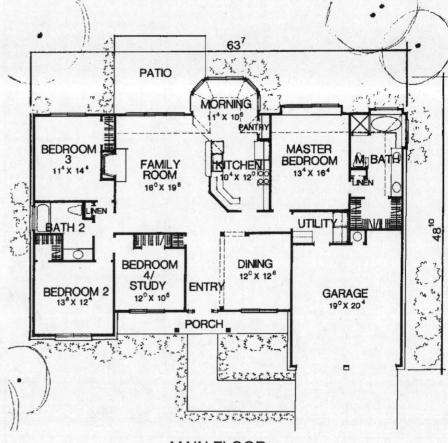

MAIN FLOOR

Plan DD-1962

PRICES AND DETAILS ON PAGES 12-15

Interior Angles Add Excitement

- Interior angles add a touch of excitement to this one-story home.
- A pleasantly charming exterior combines wood and stone to give the plan a solid, comfortable look for any neighborhood.
- Formal living and dining rooms flank the entry, which leads into the large family room, featuring a fireplace, a 19-ft. high vaulted ceiling and built-in bookshelves. A covered porch and a sunny patio are just steps away.
- The adjoining eating area with a built-in china cabinet angles off the spacious kitchen. Note the pantry and the convenient utility room.
- The master bedroom suite is both spacious and private, and includes a dressing room, a large walk-in closet and a deluxe bath.
- The three secondary bedrooms are also zoned for privacy, and share a second full bath.

Plan E-1904	
Bedrooms: 4	**Baths:** 2½
Living Area:	
Main floor	1,997 sq. ft.
Total Living Area:	**1,997 sq. ft.**
Garage	484 sq. ft.
Storage	104 sq. ft.
Exterior Wall Framing:	2x4

Foundation Options:

Crawlspace

Slab

(All plans can be built with your choice of foundation and framing. A generic conversion diagram is available. See order form.)

BLUEPRINT PRICE CODE:	B

MAIN FLOOR

European Charm

- This distinguished European home offers today's most luxurious features.
- In the formal living and dining rooms, 15-ft. vaulted ceilings add elegance.
- The informal areas are oriented to the rear of the home, entered through French doors in the foyer. The family room features a 12-ft. tray ceiling, a fireplace with an adjoining media center and a view of a backyard deck.

- The open kitchen and breakfast area is bright and cheerful, with a window wall and French-door deck access.
- Double doors lead into the luxurious master suite, which showcases a 14-ft. vaulted ceiling and a see-through fireplace that is shared with the spa bath. The splashy bath includes a dual-sink vanity, a separate shower and a wardrobe closet and dressing area.
- Two more bedrooms, one with private deck access, and a full bath are located on the opposite side of the home.
- Unless otherwise mentioned, 9-ft. ceilings enhance every room.

Plan APS-2006	
Bedrooms: 3	**Baths:** 2
Living Area:	
Main floor	2,006 sq. ft.
Total Living Area:	**2,006 sq. ft.**
Daylight basement	2,006 sq. ft.
Garage	448 sq. ft.
Exterior Wall Framing:	2x4

Foundation Options:
Daylight basement
Slab
(All plans can be built with your choice of foundation and framing. A generic conversion diagram is available. See order form.)

BLUEPRINT PRICE CODE:	C

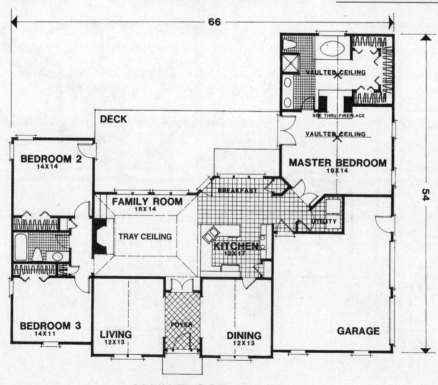

MAIN FLOOR

TO ORDER THIS BLUEPRINT, CALL TOLL-FREE 1-800-820-1283

Plan APS-2006

PRICES AND DETAILS ON PAGES 12-15

French Garden Design

- A creative, angular design gives this traditional French garden home an exciting, open and airy floor plan.
- Guests enter through a covered, columned porch that opens into the large, angled living and dining rooms.
- High 12-ft. ceilings highlight the living and dining area, which also features corner windows, a wet bar, a cozy fireplace and access to a huge covered backyard porch.
- The angled walk-through kitchen, also with a 12-ft.-high ceiling, offers plenty of work space and an adjoining informal eating nook that faces a delightful private courtyard. The nearby utility area has extra freezer space, a walk-in pantry and garage access.
- The home's bedrooms are housed in two separate wings. One wing boasts a luxurious master suite, which features a large walk-in closet, an angled tub and a separate shower.
- Two large bedrooms in the other wing share a hall bath. Each bedroom has a walk-in closet.

Plan E-2004

Bedrooms: 3	Baths: 2

Living Area:	
Main floor	2,023 sq. ft.
Total Living Area:	**2,023 sq. ft.**
Garage	484 sq. ft.
Storage	87 sq. ft.
Exterior Wall Framing:	2x6

Foundation Options:

Crawlspace

Slab

(All plans can be built with your choice of foundation and framing. A generic conversion diagram is available. See order form.)

BLUEPRINT PRICE CODE: C

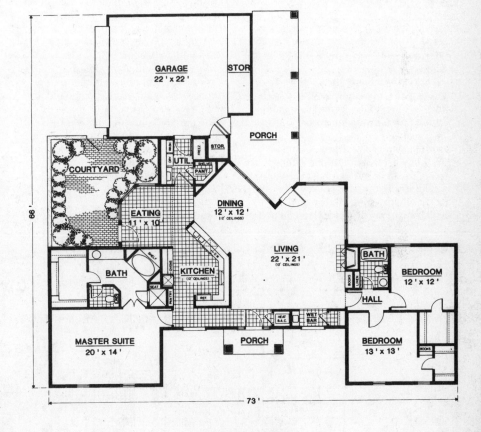

MAIN FLOOR

TO ORDER THIS BLUEPRINT, CALL TOLL-FREE 1-800-820-1283

Plan E-2004

PRICES AND DETAILS ON PAGES 12-15

Sought-After Elegance

- Decorative corner quoins, copper accents and gorgeous windows take the brick and stucco facade of this home to the height of elegance.
- Luxurious appointments continue inside, with a sidelighted 11-ft.-high foyer leading to the formal living and dining rooms. The living room boasts a 14-ft. vaulted ceiling, while the dining room has an 11-ft. ceiling.
- Smoothly accessed from the dining room, the flow-through kitchen offers a serving counter to the breakfast nook. Bright windows light the two areas, which share an 11-ft. vaulted ceiling.

- Adjacent to the nook, the luxurious family room sports a handsome fireplace and access to a sprawling backyard deck. A fancy fan hangs from the soaring 14-ft. vaulted ceiling.
- Just off the family room, two roomy secondary bedrooms share a nice compartmentalized bath.
- The sumptuous master bedroom flaunts its own deck access, a quaint morning porch for quiet cups of coffee and a large walk-in closet.
- The master bath is highlighted by a plant shelf, a garden tub and a separate shower. An 11-ft. ceiling crowns the master bedroom and bath.
- Unless otherwise noted, all rooms have 9-ft. ceilings.
- A bonus room above the garage offers expansion possibilities.

Plan APS-2018	
Bedrooms: 3+	**Baths:** 2½
Living Area:	
Main floor	2,088 sq. ft.
Total Living Area:	**2,088 sq. ft.**
Bonus room (unfinished)	282 sq. ft.
Daylight basement	2,088 sq. ft.
Garage	460 sq. ft.
Storage	35 sq. ft.
Exterior Wall Framing:	2x4

Foundation Options:

Daylight basement
(All plans can be built with your choice of foundation and framing. A generic conversion diagram is available. See order form.)

BLUEPRINT PRICE CODE:	C

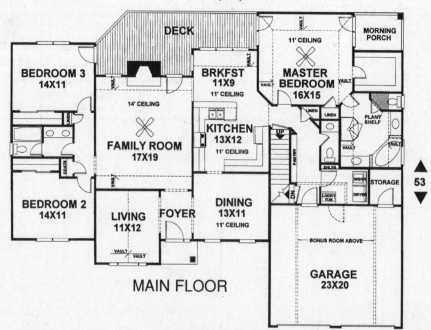

MAIN FLOOR

Wonderful Windows

- This one-story's striking stucco and stone facade is enhanced by great gables and wonderful windows.
- A beautiful bay augments the living room/den, which can be closed off.
- A wall of windows lets sunbeams brighten the exquisite formal dining room, which is defined by decorative columns and a high 14-ft. ceiling.
- The spacious family room offers a handsome fireplace flanked by glass.
- The kitchen boasts a large pantry, a corner sink and two convenient serving bars. A 13-ft. vaulted ceiling presides over the adjoining breakfast room.
- A lovely window seat highlights one of the two secondary bedrooms, which are serviced by a full bath with a 13-ft., 10-in. vaulted ceiling.
- The magnificent master suite features a symmetrical tray ceiling that sets off an attractive round-top window. The elegant master bath offers a 15-ft.-high vaulted ceiling, a garden tub and dual vanities, one with knee space.
- Ceilings not specified are 9 ft. high.

Plan FB-5009-CHAD

Bedrooms: 3	Baths: 2
Living Area:	
Main floor	2,115 sq. ft.
Total Living Area:	**2,115 sq. ft.**
Daylight basement	2,115 sq. ft.
Garage and storage	535 sq. ft.
Exterior Wall Framing:	2x4

Foundation Options:

Daylight basement

Slab

(All plans can be built with your choice of foundation and framing. A generic conversion diagram is available. See order form.)

BLUEPRINT PRICE CODE:	C

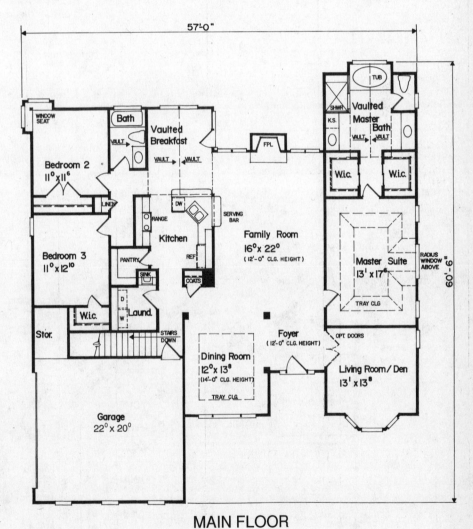

MAIN FLOOR

A Taste of Europe

- This tasteful one-story home is characterized by a European exterior and an ultra-modern interior.
- High 10-ft. ceilings grace the central living areas, from the foyer to the Great Room, and from the nook through the kitchen to the dining room.
- The inviting Great Room showcases a fireplace framed by glass that overlooks the covered back porch.
- A snack bar unites the Great Room with the bayed nook and the galley-style kitchen. A spacious utility room is just off the kitchen and accessible from the two-car garage as well.
- The secluded master suite boasts a luxurious private bath and French doors that open to the covered backyard porch.
- The master bath features a raised garden spa tub set into an intimate corner, with a separate shower nearby. A large walk-in closet and two sinks separated by a built-in makeup table are also included.
- Two additional bedrooms, a second full bath and a front study or home office make up the remainder of this up-to-date design.

Plan VL-2162

Bedrooms: 3	**Baths:** 2

Living Area:

Main floor	2,162 sq. ft.
Total Living Area:	**2,162 sq. ft.**
Garage	498 sq. ft.
Exterior Wall Framing:	2x4

Foundation Options:

Crawlspace
Slab
(All plans can be built with your choice of foundation and framing. A generic conversion diagram is available. See order form.)

BLUEPRINT PRICE CODE: C

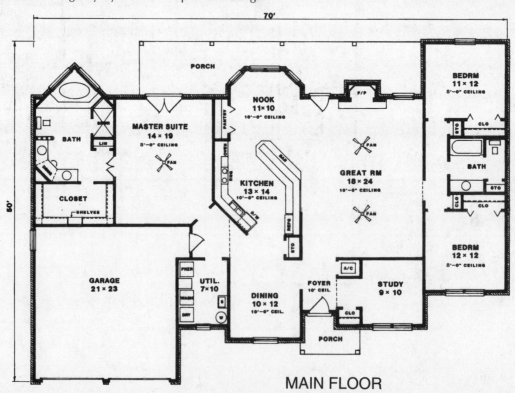

MAIN FLOOR

Captivating Facade

- This home attracts the eye with stately columns, half-round transoms and a sidelighted entry.
- A tall, barrel-vaulted foyer flows between the radiant formal areas at the front of the home.
- The barrel vault opens from the foyer to an overwhelming 14½-ft. vaulted family room, where a striking fireplace and a media center are captivating features.
- The central kitchen offers a dramatic 14½-ft. vaulted ceiling and a snack bar to the breakfast nook and family room. The nook's bay window overlooks a covered backyard patio.
- Formal occasions are hosted in the dining room, which boasts its own bay window and a 10½-ft. vaulted ceiling.
- The secluded master bedroom opens to the patio and flaunts an 11-ft. vaulted ceiling. A large walk-in closet and a posh bath with a step-up garden tub and a separate shower are also featured. On the other side of the home are three additional vaulted bedrooms and two more full baths.

Plan HDS-90-807

Bedrooms: 4	Baths: 3

Living Area:

Main floor	2,171 sq. ft.
Total Living Area:	**2,171 sq. ft.**
Garage	405 sq. ft.

Exterior Wall Framing:
2x4 and 8-in. concrete block

Foundation Options:
Slab
(All plans can be built with your choice of foundation and framing. A generic conversion diagram is available. See order form.)

BLUEPRINT PRICE CODE: C

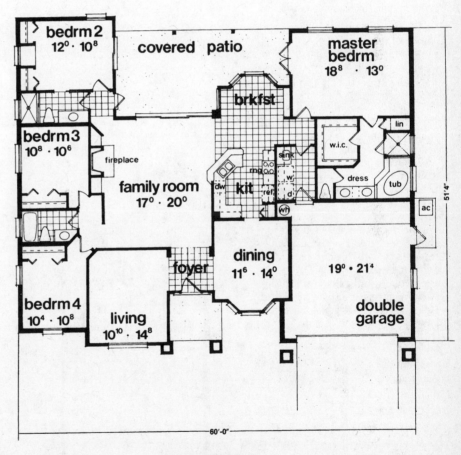

MAIN FLOOR

Luxurious Master Suite

- The inviting facade of this gorgeous one-story design boasts a sheltered porch, symmetrical architecture and elegant window treatments.
- Inside, beautiful arched openings frame the living room, which features a 12-ft. ceiling, a dramatic fireplace and a wet bar that is open to the deluxe kitchen.
- The roomy kitchen is highlighted by an island cooktop, a built-in desk and a snack bar that faces the bayed eating area and the covered back porch.
- Isolated to the rear of the home, the master suite is a romantic retreat, offering an intimate sitting area and a luxurious bath. Entered through elegant double doors, the private bath showcases a skylighted corner tub, a separate shower, his-and-hers vanities, and a huge walk-in closet.
- The two remaining bedrooms have walk-in closets and share a hall bath.
- Unless otherwise specified, the home has 9-ft. ceilings throughout.

Plan E-2106

Bedrooms: 3	**Baths:** 2

Living Area:	
Main floor	2,177 sq. ft.
Total Living Area:	**2,177 sq. ft.**
Standard basement	2,177 sq. ft.
Garage and storage	570 sq. ft.
Exterior Wall Framing:	2x4

Foundation Options:

Standard basement

Crawlspace

Slab

(All plans can be built with your choice of foundation and framing. A generic conversion diagram is available. See order form.)

BLUEPRINT PRICE CODE: C

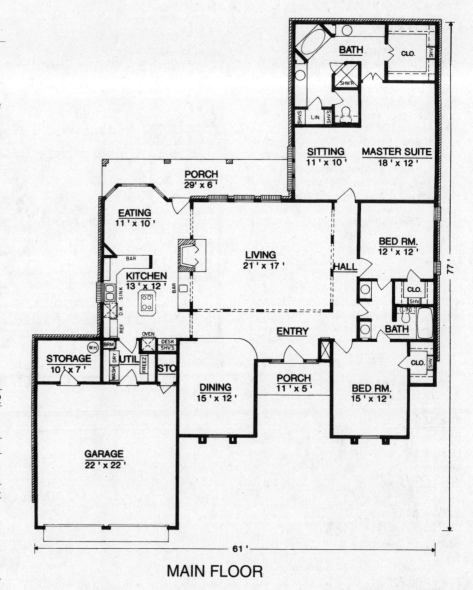

MAIN FLOOR

Plan E-2106

TO ORDER THIS BLUEPRINT, CALL TOLL-FREE 1-800-820-1283

PRICES AND DETAILS ON PAGES 12-15

Quiet Relaxation

- This elegant brick one-story home features a stunning master bedroom with a sunny morning porch for quiet relaxation. The bedroom's 11-ft. vaulted ceiling extends into the master bath, which boasts a corner garden tub and an attractive plant shelf.
- A few steps away, the open kitchen shares its 11-ft. ceiling and handy snack bar with the bright breakfast nook.
- A handsome fireplace warms the spacious family room, which is enhanced by a soaring 14-ft. ceiling. A striking French door provides access to a roomy deck that may also be reached from the master bedroom.
- The formal living areas flank the sidelighted foyer. The living room shows off a 14-ft. cathedral ceiling.
- Three secondary bedrooms with 9-ft. ceilings have easy access to a split bath. The center bedroom features a built-in desk with shelves above. Two of the bedrooms have walk-in closets.
- A convenient half-bath and a good-sized laundry room are located near the two-car garage, which offers additional storage space and excellent lighting from three bright windows.

Plan APS-2117	
Bedrooms: 4	**Baths:** 2½
Living Area:	
Main floor	2,187 sq. ft.
Total Living Area:	**2,187 sq. ft.**
Garage	460 sq. ft.
Exterior Wall Framing:	2x4

Foundation Options:

Crawlspace
(All plans can be built with your choice of foundation and framing. A generic conversion diagram is available. See order form.)

BLUEPRINT PRICE CODE:	C

MAIN FLOOR

DECK

MORNING PORCH

BEDRM 4 11X12

BRKFST 11X9

MASTER BEDROOM 16X15

BEDRM 3 11X12

FAMILY ROOM 17X19

KITCHEN 13X12

LINEN SINK WSHR DRYER

PLANT SHELF

PANTRY

BEDRM 2 12X11

LIVING 11X12

FOYER

DINING 13X11

STORAGE / MECH.

GARAGE 23X20

47

70

Peace of Mind

- Peace and privacy were the inspiration for this tranquil home.
- Past the inviting columned entry, the bright foyer flows into the spacious 13½-ft.-high vaulted living room, which includes a wet bar.
- The gourmet kitchen enjoys a 14-ft. vaulted ceiling and includes an angled snack counter and a large pantry. Sliding glass doors in the adjoining breakfast nook lead to a covered patio with a functional summer kitchen.
- The adjacent family room boasts a 15-ft. vaulted ceiling and a handsome window-flanked fireplace.
- The master suite offers an 11½-ft. vaulted ceiling, a windowed sitting area and patio access. His-and-hers walk-in closets flank the entrance to the plush master bath, which is highlighted by a garden tub overlooking a privacy yard.
- Three more bedrooms have vaulted ceilings that are at least 11½ ft. high. With a nearby full bath and back door entrance, the rear bedroom could be made into a great guest or in-law suite.

Plan HDS-99-157

Bedrooms: 4	Baths: 3

Living Area:

Main floor	2,224 sq. ft.
Total Living Area:	**2,224 sq. ft.**
Garage	507 sq. ft.

Exterior Wall Framing:
2x4 and concrete block

Foundation Options:
Slab
(All plans can be built with your choice of foundation and framing. A generic conversion diagram is available. See order form.)

BLUEPRINT PRICE CODE:	**C**

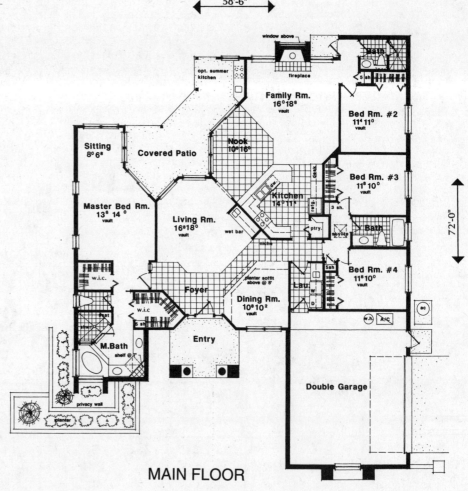

MAIN FLOOR

Plan HDS-99-157

PRICES AND DETAILS ON PAGES 12-15

Deluxe Suite!

- Decorative corner quoins, arched windows and a sleek hip roofline give this charming home a European look.
- The inviting foyer extends its 12-ft. ceiling into the formal spaces. The airy living room is brightened by high half- and quarter-round windows.
- The adjoining formal dining room is set off with elegant columned openings and high plant shelves.
- The island kitchen features a pantry and a sunny breakfast bay. A pass-through over the sink serves the family room.
- Boasting a 17-ft. vaulted ceiling and a glass-flanked fireplace, the family room also enjoys backyard access.
- The deluxe master suite includes a private sitting room. Both the bedroom and the sitting room have an 11-ft. tray ceiling and a view of a romantic two-sided fireplace. The master bath boasts a 13½-ft. vaulted ceiling, a garden tub, a three-sided mirror and a dual-sink vanity with knee space.
- A second bath is shared by the two remaining bedrooms.
- Unless otherwise noted, all rooms have 9-ft. ceilings.

Plan FB-5154-GEOR

Bedrooms: 3	**Baths:** 2½

Living Area:	
Main floor	2,236 sq. ft.
Total Living Area:	**2,236 sq. ft.**
Daylight basement	2,236 sq. ft.
Garage	483 sq. ft.
Exterior Wall Framing:	2x4

Foundation Options:
Daylight basement
Crawlspace
(All plans can be built with your choice of foundation and framing. A generic conversion diagram is available. See order form.)

BLUEPRINT PRICE CODE: C

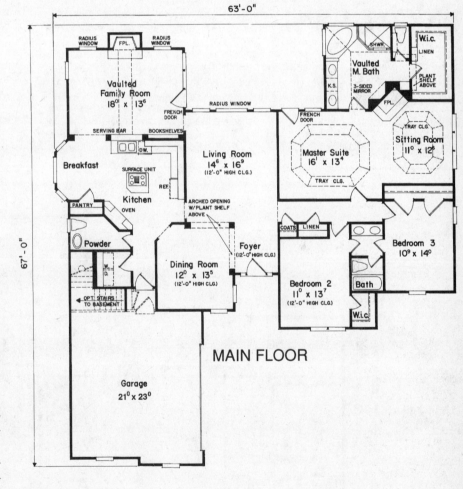

MAIN FLOOR

Luxurious Living on One Level

- The elegant exterior of this spacious one-story presents a classic air of quality and distinction.
- Three French doors brighten the inviting entry, which flows into the spacious living room. Boasting a 13-ft. ceiling, the living room enjoys a fireplace with a wide hearth and adjoining built-in bookshelves. A wall of glass, including a French door, provides views of the sheltered backyard porch.
- A stylish angled counter joins the spacious kitchen to the sunny bay-windowed eating nook.
- Secluded for privacy, the master suite features a nice dressing area, a large walk-in closet and private backyard access. A convenient laundry/utility room is adjacent to the master bath.
- At the opposite end of the home, double doors lead to three more bedrooms, a compartmentalized bath and lots of closet space.

Plan E-2208

Bedrooms: 4	**Baths:** 2
Living Area:	
Main floor	2,252 sq. ft.
Total Living Area:	**2,252 sq. ft.**
Standard basement	2,252 sq. ft.
Garage and storage	592 sq. ft.
Exterior Wall Framing:	2x6

Foundation Options:
Standard basement
Crawlspace
Slab
(All plans can be built with your choice of foundation and framing. A generic conversion diagram is available. See order form.)

BLUEPRINT PRICE CODE: C

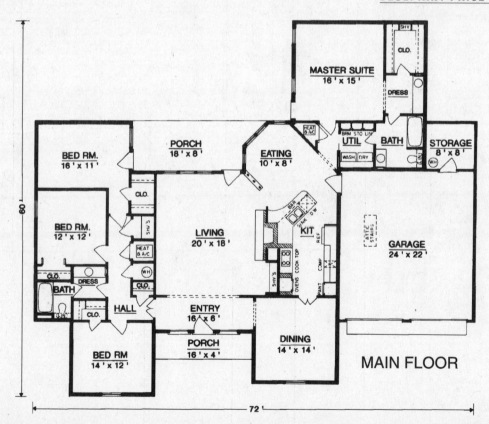

MAIN FLOOR

Plan E-2208

PRICES AND DETAILS ON PAGES 12-15

Ultra-Modern Interior

- The traditional exterior of this home conceals an ultra-modern floor plan.
- The foyer, brightened by sidelights and a transom window, reveals the sunken living room with an 11-ft. ceiling and a rear window wall. The formal dining room is entered through elegant arches.
- The fantastic family living spaces include an island kitchen, a gazebo-like breakfast room with a tray ceiling and a vaulted family room with a fireplace and access to the backyard.
- The regal master suite boasts a tray ceiling, private access to the backyard and a vaulted bath filled with all the latest luxuries.
- Two more bedrooms, two full baths and a vaulted bedroom or optional sitting room complete this unique design.

Plan FB-5010-GRAN

Bedrooms: 3+	Baths: 3
Living Area:	
Main floor	2,282 sq. ft.
Total Living Area:	**2,282 sq. ft.**
Daylight basement	2,282 sq. ft.
Garage	441 sq. ft.
Storage	70 sq. ft.
Exterior Wall Framing:	2x4

Foundation Options:
Daylight basement
Crawlspace
Slab
(Typical foundation & framing conversion diagram available—see order form.)

BLUEPRINT PRICE CODE:	C

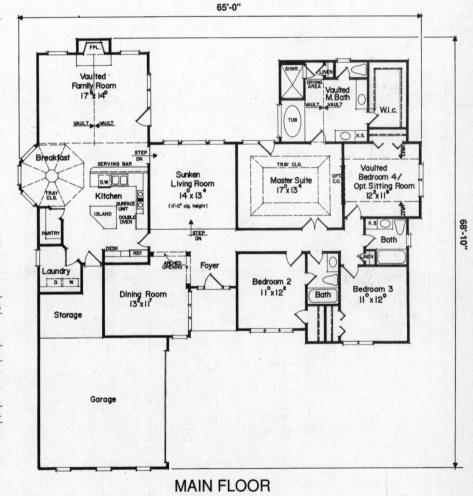

MAIN FLOOR

Elegant and Stylish

- An elegant brick exterior sets the tone for this stylish design.
- A raised foyer leads visitors to a formal dining room with a coffered ceiling or to a spacious living room.
- A double-sided fireplace is shared between the living room and the game room, which both feature cathedral ceilings.
- The large kitchen includes a work island, a pantry and abundant counter space.
- A magnificent master suite includes a luxurious master bath, two large closets and a multi-sided, multi-windowed sleeping area.
- Two secondary bedrooms share another full bath with two sinks.
- Also note the utility room off the breakfast nook.

MAIN FLOOR

Plan KY-2328	
Bedrooms: 3	Baths: 2
Living Area:	
Main floor	2,328 sq. ft.
Total Living Area:	**2,328 sq. ft.**
Garage	460 sq. ft.
Exterior Wall Framing:	2x4
Foundation Options:	
Slab	
(Typical foundation & framing conversion diagram available—see order form.)	
BLUEPRINT PRICE CODE:	C

TO ORDER THIS BLUEPRINT, CALL TOLL-FREE 1-800-820-1283

Plan KY-2328

PRICES AND DETAILS ON PAGES 12-15

High Luxury in One Story

- Beautiful arched windows lend a luxurious feeling to the exterior of this one-story home.
- Soaring 12-ft. ceilings add volume to both the wide entry area and the central living room, which boasts a large fireplace and access to a covered porch and the patio beyond.
- Double doors separate the formal dining room from the corridor-style kitchen. Features of the kitchen include a pantry and an angled eating bar. The sunny, bayed eating area is perfect for casual family meals.
- The plush master suite has amazing amenities: a walk-in closet, a skylighted, angled whirlpool tub, a separate shower and private access to the laundry/utility room and the patio.
- Three good-sized bedrooms and a full bath are situated across the home.

Plan E-2302

Bedrooms: 4	Baths: 2
Living Area:	
Main floor	2,396 sq. ft.
Total Living Area:	**2,396 sq. ft.**
Standard basement	2,396 sq. ft.
Garage	484 sq. ft.
Exterior Wall Framing:	2x6

Foundation Options:

Standard basement

Crawlspace

Slab

(All plans can be built with your choice of foundation and framing. A generic conversion diagram is available. See order form.)

BLUEPRINT PRICE CODE:	C

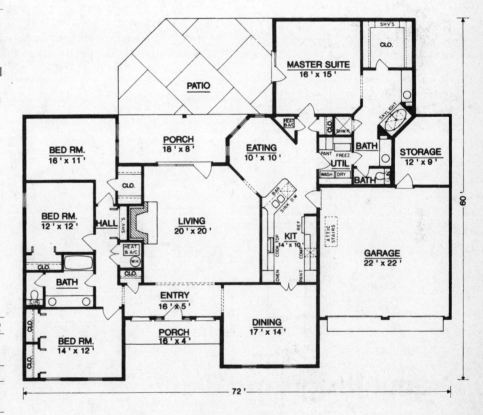

MAIN FLOOR

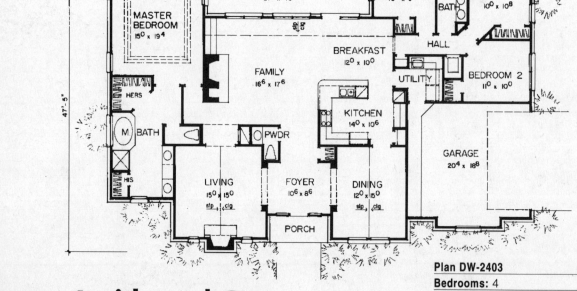

Drama Inside and Out

- Dramatic arched top windows, a brick chimney and rear lanai accent the exterior of this stylish transitional one-story.
- Vaulted living and dining areas flank the spacious foyer.
- Off the open kitchen and breakfast area is the central family room with 10' sloped ceiling, fireplace and built-in entertainment center.
- The secluded master suite offers a coffered ceiling, angled wall with access to the lanai, and private bath with separate closets, vanities and tub and shower.
- Three additional bedrooms share a second full bath at the opposite end of the home.

Plan DW-2403	
Bedrooms: 4	Baths: 2 ½
Space:	
Main floor	2,403 sq. ft.
Total Living Area	**2,403 sq. ft.**
Basement	2,403 sq. ft.
Garage	380 sq. ft.
Exterior Wall Framing	2x4
Foundation options:	
Standard Basement	
Crawlspace	
Slab	
(Foundation & framing conversion diagram available—see order form.)	
Blueprint Price Code	C

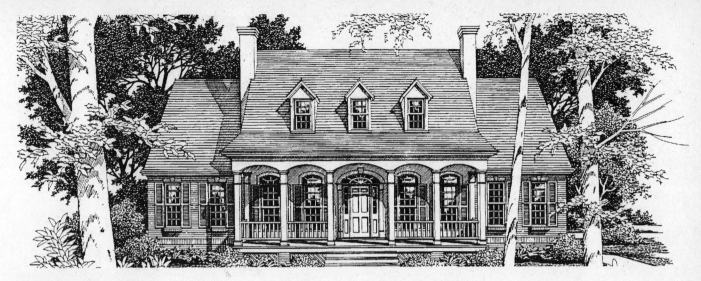

Wonderful Detailing

- The wonderfully detailed front porch, with its graceful arches, columns and railings, gives this home a character all its own. Dormer windows and arched transoms further accentuate the porch.
- The floor plan features a central living room with a 10-ft.-high ceiling and a fireplace framed by French doors. These doors open to a covered porch or a sun room, and a sheltered deck beyond.
- Just off the living room, the island kitchen and breakfast area provide a spacious place for family or guests. The nearby formal dining room has arched transom windows and a 10-ft. ceiling, as does the bedroom off the foyer. All of the remaining rooms have 9-ft. ceilings.
- The unusual master suite includes a window alcove, access to the porch and a fantastic bath with a garden tub.
- A huge utility room, a storage area off the garage and a 1,000-sq.-ft. attic space are other bonuses of this design.

Plan J-90019

Bedrooms: 3	Baths: 2½
Living Area:	
Main floor	2,410 sq. ft.
Total Living Area:	**2,410 sq. ft.**
Standard basement	2,410 sq. ft.
Garage	512 sq. ft.
Storage	86 sq. ft.
Exterior Wall Framing:	2x6

Foundation Options:

Standard basement
Crawlspace
Slab
(All plans can be built with your choice of foundation and framing. A generic conversion diagram is available. See order form.)

BLUEPRINT PRICE CODE: **C**

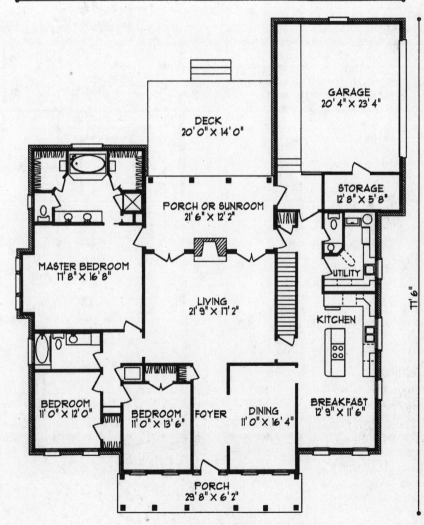

MAIN FLOOR

Easy Elegance

- Beautiful details combine with many traditional elements to give this home an easy but elegant feel.

- Inside, a 14-ft. ceiling tops the entry. Two half-walls with built-in shelves and natural wood columns introduce the dining room and a quiet study. The dining room features an 11-ft. ceiling, while the study has a 9-ft. ceiling and a neat built-in desk with shelves above.

- Beyond two more wood columns, the stunning living room shows off a 10-ft. stepped ceiling.

- A butler's pantry and a step-in pantry are nestled between the dining room and the gourmet kitchen. The kitchen's high counter extends to the adjacent family room, while the sunny breakfast nook overlooks a back porch.

- The family room includes a 10-ft. stepped ceiling, a media center and French doors to the porch.

- Two secondary bedrooms nearby are serviced by a full bath.

- Across the home, a 10-ft. stepped ceiling and a sitting area highlight the master bedroom. Two walk-in closets lead to the private bath, where two vanities make life a little easier.

Plan RD-2448

Bedrooms: 3+	Baths: 3
Living Area:	
Main floor	2,448 sq. ft.
Total Living Area:	**2,448 sq. ft.**
Garage and storage	539 sq. ft.
Exterior Wall Framing:	2x4

Foundation Options:

Crawlspace

Slab

(All plans can be built with your choice of foundation and framing. A generic conversion diagram is available. See order form.)

BLUEPRINT PRICE CODE: C

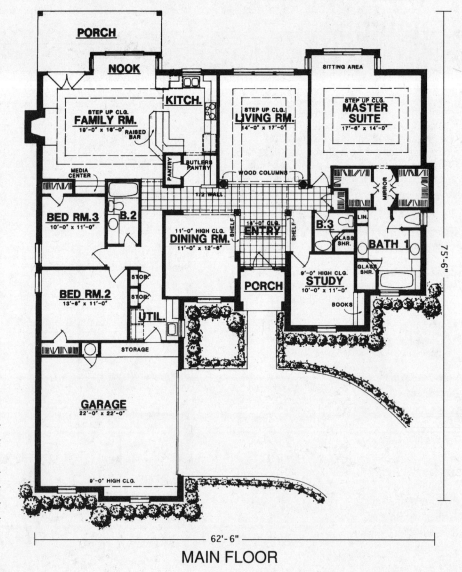

MAIN FLOOR

Plan RD-2448

PRICES AND DETAILS ON PAGES 12-15

Sophisticated One-Story

- Beautiful windows accentuated by elegant keystones highlight the exterior of this sophisticated one-story design.
- An open floor plan is the hallmark of the interior, beginning with the foyer that provides instant views of the study as well as the dining and living rooms.
- The spacious living room boasts a fireplace with built-in bookshelves and a rear window wall that stretches into the morning room.
- The sunny morning room has a snack bar to the kitchen. The island kitchen includes a walk-in pantry, a built-in desk and easy access to the utility room and the convenient half-bath.
- The master suite features private access to a nice covered patio, plus an enormous walk-in closet and a posh bath with a spa tub and glass-block shower.
- A hall bath serves the two secondary bedrooms. These three rooms, plus the utility area, have standard 8-ft. ceilings. Other ceilings are 10 ft. high.

Plan DD-2455

Bedrooms: 3+	Baths: 2½
Living Area:	
Main floor	2,457 sq. ft.
Total Living Area:	**2,457 sq. ft.**
Standard basement	2,457 sq. ft.
Garage	585 sq. ft.
Exterior Wall Framing:	2x4

Foundation Options:
Standard basement
Crawlspace
Slab
(All plans can be built with your choice of foundation and framing. A generic conversion diagram is available. See order form.)

BLUEPRINT PRICE CODE: C

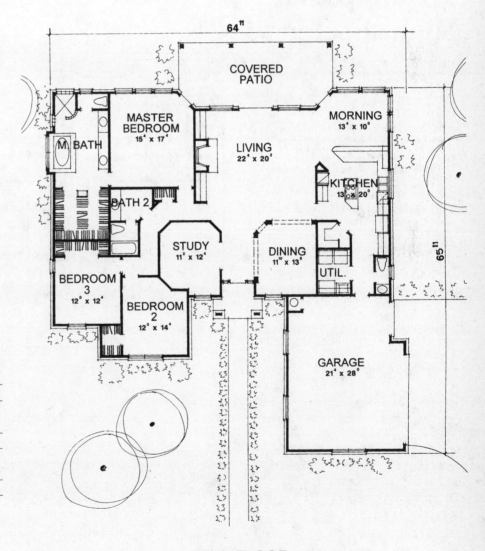

MAIN FLOOR

Stunning and Sophisticated

- A well-balanced blend of brick, stucco, and glass gives this stunning one-story home a sophisticated look.

- Past the recessed entry, the 16-ft.-high foyer is highlighted by a round-topped transom window. An arched opening introduces the formal dining room.

- The spectacular living room boasts an elegant 16-ft. coffered ceiling and is brightened by a trio of tall windows topped by a radius transom.

- The spacious island kitchen includes a roomy corner pantry and a built-in desk. A serving bar is convenient to the family room and the sunny breakfast area.

- A window-flanked fireplace is the focal point of the family room, which features a 16-ft. vaulted ceiling.

- A tray ceiling adorns the luxurious master suite. The vaulted master bath has a 16-ft. ceiling and includes a garden tub, a separate shower and his-and-hers vanities and walk-in closets.

Plan FB-5074-ARLI

Bedrooms: 3+	Baths: 2½
Living Area:	
Main floor	2,492 sq. ft.
Total Living Area:	**2,492 sq. ft.**
Daylight basement	2,492 sq. ft.
Garage	400 sq. ft.
Exterior Wall Framing:	2x4

Foundation Options:

Daylight basement

Crawlspace

(All plans can be built with your choice of foundation and framing. A generic conversion diagram is available. See order form.)

BLUEPRINT PRICE CODE: C

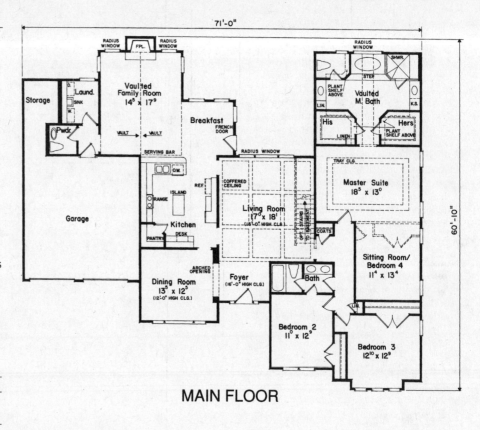

MAIN FLOOR

Plan FB-5074-ARLI

Creative Luxury

- A stunning facade and a creative floor plan combine to produce a truly luxurious home.
- The 17-ft., 10-in.-high foyer is flanked by a den with a nearby full bath, and the sunken formal dining room. Both rooms offer 13-ft. ceilings.
- Straight ahead, the sunken living room is topped by a 13-ft. ceiling and offers access to a covered patio through sliding glass doors. A summer kitchen services the patio on warm evenings.
- Patio access through sliding glass doors enhances the master bedroom.
- Twin walk-in closets with plant shelves above line the path to the sunken master bath. Here, amenities include a raised tub and a glass-block shower.
- Connected to the living room by a wet bar, the open kitchen is bordered by a quaint breakfast nook. From the nook, French and sliding doors open to the summer kitchen and patio.
- A beautiful fireplace warms the family room, while window-lined walls let in cheery sunlight.
- Two large secondary bedrooms flaunt exotic plant shelves and private access to a split bath.
- Unless otherwise noted, all rooms have 11-ft. ceilings.

Plan HDS-99-237

Bedrooms: 3+	Baths: 3
Living Area:	
Main floor	2,636 sq. ft.
Total Living Area:	**2,636 sq. ft.**
Garage	536 sq. ft.
Exterior Wall Framing:	8-in. concrete block

Foundation Options:

Slab

(All plans can be built with your choice of foundation and framing. A generic conversion diagram is available. See order form.)

BLUEPRINT PRICE CODE: D

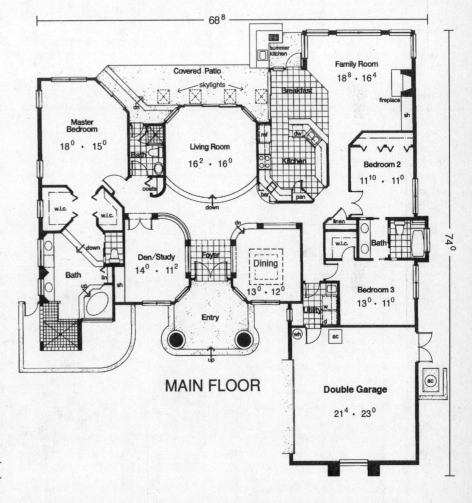

MAIN FLOOR

Dramatic Entry

- A dramatic entry accented by columns and arched window arrangements greets visitors to this beautiful home.
- Inside, the elegant columned foyer separates the sunken formal living room from the serene dining room. A striking 12-ft. ceiling soars over all three rooms.
- Handy cabinets flank a fireplace in the family room, where sliding glass doors open to a covered patio. A neat summer kitchen on the patio makes warm-weather gatherings a blast.

- An angled serving bar and a 15-ft. vaulted ceiling are shared by the family room and the kitchen. The breakfast nook is a perfect spot for casual meals.
- The master suite boasts a 12-ft., 8-in. ceiling and private patio access. The master bath features a raised tub and a separate sit-down shower.
- Across the home, two bedrooms share a split bath. The front room boasts a 12-ft. ceiling, and the other a 15-ft. ceiling. A quiet fourth bedroom with a 12-ft. vaulted ceiling is serviced by a bath near the patio.

Plan HDS-99-238	
Bedrooms: 4	Baths: 3
Living Area:	
Main floor	2,654 sq. ft.
Total Living Area:	2,654 sq. ft.
Garage	544 sq. ft.
Exterior Wall Framing:	8-in. concrete block
Foundation Options:	

Slab
(All plans can be built with your choice of foundation and framing. A generic conversion diagram is available. See order form.)

BLUEPRINT PRICE CODE:	D

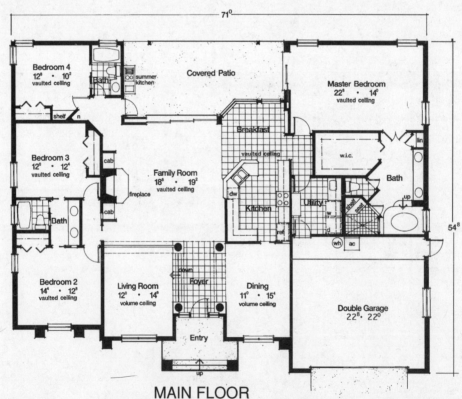

MAIN FLOOR

Plan HDS-99-238
PRICES AND DETAILS ON PAGES 12-15

Enjoyable Porch

- This stylish home offers an exciting four-season porch and a large deck. Transom windows adorn the exterior and allow extra light into the interior.
- The airy 17-ft., 4-in.-high foyer provides views into all of the living areas.
- The sunken Great Room boasts a see-through fireplace, a Palladian window and a 13-ft., 4-in. cathedral ceiling.
- An island cooktop highlights the corner kitchen, which is open to both the formal dining room and the casual dinette. Double doors access the porch, with its 12-ft. vaulted ceiling and French door to the inviting deck.
- The master bedroom is enhanced by a 10-ft., 3-in. tray ceiling and the see-through fireplace. The master bath has a whirlpool tub and a separate shower, each with striking glass-block walls.
- The front bedroom boasts an arched window under an 11-ft., 9-in. ceiling.
- The den off the foyer may be used to accommodate overnight guests.
- Unless otherwise noted, all rooms have 9-ft. ceilings.

Plan PI-92-535	
Bedrooms: 2+	**Baths:** 2½
Living Area:	
Main floor	2,302 sq. ft.
Four-season porch	208 sq. ft.
Total Living Area:	**2,510 sq. ft.**
Daylight basement	2,302 sq. ft.
Garage	912 sq. ft.
Exterior Wall Framing:	2x6
Foundation Options:	

Daylight basement

(All plans can be built with your choice of foundation and framing. A generic conversion diagram is available. See order form.)

BLUEPRINT PRICE CODE:	D

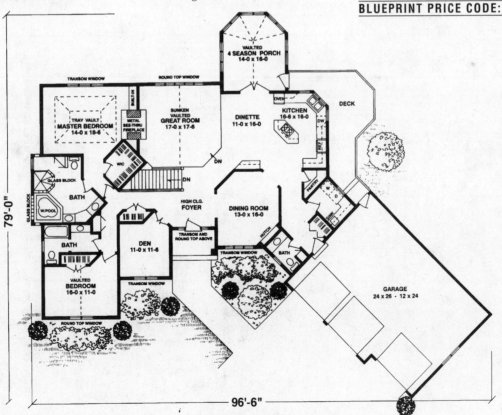

MAIN FLOOR

Room to Move

- Large rooms and high ceilings give this French-style home an expansive feel, and ceiling fans in the main living spaces add atmosphere and grace.
- Accessed from the 12-ft.-high entry, the living and dining rooms boast 11-ft. ceilings. Lovely windows with arched transoms flood each room with natural light. A central fireplace and built-in bookshelves grace the living room.
- In the dining room, double doors lead to the kitchen, which sports island cabinets, a large serving bar and a built-in desk. Two boxed-out windows let in the sun. Just past the serving bar, a bayed breakfast nook adds charm.
- A 10-ft. stepped ceiling rises over the secluded master bedroom, which offers private access to a covered porch. A see-through fireplace is shared with the private bath. The bath has a garden tub, a separate shower and walk-in closets.
- Three secondary bedrooms on the other side of the home have 10-ft. ceilings and share a skylighted hall bath.
- A bonus room above the garage may be finished for an additional bedroom or a quiet office space.

Plan RD-2240	
Bedrooms: 4+	**Baths:** 2½
Living Area:	
Main floor	2,240 sq. ft.
Bonus room	349 sq. ft.
Total Living Area:	**2,589 sq. ft.**
Garage	737 sq. ft.
Exterior Wall Framing:	2x4

Foundation Options:
Crawlspace
Slab
(All plans can be built with your choice of foundation and framing. A generic conversion diagram is available. See order form.)

BLUEPRINT PRICE CODE:	**D**

BONUS ROOM

MAIN FLOOR

Plan RD-2240

PRICES AND DETAILS ON PAGES 12-15

Patio Living

- A well-executed floor plan sets this impeccable design apart from the ordinary. Rooms of various shapes are arranged to maintain openness and to take advantage of a wonderful patio.
- The granite-paved foyer is open to the large living room, which provides a terrific view of the covered patio.
- The octagonal dining room and den or study flank the foyer and also face the living room.
- The uniquely shaped family room, with a fireplace centered between a wall of built-ins, has a dynamic view of the outdoors and is open to the kitchen.
- The spacious kitchen has an island range, a pantry and an octagonal nook.
- All of the living areas are enhanced by 11-ft.-high volume ceilings.
- Two nicely placed bedrooms allow for privacy. They have 9-ft., 4-in. ceilings and share a full bath, which is also accessible from the patio.
- The master suite is a wing in itself. The bedroom boasts a fireplace, walls of glass and a 9-ft., 8-in. ceiling. The posh bath includes a whirlpool tub, a corner shower and separate dressing areas.

Plan HDS-99-137

Bedrooms: 3	**Baths:** 2½

Living Area:

Main floor	2,656 sq. ft.
Total Living Area:	**2,656 sq. ft.**
Garage	503 sq. ft.

Exterior Wall Framing:
2x4 and 8-in. concrete block

Foundation Options:
Slab
(All plans can be built with your choice of foundation and framing. A generic conversion diagram is available. See order form.)

BLUEPRINT PRICE CODE:	**D**

MAIN FLOOR

- A/C
- Window Seat
- Bed Rm. 3 11⁰x 14⁸
- Bed Rm. 2 12⁰x 11⁰
- Bath
- blt-ins
- La.
- 36" fireplace
- 2 Car Garage 20⁰x 24⁴
- Hw.
- DW
- A/H
- wh
- Kit. 14⁰x 17⁰
- Family Rm. 21⁰x 17⁰
- Nook 10⁰x 10⁰
- covered patio
- Dining Rm. 11⁰x 11⁰
- Living Rm. 13⁰x 19⁰
- Foyer
- Entry
- Den/Study 11⁰x 11⁰
- Master Suite 18⁰x 18⁰
- wic
- wic
- A/C
- Ma. Bath

92'-0"

69'-0"

Living Room Overlooks Deck

- This stylish, updated home offers an open floor plan that revolves around a spacious living room; an inviting deck is visible through a spectacular rear window wall. A fireplace flanked by bookshelves adds more drama to this attention center.
- An island kitchen, a morning room with a bow window and a family room combine for convenient family dining or entertaining.
- The formal dining room is also handy for meal serving.
- The sleeping wing includes three bedrooms, two baths and an elegant master suite. Adjoining window seats, a gambrel ceiling and a private bath with dual closets and vanities are highlights of the master suite.
- The entire home is expanded by soaring 10-ft. ceilings.

Plan DD-2755

Bedrooms: 4	Baths: 3
Living Area:	
Main floor	2,868 sq. ft.
Total Living Area:	**2,868 sq. ft.**
Standard basement	2,800 sq. ft.
Garage	496 sq. ft.
Exterior Wall Framing:	2x4

Foundation Options:

Standard basement

Crawlspace

Slab

(All plans can be built with your choice of foundation and framing. A generic conversion diagram is available. See order form.)

BLUEPRINT PRICE CODE: D

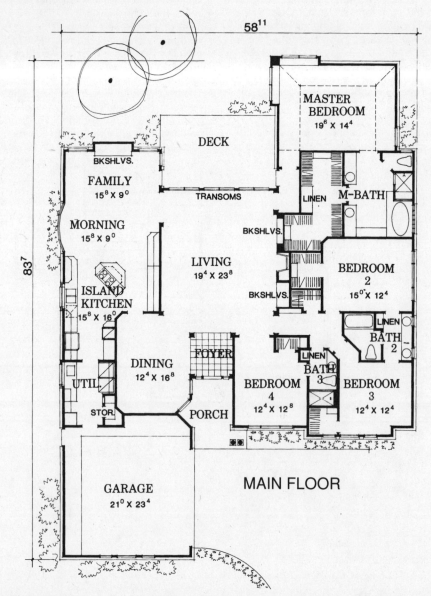

MAIN FLOOR

Plan DD-2755

PRICES AND DETAILS ON PAGES 12-15

Designed with the Master in Mind

- This elegant stucco home is designed with the master of the home in mind.
- Over 600 sq. ft. has been reserved for the master bedroom with an angled sitting area and patio access and a private bath with a large Jacuzzi, a private toilet room, dual dressing areas and an elegant double-doored entry.
- The formal living areas extend from the foyer. The central living room features a vaulted ceiling and a spectacular window wall overlooking the adjoining covered patio with a summer kitchen.
- The large gourmet kitchen merges with a breakfast area and a spacious family room. The breakfast area boasts a fascinating curved glass wall and opens to the patio. A handy snack bar serves refreshments to guests in the family room, which features a volume ceiling and a warming fireplace.
- Two secondary bedrooms, a den or guest room, and a hall or pool bath complete this unique floor plan.

Plan HDS-99-178

Bedrooms: 3-4	Baths: 3
Living Area:	
Main floor	2,931 sq. ft.
Total Living Area:	**2,931 sq. ft.**
Garage	703 sq. ft.
Exterior Wall Framing:	8-in. concrete block

Foundation Options:

Slab

(Typical foundation & framing conversion diagram available—see order form.)

BLUEPRINT PRICE CODE: **D**

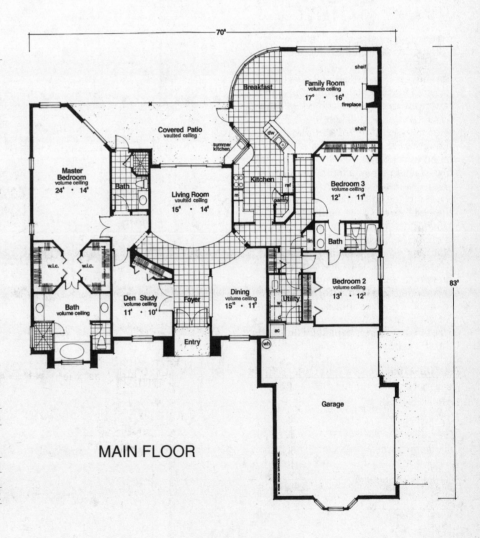

MAIN FLOOR

Master Suite
Fit for a King

- This sprawling one-story features an extraordinary master suite that stretches from the front of the home to the back.
- Eye-catching windows and columns introduce the foyer, which flows back to the Grand Room. French doors open to the covered veranda, which offers a fabulous summer kitchen.
- The kitchen and bayed morning room are nestled between the Grand Room and a warm Gathering Room. A striking fireplace, an entertainment center and an ale bar are found here. This exciting core of living spaces also offers dramatic views of the outdoors.
- The isolated master suite features a stunning two-sided fireplace and an octagonal lounge area with veranda access. His-and-hers closets, separate dressing areas and a garden tub are other amenities. Across the home, three additional bedroom suites have private access to one of two more full baths.
- The private dining room at the front of the home has a 13-ft. coffered ceiling and a niche for a china cabinet.
- An oversized laundry room is located across from the kitchen and near the entrance to the three-car garage.

Plan EOF-60	
Bedrooms: 4	**Baths:** 3
Living Area:	
Main floor	3,002 sq. ft.
Total Living Area:	**3,002 sq. ft.**
Garage	660 sq. ft.
Exterior Wall Framing:	2x6
Foundation Options:	

Slab
(All plans can be built with your choice of foundation and framing. A generic conversion diagram is available. See order form.)

BLUEPRINT PRICE CODE: E

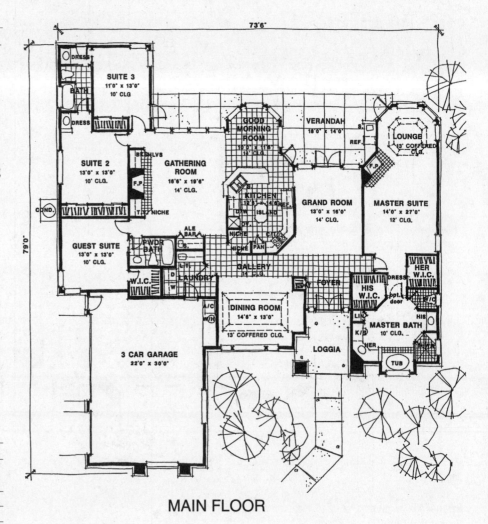

MAIN FLOOR

Plan EOF-60

PRICES AND DETAILS
ON PAGES 12-15

One-Floor Gracious Living

- An impressive roofscape, stately brick with soldier coursing and an impressive columned entry grace the exterior of this exciting single-story home.
- The entry opens to the the free-flowing interior, where the formal areas merge near the den, or guest room.
- The living room offers a window wall to a wide backyard deck, and the dining room is convenient to the kitchen.

- The octagonal island kitchen area offers a sunny breakfast nook with a large corner pantry.
- The spacious family room adjoins the kitchen and features a handsome fireplace and deck access. Laundry facilities and garage access are nearby.
- The lavish master suite with a fireplace and a state-of-the-art bath is privately situated in the left wing.
- Three secondary bedrooms have abundant closet space and share two baths on the right side of the home.
- The entire home features expansive 9-ft. ceilings.

Plan DD-3076

Bedrooms: 4+	**Baths:** 3

Living Area:	
Main floor	3,076 sq. ft.
Total Living Area:	**3,076 sq. ft.**
Standard basement	3,076 sq. ft.
Garage	648 sq. ft.
Exterior Wall Framing:	2x4

Foundation Options:

Standard basement
Crawlspace
Slab
(All plans can be built with your choice of foundation and framing. A generic conversion diagram is available. See order form.)

BLUEPRINT PRICE CODE:	E

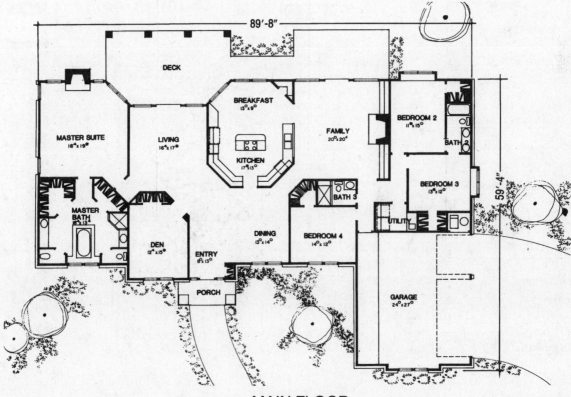

MAIN FLOOR

Distinguished Living

- Beautiful arches, sweeping rooflines and a dramatic entry court distinguish this one-story from all the rest.
- Elegant columns outline the main foyer. To the right, the dining room has a 13-ft. coffered ceiling and an ale bar with a wine rack.
- The centrally located Grand Room can be viewed from the foyer and gallery. French doors and flanking windows allow a view of the veranda as well.
- A large island kitchen and sunny morning room merge with the casual Gathering Room. The combination offers a big fireplace, a TV niche, bookshelves and a handy snack bar.
- The extraordinary master suite flaunts a 12-ft. ceiling, an exciting three-sided fireplace and a TV niche shared with the private bayed lounge. A luxurious bath, a private library and access to the veranda are also featured.
- The two smaller bedroom suites have private baths and generous closets.

Plan EOF-62

Bedrooms: 3	Baths: 3½
Living Area:	
Main floor	3,090 sq. ft.
Total Living Area:	**3,090 sq. ft.**
Garage	660 sq. ft.
Exterior Wall Framing:	2x6

Foundation Options:

Slab

(All plans can be built with your choice of foundation and framing. A generic conversion diagram is available. See order form.)

BLUEPRINT PRICE CODE: E

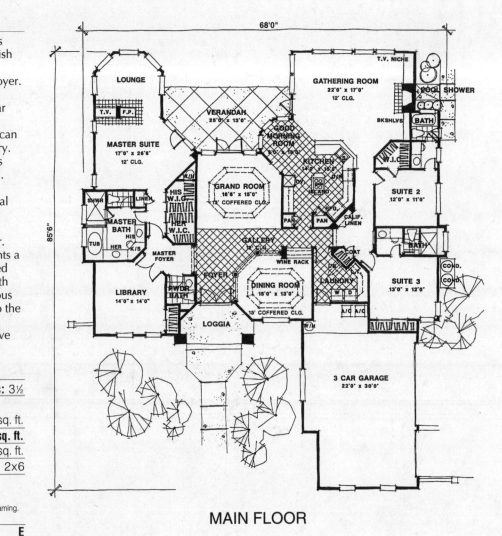

MAIN FLOOR

TO ORDER THIS BLUEPRINT,
CALL TOLL-FREE 1-800-820-1283

Plan EOF-62

PRICES AND DETAILS
ON PAGES 12-15

Design Excellence

- This stunning one-story home features dramatic detailing and an exceptionally functional floor plan.
- The brick exterior and exciting window treatments beautifully hint at the spectacular interior design.
- High ceilings, a host of built-ins and angled window walls are just some of the highlights.
- The family room showcases a curved wall of windows and a three-way fireplace that can be enjoyed from the adjoining kitchen and breakfast room.
- The octagonal breakfast room offers access to a lovely porch and a handy half-bath. The large island kitchen boasts a snack bar and a unique butler's pantry that connects with the dining room. The sunken living room includes a second fireplace and a window wall.
- The master suite sports a coffered ceiling, a private sitting area and a luxurious bath with a gambrel ceiling.
- Each of the four possible bedrooms has private access to a bath.

Plan KLF-922

Bedrooms: 3+	Baths: 3½
Living Area:	
Main floor	3,450 sq. ft.
Total Living Area:	**3,450 sq. ft.**
Garage	698 sq. ft.
Exterior Wall Framing:	2x4

Foundation Options:

Slab
(All plans can be built with your choice of foundation and framing. A generic conversion diagram is available. See order form.)

BLUEPRINT PRICE CODE: **E**

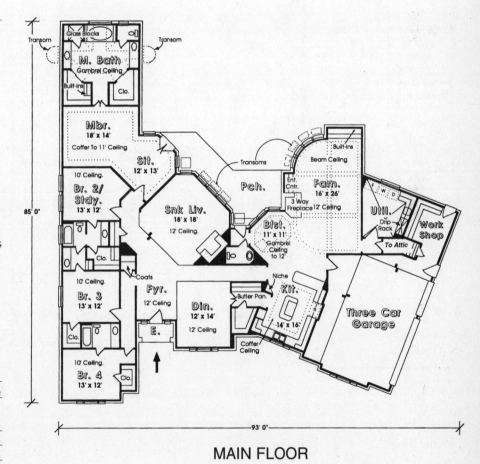

MAIN FLOOR

TO ORDER THIS BLUEPRINT,
CALL TOLL-FREE 1-800-820-1283

Plan KLF-922

PRICES AND DETAILS
ON PAGES 12-15

103

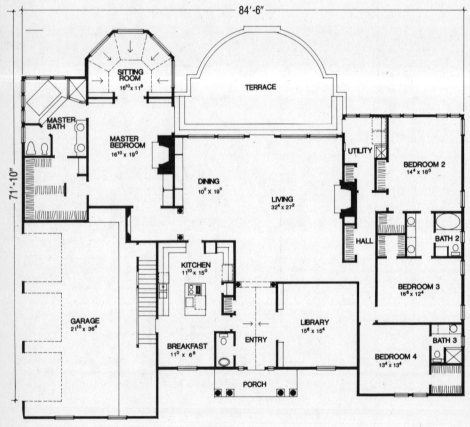

For Luxurious Living

- A high, sweeping roofline with dormers, an important-looking arched entry with support columns, and half-round window details all give a formal, estate look to this one-story plan.
- A cathedral ceilinged entryway leads past the island kitchen/breakfast and library room into the grand living room.
- With 10' ceilings, a fireplace, and glasswall views to the rear terrace, the combination living/formal dining room can accommodate large, formal gatherings or day-to-day family life equally well.
- The stunning master suite features a fireplace with built-ins, a cozy octagonal sitting room, lavish master bath and an enormous walk-in closet.
- The three secondary bedrooms offer abundant closet space and are served by two more baths.

Plan DD-3512-A

Bedrooms: 4	Baths: 3½
Space:	
Main floor	3,512 sq. ft.
Total Living Area	**3,512 sq. ft.**
Basement	3,512 sq. ft.
Garage	793 sq. ft.
Exterior Wall Framing	2x6
Ceiling Heights:	
Main floor	9'-10'

Foundation options:
Standard Basement
Crawlspace
Slab
(Foundation & framing conversion diagram available—see order form.)

Blueprint Price Code	F

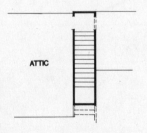

Prominent Portico

- A prominent portico accented by dramatic windows and a Spanish tile roof draws attention to this home. Grand double doors open into a foyer with an airy 14-ft. ceiling.
- Straight ahead, an elegant curved gallery frames the living room, which opens to a skylighted patio. Arched openings along one wall add high style.
- The quiet den and the formal dining room feature striking 12-ft. ceilings.
- The island kitchen boasts a big pantry and a neat pass-through to the patio, which offers a summer kitchen with a bar sink. A powder room is nearby.
- A 14-ft. vaulted ceiling, plus a fireplace set into a media wall make the family room a fun indoor gathering place.
- Two secondary bedrooms share a split bath with a dual-sink vanity.
- Across the home, a three-way fireplace and an entertainment center separate the master bedroom from its bayed sitting room. An exercise area, a wet bar and a posh bath are other pleasures!
- Unless otherwise mentioned, every room features a 10-ft. ceiling.

Plan HDS-99-242

Bedrooms: 3+	Baths: 3½
Living Area:	
Main floor	3,556 sq. ft.
Total Living Area:	**3,556 sq. ft.**
Garage	809 sq. ft.
Exterior Wall Framing:	8-in. concrete block

Foundation Options:

Slab

(All plans can be built with your choice of foundation and framing. A generic conversion diagram is available. See order form.)

BLUEPRINT PRICE CODE:	F

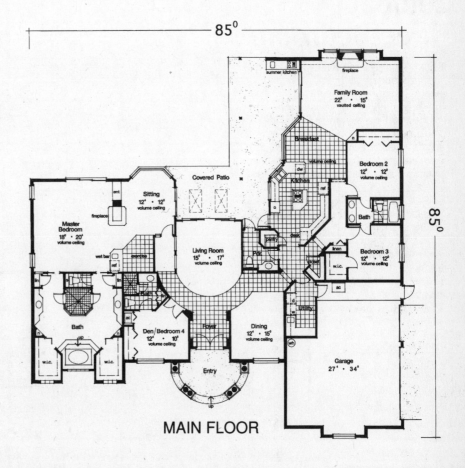

MAIN FLOOR

TO ORDER THIS BLUEPRINT,
CALL TOLL-FREE 1-800-820-1283

Plan HDS-99-242

PRICES AND DETAILS
ON PAGES 12-15

105

Compact Three-Bedroom

- Both openness and privacy are possible in this economical three-bedroom home design.
- The bright living room boasts a 17-ft. vaulted ceiling, a warming fireplace and a corner window. A high clerestory window lets in additional natural light.
- The modern, U-shaped kitchen features a handy corner pantry and a versatile snack bar.
- The adjacent open dining area provides access to a backyard deck through sliding glass doors.
- A lovely corner window brightens the secluded master bedroom, which also includes a roomy walk-in closet and private access to a compartmentalized hall bath.
- Upstairs, two good-sized bedrooms share a second split bath.

Plan B-101-8501

Bedrooms: 3	Baths: 2
Living Area:	
Upper floor	400 sq. ft.
Main floor	846 sq. ft.
Total Living Area:	**1,246 sq. ft.**
Garage	400 sq. ft.
Standard basement	846 sq. ft.
Exterior Wall Framing:	2x4

Foundation Options:

Standard basement

(All plans can be built with your choice of foundation and framing. A generic conversion diagram is available. See order form.)

BLUEPRINT PRICE CODE: A

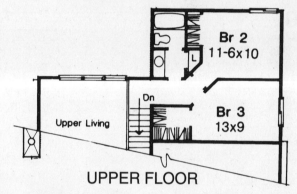

UPPER FLOOR

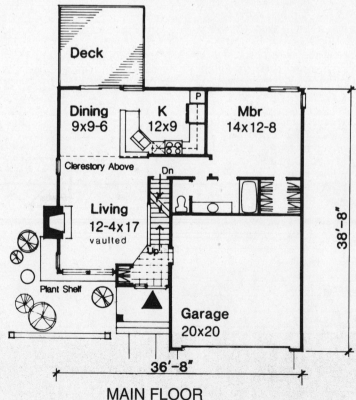

MAIN FLOOR

TO ORDER THIS BLUEPRINT, CALL TOLL-FREE 1-800-820-1283

Plan B-101-8501

PRICES AND DETAILS ON PAGES 12-15

Pleasantly Peaceful

- The covered front porch of this lovely two-story traditional home offers a pleasant and peaceful welcome.
- Off the open foyer is an oversized family room, drenched with sunlight through a French door and surrounding windows. A handsome fireplace adds further warmth.
- The neatly arranged kitchen is conveniently nestled between the formal dining room and the sunny breakfast room. A pantry and a powder room are also within easy reach.
- A stairway off the family room accesses the upper floor, which houses three bedrooms. The isolated master bedroom features a 10-ft. tray ceiling, a huge walk-in closet and a private bath offering a vaulted ceiling, an oval garden tub and a separate shower.
- The two secondary bedrooms share another full bath.

Plan FB-1466

Bedrooms: 3	Baths: 2½
Living Area:	
Upper floor	703 sq. ft.
Main floor	763 sq. ft.
Total Living Area:	**1,466 sq. ft.**
Daylight basement	763 sq. ft.
Garage	426 sq. ft.
Storage	72 sq. ft.
Exterior Wall Framing:	2x4

Foundation Options:
Daylight basement
Crawlspace
(All plans can be built with your choice of foundation and framing. A generic conversion diagram is available. See order form.)

BLUEPRINT PRICE CODE:	**A**

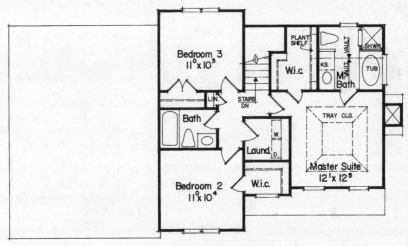

UPPER FLOOR

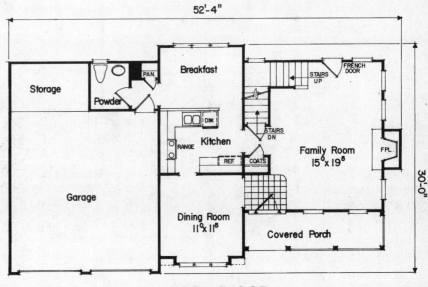

MAIN FLOOR

City House, Country Home

- Gingerbread detailing and a covered front porch give this charming home a country-style feel, while its modest width makes it suitable for a city lot.
- The inviting entry leads directly into the spacious Great Room, which boasts a 14-ft. vaulted ceiling. An impressive brick fireplace adds warmth and atmosphere.

- A French door in the adjoining dining area opens to a covered back porch.
- The efficient L-shaped kitchen is open to the dining area and brightened by a window above the sink. The nearby laundry room also accesses the porch.
- The quiet master bedroom is furnished with a roomy walk-in closet. The central full bath is just steps away.
- An elegant open-railed stairway overlooks the entry and leads to the upper floor, where two additional bedrooms share a hallway linen closet and a second full bath.

Plan V-1098	
Bedrooms: 3	Baths: 2
Living Area:	
Upper floor	396 sq. ft.
Main floor	702 sq. ft.
Total Living Area:	**1,098 sq. ft.**
Exterior Wall Framing:	2x6
Foundation Options:	
Crawlspace	

(All plans can be built with your choice of foundation and framing. A generic conversion diagram is available. See order form.)

BLUEPRINT PRICE CODE:	A

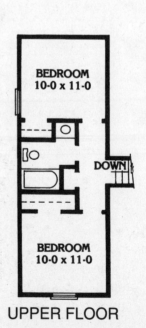

MAIN FLOOR

UPPER FLOOR

TO ORDER THIS BLUEPRINT, CALL TOLL-FREE 1-800-820-1283

Plan V-1098

PRICES AND DETAILS ON PAGES 12-15

Striking Stone Chimney

- With tall windows and a rustic stone chimney, the striking facade of this home demands attention.
- The sheltered entry leads into a raised foyer, which steps down to the sunny living room and its dramatic 16-ft. vaulted ceiling.
- A handsome fireplace warms the living room and the adjoining dining room, which offers access to an inviting deck.
- A cozy breakfast nook is included in the efficient, open-design kitchen. A special feature is the convenient pass-through to the dining room.
- A skylighted staircase leads upstairs to the master suite, with its private bath and large walk-in closet.
- A second bedroom shares another full bath with a loft or third bedroom.
- A dramatic balcony overlooks the living room below.

Plan B-224-8512

Bedrooms: 2+	Baths: 2½
Living Area:	
Upper floor	691 sq. ft.
Main floor	668 sq. ft.
Total Living Area:	**1,359 sq. ft.**
Standard basement	668 sq. ft.
Garage	458 sq. ft.
Exterior Wall Framing:	2x4

Foundation Options:

Standard basement

(All plans can be built with your choice of foundation and framing. A generic conversion diagram is available. See order form.)

BLUEPRINT PRICE CODE:	**A**

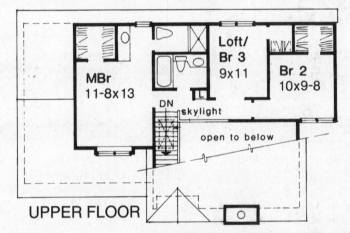

UPPER FLOOR

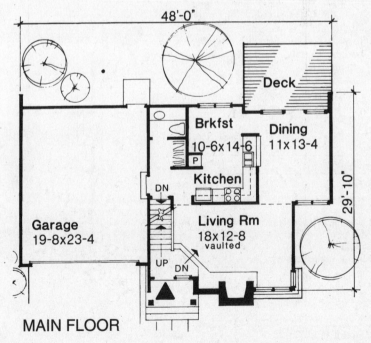

MAIN FLOOR

TO ORDER THIS BLUEPRINT,
CALL TOLL-FREE 1-800-820-1283

Plan B-224-8512

PRICES AND DETAILS
ON PAGES 12-15

109

Deluxe Master Bedroom Suite in Compact Two-Story

- Plenty of luxuries are found in this compact two-story.
- A massive corner fireplace, corner window, vaulted ceiling and library alcove highlight the living room.
- A rear window wall in the dining room overlooks a rear deck that joins the bayed breakfast area and kitchen.
- The vaulted master suite offers corner window, plant shelf and a private bath.
- Up one step are two extra bedrooms and the hall loft that views the living room and entryway below.

Plan B-88002

Bedrooms: 3	Baths: 2½
Space:	
Upper floor:	833 sq. ft.
Main floor:	744 sq. ft.
Total living area:	1,577 sq. ft.
Garage:	528 sq. ft.
Exterior Wall Framing:	2x4

Foundation options:
Standard basement.
(Foundation & framing conversion diagram available — see order form.)

Blueprint Price Code: B

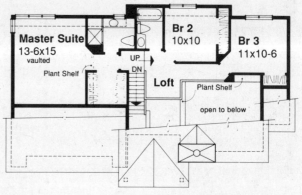

UPPER FLOOR

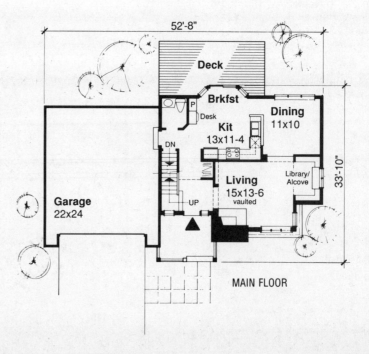

MAIN FLOOR

Plan B-88002

Luxury and Livability

- Big on style, this modest-sized home features a quaint Colonial exterior and an open interior.
- The covered front porch leads to a two-story foyer that opens to the formal living and dining rooms. A coat closet, an attractive display niche and a powder room are centrally located, as is the stairway to the upper floor.
- The kitchen, breakfast nook and family room are designed so that each room has its own definition yet also functions as part of a whole. The angled sink separates the kitchen from the breakfast nook, which is outlined by a bay window. The large family room includes a fireplace.
- The upper floor has an exceptional master suite, featuring an 8-ft., 6-in. tray ceiling in the sleeping area and an 11-ft. vaulted ceiling in the spa bath.
- Two more bedrooms and a balcony hall add to this home's luxury and livability.

Plan FB-1600

Bedrooms: 3	**Baths:** 2½

Living Area:	
Upper floor	772 sq. ft.
Main floor	828 sq. ft.
Total Living Area:	**1,600 sq. ft.**
Daylight basement	828 sq. ft.
Garage	473 sq. ft.
Exterior Wall Framing:	**2x4**

Foundation Options:

Daylight basement

Crawlspace

Slab

(All plans can be built with your choice of foundation and framing. A generic conversion diagram is available. See order form.)

BLUEPRINT PRICE CODE: B

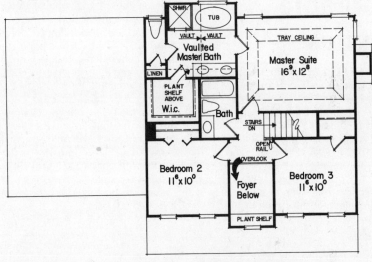

UPPER FLOOR

MAIN FLOOR

Affordable Luxuries

- An attractive stucco exterior introduces a cozy home packed with luxuries.
- A bright French door in the covered entry opens into the dramatic foyer, which is highlighted by a soaring 17-ft. vaulted ceiling.
- An inviting archway, a half-wall and a 10-ft., 3-in. vaulted ceiling frame the sunken living/dining room.
- A large family room with a cozy fireplace highlights the casual living

areas at the rear of the home. A wall of windows brightens both the family room and the breakfast nook. A French door opens to a backyard patio.

- In the kitchen, a neat island with a cooktop and an eating bar for three makes casual and formal meals a snap.
- Upstairs, a sun-drenched loft with a skylight looks over the foyer below.
- A peaceful sitting area in the master suite serves as a welcome refuge after harried days. The compartmentalized master bath boasts a bright skylight and a dual-sink vanity.
- Two more good-sized bedrooms share a second full bath.

Plan S-70794

Bedrooms: 3	Baths: 2½
Living Area:	
Upper floor	714 sq. ft.
Main floor	947 sq. ft.
Total Living Area:	**1,661 sq. ft.**
Partial basement	608 sq. ft.
Garage	451 sq. ft.
Exterior Wall Framing:	2x6

Foundation Options:

Partial basement
Crawlspace
Slab
(All plans can be built with your choice of foundation and framing. A generic conversion diagram is available. See order form.)

BLUEPRINT PRICE CODE:	B

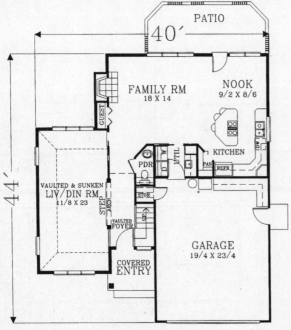

MAIN FLOOR

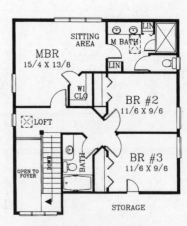

UPPER FLOOR

TO ORDER THIS BLUEPRINT,
CALL TOLL-FREE 1-800-820-1283

Plan S-70794

PRICES AND DETAILS
ON PAGES 12-15

Compact Three-Bedroom Home

- A stylish blend of traditional and contemporary architecture emanates from this compact, three-bedroom home.
- Two bedrooms and an adjoining bath occupy one corner of the main level, segregated from the living areas by a central hallway.
- Large living and dining area has sloped ceilings, wood stove, and access to side deck.
- Master suite occupies entire 516 sq. ft. second floor, features sloped ceilings, and overlooks the living room below.

LIVING ROOM 20/8 x13/6
WOOD STOVE
SLOPED CEILING
DINING 10/3 x12/0
SLOPED CEILING
DECK
BEDROOM 11/0x10/0
CLOSET
CLOSET
CLOSET 4/0
LIN
BATH
down
R/O
D W
KITCHEN 9/8 x9/0
REF
STOR
up
LAUNDRY
furnace
WH
GARAGE 22/4x23/9
SEAT
Tub w/ Shower
ENTRY
W D
BEDROOM 11/0x10/0
CLOSET 6/0
SEAT
50'-0"
52'-6"

MAIN FLOOR

SLOPED CEILING
BALCONY RAILING
down
BEDROOM 17/5 x13/3
SLOPED CEILING
Shower
BATHTUB
WALK-IN CLOSET
11/0
11/0
BATH

UPPER FLOOR

STOR **PLAN H-947-2A**
WITHOUT BASEMENT

PLAN H-947-2B
WITH DAYLIGHT BASEMENT

Plans H-947-2A & -2B	
Bedrooms: 3	Baths: 2

Space:

Upper floor:	516 sq. ft.
Main floor:	1,162 sq. ft.
Total living area:	**1,678 sq. ft.**
Basement:	approx. 1,162 sq. ft.
Garage:	530 sq. ft.

Exterior Wall Framing: 2x6

Foundation options:
Daylight basement (Plan H-947-2B).
Crawlspace (Plan H-947-2A).
(Foundation & framing conversion diagram available — see order form.)

Blueprint Price Code: B

Plenty of Presence

- A stucco facade complemented by fieldstone, a dramatic roofline and handsome keystones accenting the window treatments gives this home plenty of presence.

- Inside, the two-story foyer boasts an open stairway with a balcony overlook. Straight ahead, the huge family room is expanded by a 16½-ft. vaulted ceiling, plus a tall window and a French door that frame the fireplace.

- The adjoining dining room flows into the kitchen and breakfast room, which feature an angled serving bar, a bright window wall and a French door that opens to a covered patio.

- The main-floor master suite is the pride of the floor plan, offering a 10-ft. tray ceiling. The deluxe master bath has a 14-ft. vaulted ceiling, a garden tub and a spacious walk-in closet.

- The upper floor offers two more bedrooms, a full bath and attic space.

Plan FB-1681

Bedrooms: 3	Baths: 2½
Living Area:	
Upper floor	449 sq. ft.
Main floor	1,232 sq. ft.
Total Living Area:	**1,681 sq. ft.**
Daylight basement	1,232 sq. ft.
Garage and storage	435 sq. ft.
Exterior Wall Framing:	2x4
Foundation Options:	
Daylight basement	
Crawlspace	

(All plans can be built with your choice of foundation and framing. A generic conversion diagram is available. See order form.)

BLUEPRINT PRICE CODE: B

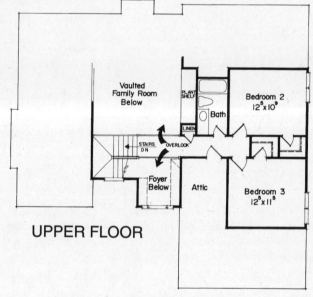

UPPER FLOOR

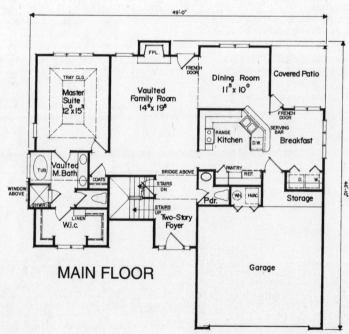

MAIN FLOOR

TO ORDER THIS BLUEPRINT, CALL TOLL-FREE 1-800-820-1283

Plan FB-1681

PRICES AND DETAILS ON PAGES 12-15

Windows of Opportunity

- This handsome home features a wide assortment of windows, flooding the interior with light and accentuating the open, airy atmosphere.
- The two-story-high entry is brightened by a beautiful Palladian window above. Just ahead, the vaulted Great Room also showcases a Palladian window. The adjoining dining area offers sliding glass doors that open to a large deck.
- The centrally located kitchen includes a boxed-out window over the sink, providing a nice area for plants.
- The family/breakfast area hosts a snack bar and a wet bar, in addition to a fireplace that warms the entire area.
- Upstairs, the master suite boasts corner windows, a large walk-in closet and a compartmentalized bath with a dual-sink vanity. A balcony overlooking the foyer and the Great Room leads to two more bedrooms and a full bath.

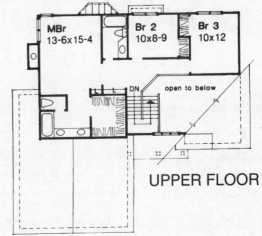

UPPER FLOOR

Plan B-129-8510

Bedrooms: 3	Baths: 2½
Living Area:	
Upper floor	802 sq. ft.
Main floor	922 sq. ft.
Total Living Area:	**1,724 sq. ft.**
Standard basement	924 sq. ft.
Garage	579 sq. ft.
Exterior Wall Framing:	2x4

Foundation Options:

Standard basement
(All plans can be built with your choice of foundation and framing. A generic conversion diagram is available. See order form.)

BLUEPRINT PRICE CODE:	**B**

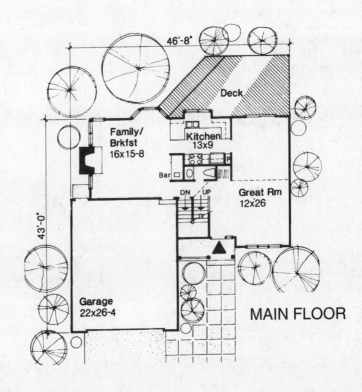

MAIN FLOOR

TO ORDER THIS BLUEPRINT,
CALL TOLL-FREE 1-800-820-1283

Plan B-129-8510

PRICES AND DETAILS
ON PAGES 12-15

115

Casual Country Living

- With its covered wraparound porch, this gracious design is ideal for warm summer days or starry evenings.
- The spacious living room boasts a handsome brick-hearth fireplace and built-in book and gun storage. A French door accesses the backyard.
- The open kitchen design provides plenty of space for food storage and preparation with its pantry and oversized central island.
- Two mirror-imaged baths service the three bedrooms on the upper floor. Each secondary bedroom features a window seat and two closets. The master bedroom has a large walk-in closet and a private bath.
- A versatile hobby or sewing room is also included.
- An optional carport off the dining room is available upon request. Please specify when ordering.

Plan J-8895

Bedrooms: 3	Baths: 2½
Living Area:	
Upper floor	860 sq. ft.
Main floor	919 sq. ft.
Total Living Area:	**1,779 sq. ft.**
Standard basement	919 sq. ft.
Optional carport	462 sq. ft.
Exterior Wall Framing:	2x4

Foundation Options:

Standard basement

Crawlspace

Slab

(All plans can be built with your choice of foundation and framing. A generic conversion diagram is available. See order form.)

BLUEPRINT PRICE CODE: **B**

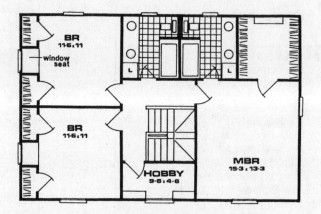

UPPER FLOOR

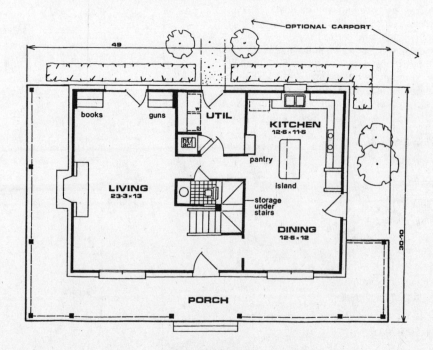

MAIN FLOOR

TO ORDER THIS BLUEPRINT, CALL TOLL-FREE 1-800-820-1283   Plan J-8895   *PRICES AND DETAILS ON PAGES 12-15*

Customize Your Floor Plan!

- An optional bonus room and a choice between a loft or a bedroom allow you to customize the floor plan of this striking two-story traditional.
- The 18-ft. vaulted foyer leads guests past a handy powder room and directly into the living areas. Straight ahead is an 18-ft. vaulted family room with a handsome centered fireplace. To the right of the foyer is the formal dining room. The spaces are pleasantly set off by a beautiful open-railed staircase.
- The sunny breakfast room is open to the island kitchen. A pantry closet, a lot of counter space and direct access to the laundry room and the garage add to the kitchen's efficiency.
- The main-floor master suite is a treasure, with its 11-ft. tray ceiling and vaulted, amenity-filled master bath.
- Upstairs, two bedrooms, a full bath and an optional loft and bonus room provide plenty of opportunity for expansion and customization.

Plan FB-1874

Bedrooms: 3+	Baths: 2½
Living Area:	
Upper floor	554 sq. ft.
Main floor	1,320 sq. ft.
Bonus room	155 sq. ft.
Total Living Area:	**2,029 sq. ft.**
Daylight basement	1,320 sq. ft.
Garage	240 sq. ft.
Storage	38 sq. ft.
Exterior Wall Framing:	2x4

Foundation Options:

Daylight basement

(All plans can be built with your choice of foundation and framing. A generic conversion diagram is available. See order form.)

BLUEPRINT PRICE CODE: C

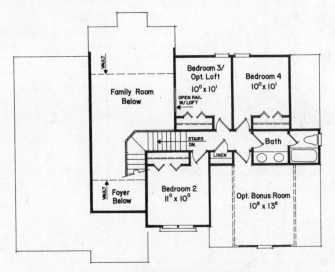

UPPER FLOOR

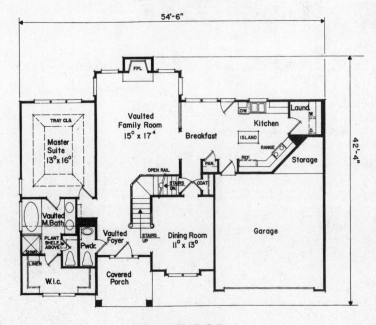

MAIN FLOOR

TO ORDER THIS BLUEPRINT,
CALL TOLL-FREE 1-800-820-1283

Plan FB-1874

PRICES AND DETAILS
ON PAGES 12-15

117

Octagonal Dining Bay

- Classic traditional styling is recreated with a covered front porch and triple dormers with half-round windows.
- Off the entry porch, double doors reveal the reception area, with a walk-in closet and a half-bath.

- The living room features a striking fireplace and leads to the dining room, with its octagonal bay.
- The island kitchen overlooks the dinette and the family room, which features a second fireplace and sliding glass doors to a rear deck.
- Upstairs, the master suite boasts a walk-in closet and a whirlpool bath. A skylighted hallway connects three more bedrooms and another full bath.

Plan K-680-R	
Bedrooms: 4	**Baths:** 2½
Living Area:	
Upper floor	853 sq. ft.
Main floor	1,047 sq. ft.
Total Living Area:	**1,900 sq. ft.**
Standard basement	1,015 sq. ft.
Garage and storage	472 sq. ft.
Exterior Wall Framing:	2x4 or 2x6
Foundation Options:	
Standard basement	
Slab	

(All plans can be built with your choice of foundation and framing. A generic conversion diagram is available. See order form.)

BLUEPRINT PRICE CODE:	B

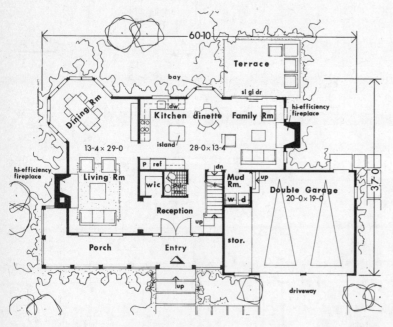

MAIN FLOOR

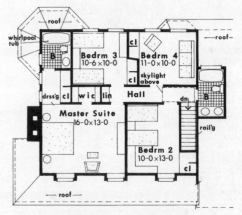

UPPER FLOOR

**VIEW INTO LIVING ROOM
AND DINING ROOM**

**TO ORDER THIS BLUEPRINT,
CALL TOLL-FREE 1-800-820-1283**

Plan K-680-R

**PRICES AND DETAILS
ON PAGES 12-15**

Farmhouse for Today

- An inviting covered porch and decorative dormer windows lend traditional warmth and charm to this attractive design.
- The up-to-date interior includes ample space for entertaining as well as for daily family activities.
- The elegant foyer is flanked on one side by the formal, sunken living room and on the other by a sunken family room with a fireplace and an entertainment center. Each room features an 8½-ft. tray ceiling and views of the porch.
- The dining room flows from the living room to increase the entertaining space.
- The kitchen/nook/laundry area forms a large expanse for casual family living and domestic chores.
- Upstairs, the grand master suite includes a large closet and a private bath with a garden tub, a designer shower and a private deck.
- A second full bath serves the two secondary bedrooms.

Plan U-87-203

Bedrooms: 3	Baths: 2½
Living Area:	
Upper floor	857 sq. ft.
Main floor	1,064 sq. ft.
Total Living Area:	**1,921 sq. ft.**
Standard basement	1,064 sq. ft.
Garage	552 sq. ft.
Exterior Wall Framing:	2x4 or 2x6

Foundation Options:

Standard basement

Crawlspace

Slab

(All plans can be built with your choice of foundation and framing. A generic conversion diagram is available. See order form.)

BLUEPRINT PRICE CODE: B

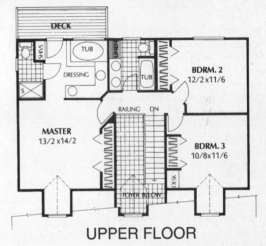

UPPER FLOOR

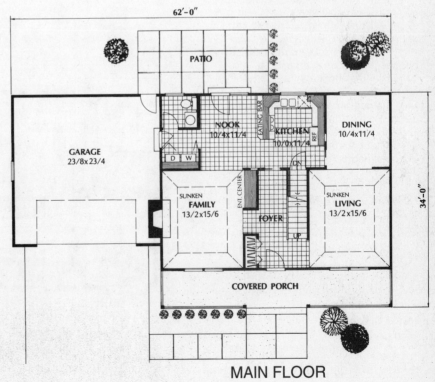

MAIN FLOOR

Irresistible Master Suite

- This traditional three-bedroom home features a main-floor master suite that is hard to resist, with an inviting window seat and a delightful bath.
- The home is introduced by a covered front entry, topped by a dormer with a half-round window.
- Just off the front entry, the formal dining room is distinguished by a tray ceiling and a large picture window overlooking the front porch.
- Straight back, the Great Room features a 16-ft.-high vaulted ceiling with a window wall facing the backyard. The fireplace can be enjoyed from the adjoining kitchen and breakfast area.
- The gourmet kitchen includes a corner sink, an island cooktop and a walk-in pantry. A 12-ft. vaulted ceiling expands the breakfast nook, which features a built-in desk and backyard deck access.
- The spacious master suite offers a 14-ft. vaulted ceiling and a luxurious private bath with a walk-in closet, a garden tub, a separate shower and a dual-sink vanity with a sit-down makeup area.
- An open-railed stairway leads up to another full bath that serves two additional bedrooms.

Plan B-89061

Bedrooms: 3	Baths: 2½
Living Area:	
Upper floor	436 sq. ft.
Main floor	1,490 sq. ft.
Total Living Area:	**1,926 sq. ft.**
Standard basement	1,490 sq. ft.
Garage	400 sq. ft.
Exterior Wall Framing:	2x4

Foundation Options:

Standard basement

(All plans can be built with your choice of foundation and framing. A generic conversion diagram is available. See order form.)

BLUEPRINT PRICE CODE: B

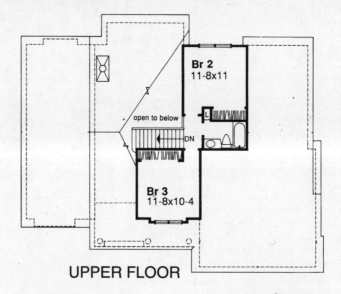

UPPER FLOOR

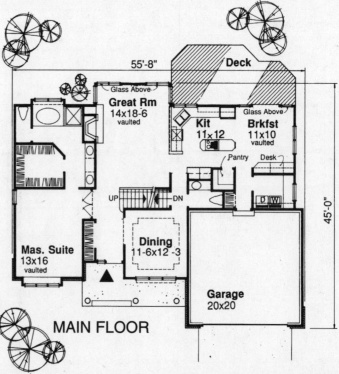

MAIN FLOOR

Plan B-89061

PRICES AND DETAILS ON PAGES 12-15

Bedroom Options

- Your choice of a three- or four-bedroom upper level is offered in this classically designed home.
- A bayed formal dining area and a cozy den flank the open foyer. Both rooms feature stunning floor-to-ceiling bay windows.
- A spacious living room with a large fireplace merges with the modern island kitchen and dinette at the rear. Sliders provide access to a future patio.
- Convenient main-floor laundry facilities and a powder room are located near the garage entrance.
- Both upper-level bedroom options are included in the plans for this home.

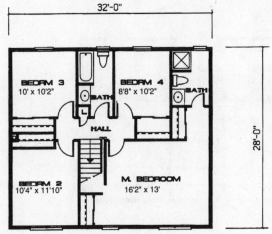

UPPER FLOOR
FOUR BEDROOMS

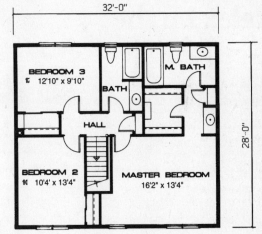

UPPER FLOOR
THREE BEDROOMS

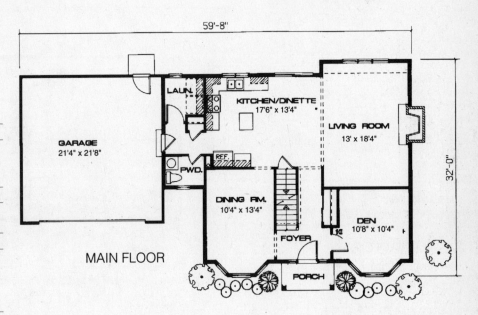

MAIN FLOOR

Plan GL-1953-P

Bedrooms: 3-4	Baths: 2 ½
Space:	
Upper floor	896 sq. ft.
Main floor	1,057 sq. ft.
Total Living Area	**1,953 sq. ft.**
Basement	1,032 sq. ft.
Garage	462 sq. ft.
Exterior Wall Framing	2x6

Foundation options:
Standard Basement
(Foundation & framing conversion diagram available—see order form.)

Blueprint Price Code	B

Relax on the Front Porch

- With its wraparound covered porch, this quaint two-story home makes summer evenings a breeze.
- Inside, a beautiful open stairway welcomes guests into the vaulted foyer, which connects the formal areas. The front-facing living and dining rooms have views of the covered front porch.
- French doors open from the living room to the family room, where a fireplace and corner windows warm and brighten this spacious activity area.
- The breakfast nook, set off by a half-wall, hosts a handy work desk and opens to the back porch.
- The country kitchen offers an oversized island, a pantry closet and illuminating windows flanking the corner sink.
- The upper-floor master suite boasts two walk-in closets and a private bath with a tub and a separate shower. Two more bedrooms, another full bath and a laundry room are also included.

Plan AGH-1997

Bedrooms: 3	Baths: 2½
Living Area:	
Upper floor	933 sq. ft.
Main floor	1,064 sq. ft.
Total Living Area:	**1,997 sq. ft.**
Standard basement	1,064 sq. ft.
Garage	662 sq. ft.
Exterior Wall Framing:	2x6

Foundation Options:

Standard basement

(All plans can be built with your choice of foundation and framing. A generic conversion diagram is available. See order form.)

BLUEPRINT PRICE CODE:	B

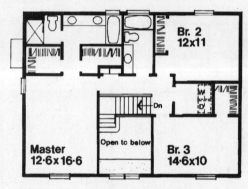

UPPER FLOOR

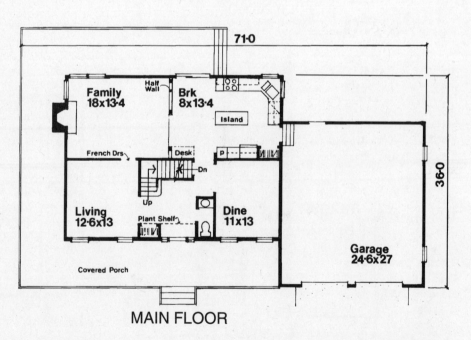

MAIN FLOOR

Plan AGH-1997

PRICES AND DETAILS ON PAGES 12-15

Aim to Relax

- Cozy spaces abound in this charming two-story, which offers many choices for relaxation.
- A wide covered porch enhances the facade and provides a wonderful area for outdoor conversations.
- Inside, the sidelighted foyer spills into the formal living and dining rooms. A boxed-out window graces the living room, while the dining room overlooks a comfortable backyard porch.
- The porch is accessed through the dinette, where a handy built-in desk allows a child to concentrate on homework under a parent's watchful

eye. The island kitchen has speedy access to the two-car garage to make unloading groceries easier. A laundry room and a half-bath are nearby.
- A magnificent 13½-ft. cathedral ceiling crowns the spacious family room. Flanked by cheery windows, a handsome central fireplace creates warmth and atmosphere.
- Upstairs, the master bedroom flaunts a 12½-ft. cathedral ceiling, a stylish Palladian window arrangement, a roomy walk-in closet and a private bath with a dual-sink vanity.
- Two secondary bedrooms are bathed in natural light and share a full bath with a nearby linen closet.

Plan GL-2042	
Bedrooms: 3	**Baths: 2½**
Living Area:	
Upper floor	839 sq. ft.
Main floor	1,203 sq. ft.
Total Living Area:	**2,042 sq. ft.**
Standard basement	1,191 sq. ft.
Garage	440 sq. ft.
Exterior Wall Framing:	2x4

Foundation Options:

Standard basement
(All plans can be built with your choice of foundation and framing. A generic conversion diagram is available. See order form.)

BLUEPRINT PRICE CODE:	**C**

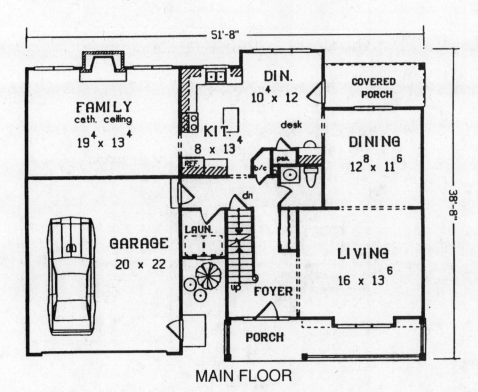

MAIN FLOOR

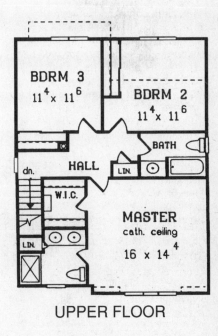

UPPER FLOOR

TO ORDER THIS BLUEPRINT,
CALL TOLL-FREE 1-800-820-1283

Plan GL-2042

PRICES AND DETAILS
ON PAGES 12-15

123

Great Spaces

- Open, airy casual living spaces and intimate formal areas are the hallmarks of this intriguing home.
- A two-story-high foyer introduces the the living room, where French doors open to a veranda. On the opposite side of the foyer is a spacious dining room with a delightful bay window.
- The casual areas combine at the back of the home. The family room features a two-story-high ceiling and a fireplace framed with glass, including a French door that opens to the backyard.
- A half-wall is all that separates the family room from the inviting bay-windowed breakfast nook. An angled serving counter/snack bar keeps the kitchen open to the activity areas.
- A walk-in pantry and a laundry room are nearby, just off the garage entrance.
- Upstairs, the luxurious master suite features an elegant 9-ft. tray ceiling. The master bath boasts a 12-ft. vaulted ceiling, an oval garden tub, a private toilet compartment and a walk-in closet adorned with a plant shelf.
- Two more bedrooms, a versatile loft and a hall bath complete the upper floor.

Plan FB-5056-MAGU

Bedrooms: 3+	Baths: 2½
Living Area:	
Upper floor	1,019 sq. ft.
Main floor	1,034 sq. ft.
Total Living Area:	**2,053 sq. ft.**
Daylight basement	1,034 sq. ft.
Garage and storage	465 sq. ft.
Exterior Wall Framing:	2x4

Foundation Options:

Daylight basement

(All plans can be built with your choice of foundation and framing. A generic conversion diagram is available. See order form.)

BLUEPRINT PRICE CODE: C

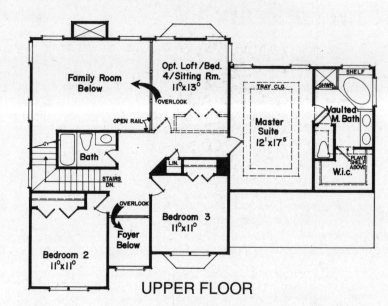

UPPER FLOOR

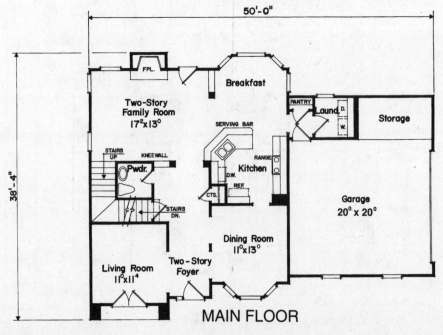

MAIN FLOOR

TO ORDER THIS BLUEPRINT, CALL TOLL-FREE 1-800-820-1283

Plan FB-5056-MAGU

PRICES AND DETAILS ON PAGES 12-15

Ornate Colonial

- The symmetrical windows of this traditional two-story are adorned with decorative shutters and gabled dormers.
- At the center of the inviting porch, the home's main entrance opens to a tiled two-story-high foyer that directs traffic to each of the living areas.
- The formal areas are located at the front of the home and are great for receiving and entertaining guests. A handsome fireplace is featured in the living room.
- The informal areas merge at the rear of the home and overlook a large terrace.
- French doors off the central dinette open to the terrace. The kitchen's U-shaped design includes a serving bar, while the family room's open plan is versatile enough for any activity.
- A charming balcony overlooks the foyer and bridges the four upstairs bedrooms.
- The spacious master suite boasts a 12-ft.-high cathedral ceiling and a relaxing window seat. Two walk-in closets and a private bath with a dual-sink vanity and a whirlpool tub under corner glass are also featured.

Plan AHP-9460

Bedrooms: 4	Baths: 2½
Living Area:	
Upper floor	1,026 sq. ft.
Main floor	1,112 sq. ft.
Total Living Area:	**2,138 sq. ft.**
Standard basement	1,112 sq. ft.
Garage and storage	494 sq. ft.
Exterior Wall Framing:	2x4 or 2x6

Foundation Options:
Standard basement
Crawlspace
Slab
(All plans can be built with your choice of foundation and framing. A generic conversion diagram is available. See order form.)

BLUEPRINT PRICE CODE: C

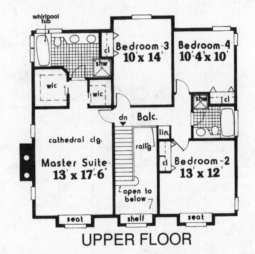

UPPER FLOOR

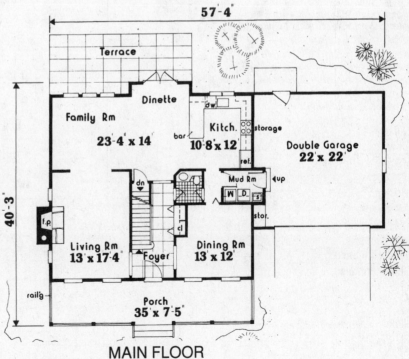

MAIN FLOOR

Today's Tradition

- This two-story country home combines traditional standards with the exciting new designs of today.
- Visitors are welcomed by the wrap-around porch and the symmetrical bay windows of the living and dining rooms.
- The front half of the main floor lends itself to entertaining as the angled entry creates a flow between the formal areas.
- French doors lead from the living room to the spacious family room, which boasts a beamed ceiling, a warm fireplace and porch access.
- The super kitchen features an island cooktop with a snack bar. A nice-sized laundry room is nearby.
- The spacious upper level hosts a master suite with two walk-in closets and a large bath with a dual-sink vanity, a tub and a separate shower. Three more bedrooms share another full bath.

Plan AGH-2143

Bedrooms: 4	Baths: 2½
Living Area:	
Upper floor	1,047 sq. ft.
Main floor	1,096 sq. ft.
Total Living Area:	**2,143 sq. ft.**
Daylight basement	1,096 sq. ft.
Garage	852 sq. ft.
Exterior Wall Framing:	2x6

Foundation Options:

Daylight basement

(All plans can be built with your choice of foundation and framing. A generic conversion diagram is available. See order form.)

BLUEPRINT PRICE CODE: C

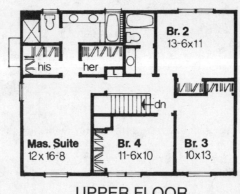

UPPER FLOOR

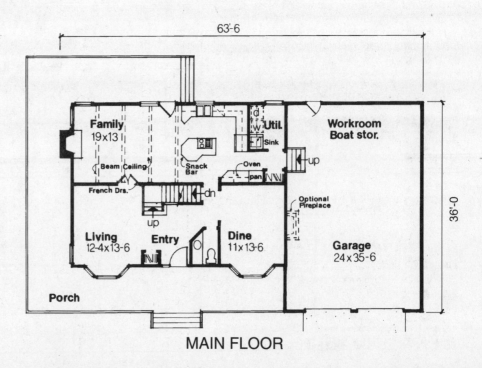

MAIN FLOOR

Plan AGH-2143

PRICES AND DETAILS
ON PAGES 12-15

Colonial for Today

- Designed for a growing family, this handsome traditional home offers four bedrooms plus a den and three complete baths. The Colonial exterior is updated by a covered front entry porch with a fanlight window above.
- The dramatic tiled foyer is two stories high and provides direct access to all of the home's living areas. The spacious living room has an inviting brick fireplace and sliding pocket doors to the adjoining dining room.
- Overlooking the backyard, the huge combination kitchen/family room is the

home's hidden charm. The kitchen features a peninsula breakfast bar with seating for six.
- The family room includes a window wall with sliding glass doors that open to an enticing terrace. A built-in entertainment center and bookshelves line another wall.
- The adjacent mudroom houses a pantry closet and the washer/dryer. A full bath and a big den complete the main floor.
- The upper floor is highlighted by a beautiful balcony that overlooks the foyer below. The luxurious master suite boasts a skylighted dressing area and two closets, including an oversized walk-in closet. The private master bath offers a whirlpool tub and a dual-sink vanity.

Plan AHP-7050	
Bedrooms: 4+	**Baths: 3**
Living Area:	
Upper floor	998 sq. ft.
Main floor	1,153 sq. ft.
Total Living Area:	**2,151 sq. ft.**
Standard basement	1,067 sq. ft.
Garage and storage	439 sq. ft.
Exterior Wall Framing:	2x6
Foundation Options:	
Standard basement	
Crawlspace	
Slab	

(All plans can be built with your choice of foundation and framing. A generic conversion diagram is available. See order form.)

BLUEPRINT PRICE CODE:	C

MAIN FLOOR

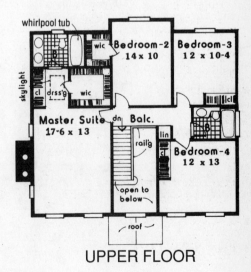

UPPER FLOOR

Front Porch Invites Visitors

- This neat and well-proportioned design exudes warmth and charm, with an inviting front porch and a decorative sunburst in the gable.
- The broad foyer flows between the formal areas for special occasions. The living room and expansive family room join together, creating additional space for larger gatherings.
- The bright and airy kitchen, dinette and family room intermingle for great casual family living.
- Upstairs, the roomy master suite is complemented by a private bath available in two configurations. The alternate master bath adds 70 sq. ft. to the home.
- Two additional bedrooms share another full bath and a sunny library that overlooks the foyer.

Plan GL-2161

Bedrooms: 3	Baths: 2½
Living Area:	
Upper floor	991 sq. ft.
Main floor	1,170 sq. ft.
Total Living Area:	**2,161 sq. ft.**
Standard basement	1,170 sq. ft.
Garage	462 sq. ft.
Exterior Wall Framing:	2x6

Foundation Options:

Standard basement

(All plans can be built with your choice of foundation and framing. A generic conversion diagram is available. See order form.)

BLUEPRINT PRICE CODE: C

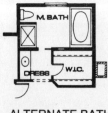

ALTERNATE BATH

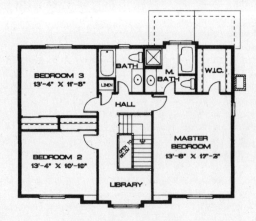

UPPER FLOOR

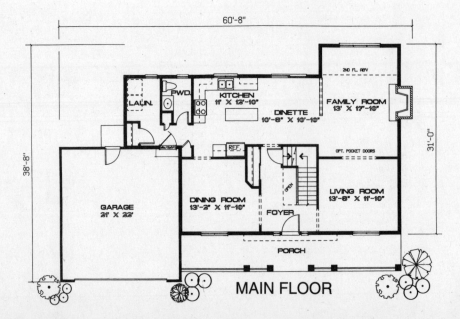

MAIN FLOOR

Plan GL-2161

PRICES AND DETAILS ON PAGES 12-15

Down-Home Country Flavor!

- Open living areas, decorative dormers and a spacious wraparound porch give this charming home its country feel.
- The main entrance opens into an enormous living room, which boasts a handsome fireplace flanked by bright windows and built-in cabinets.
- The adjoining dining room is brightened by windows on three sides. A rear French door opens to the porch.
- The modern kitchen serves the dining room over an eating bar. A half-bath and a laundry/utility area with access to the garage and porch are nearby.
- The removed master bedroom includes a roomy walk-in closet and a private bath with a corner shower and a dual-sink vanity with knee space.
- All main-floor rooms have 9-ft. ceilings.
- Two upper-floor bedrooms share a hallway bath, which is enhanced by one of three dormer windows.

Plan J-90013

Bedrooms: 3	Baths: 2½
Living Area:	
Upper floor	823 sq. ft.
Main floor	1,339 sq. ft.
Total Living Area:	**2,162 sq. ft.**
Standard basement	1,339 sq. ft.
Garage	413 sq. ft.
Storage	106 sq. ft.
Exterior Wall Framing:	2x4

Foundation Options:

Standard basement

Crawlspace

Slab

(All plans can be built with your choice of foundation and framing. A generic conversion diagram is available. See order form.)

BLUEPRINT PRICE CODE: C

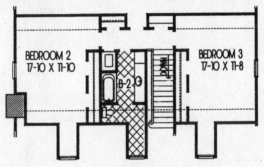

UPPER FLOOR

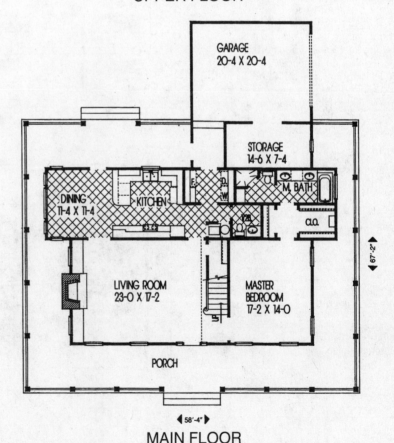

MAIN FLOOR

English Elegance

- Tradition takes on new meaning in this elegant brick and cedar two-story home, starting with the covered front entry and extending to the gracious open stairway.
- A large custom window adds light to the dramatic two-story foyer and draws visitors into a home designed for formal entertaining and casual family living.
- The spacious family room features a brick fireplace, a wall of windows overlooking the backyard and an adjoining kitchen and nook area.
- Designed for convenience, the extra-large kitchen includes an island counter, a built-in pantry and desk, and a convenient buffet counter for serving guests in the adjoining formal dining room and the informal dinette.
- All four bedrooms are on the second floor. The master suite includes a separate dressing area and a private bath with a double vanity.

Plan A-2293-DS

Bedrooms: 4	Baths: 2½
Living Area:	
Upper floor	941 sq. ft.
Main floor	1,192 sq. ft.
Total Living Area:	**2,133 sq. ft.**
Standard basement	1,192 sq. ft.
Garage	484 sq. ft.
Exterior Wall Framing:	2x6

Foundation Options:

Standard basement
(Typical foundation & framing conversion diagram available—see order form.)

BLUEPRINT PRICE CODE:	C

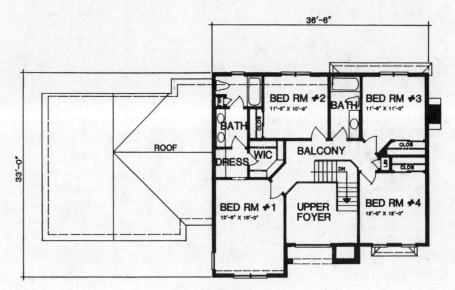

UPPER FLOOR

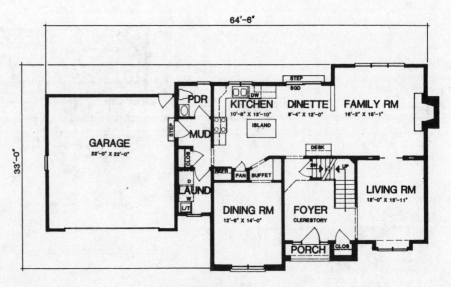

MAIN FLOOR

Plan A-2293-DS

PRICES AND DETAILS ON PAGES 12-15

Graceful Facade

- Elegant half-round transoms spruce up the wood-shuttered facade of this charming traditional two-story.
- The wide front porch opens to a two-story foyer that flows between the formal dining room and a two-story-high library or guest room. Sliding French doors close off the library from the Great Room.
- Perfect for entertaining, the spacious Great Room shows off a handsome fireplace and a TV center. Beautiful French doors on either side extend the room to a large backyard deck.
- The adjoining dinette has its own view of the backyard through a stunning semi-circular glass wall, which sheds light on the nice-sized attached kitchen.
- A pantry and a laundry room are neatly housed near the two-car garage. The adjacent full bath could be downsized to a half-bath with storage space.
- The master suite and its private whirlpool bath are isolated from the three upper-floor bedrooms and features a 14-ft.-high cathedral ceiling.
- Unless otherwise specified, all main-floor ceilings are 9 ft. high.

Plan AHP-9490

Bedrooms: 4+	Baths: 2½-3
Living Area:	
Upper floor	722 sq. ft.
Main floor	1,497 sq. ft.
Total Living Area:	**2,219 sq. ft.**
Standard basement	1,165 sq. ft.
Garage	420 sq. ft.
Exterior Wall Framing:	2x4 or 2x6

Foundation Options:
Standard basement
Crawlspace
Slab

(All plans can be built with your choice of foundation and framing. A generic conversion diagram is available. See order form.)

BLUEPRINT PRICE CODE: **C**

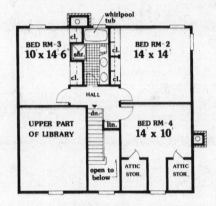

UPPER FLOOR

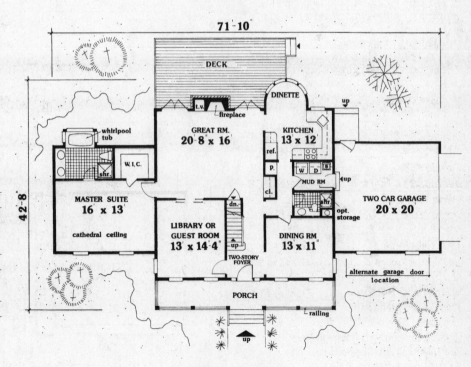

MAIN FLOOR

Distinct Formal Spaces

- This attractive traditional home boasts room for up to four bedrooms plus formal living spaces that can be closed off from the informal areas.
- The two-story foyer features two handy coat closets and a decorative upper-level plant shelf.
- A large gourmet kitchen with a work island and an adjoining breakfast room each overlook an oversized rear deck. The breakfast room opens to the family room, which features a cozy fireplace.
- The laundry closet is conveniently located on the upper level, close to the bedrooms.
- The master bedroom has a tray ceiling and a private bath. The bath boasts his-and-hers walk-in closets, separate vanities and a toilet compartment.
- The bonus room can serve as a fourth bedroom, hobby room or playroom.

Plan APS-1905

Bedrooms: 3-4	Baths: 2½
Living Area:	
Upper floor	915 sq. ft.
Main floor	1,084 sq. ft.
Bonus room/ 4th Bedroom	224 sq. ft.
Total Living Area:	**2,223 sq. ft.**
Standard basement	1,064 sq. ft.
Garage	440 sq. ft.
Exterior Wall Framing:	2x4
Foundation Options:	
Standard basement	
(Typical foundation & framing conversion diagram available—see order form.)	
BLUEPRINT PRICE CODE:	C

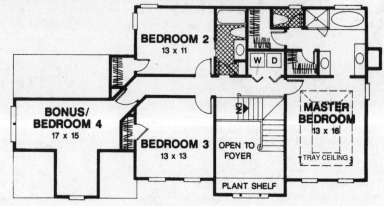

UPPER FLOOR

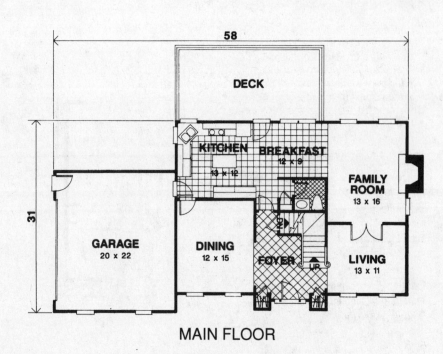

MAIN FLOOR

Plan APS-1905

PRICES AND DETAILS ON PAGES 12-15

Charming Chateau

- A two-story arched entry introduces this charming French chateau.
- To the left of the tiled foyer, the elegant formal dining room will impress friends when you entertain.
- In the kitchen, a handy island worktop and a step-in pantry take advantage of the unique space. The cheery breakfast nook is a great spot for family meals.
- A neat see-through fireplace and built-in bookshelves define the formal living room and the casual family room. Lovely French doors open to a quiet covered porch in back.
- The secluded master suite on the main floor boasts two enormous walk-in closets and a lush private bath with an inviting marble tub, a separate shower and his-and-hers vanities.
- The kitchen and the nook have 9- and 8-ft. ceilings, respectively. All other main-floor rooms are enhanced by soaring 10-ft. ceilings.
- On the upper floor, two bedrooms share a unique bath. The front bedroom offers a 10-ft. ceiling. A bonus room can be adapted to fit your future needs.

Plan RD-2225

Bedrooms: 3+	Baths: 2½
Living Area:	
Upper floor	547 sq. ft.
Main floor	1,678 sq. ft.
Total Living Area:	**2,225 sq. ft.**
Bonus room (unfinished)	136 sq. ft.
Garage and storage	519 sq. ft.
Exterior Wall Framing:	2x4
Foundation Options:	
Crawlspace	
Slab	

(All plans can be built with your choice of foundation and framing. A generic conversion diagram is available. See order form.)

BLUEPRINT PRICE CODE:	C

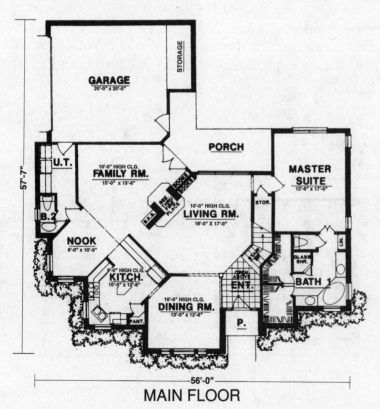

MAIN FLOOR

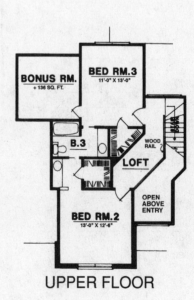

UPPER FLOOR

TO ORDER THIS BLUEPRINT,
CALL TOLL-FREE 1-800-820-1283

Plan RD-2225

PRICES AND DETAILS
ON PAGES 12-15

133

Sunny Comfort

- A covered wraparound porch and lovely arched windows give this home a comfortable country style.
- Inside, an elegant columned archway introduces the formal dining room.
- The huge Great Room features an 18-ft. vaulted ceiling, a dramatic wall of windows and two built-in wall units on either side of the fireplace.
- Ample counter space and a convenient work island allow maximum use of the roomy kitchen.
- The sunny breakfast nook opens to a porch through sliding glass doors.
- On the other side of the home, a dramatic bay window and a 10-ft. ceiling highlight the master bedroom. The enormous master bath features a luxurious whirlpool tub.
- Unless otherwise noted, all main-floor rooms have 9-ft. ceilings.
- Open stairs lead up to a balcony with a magnificent view of the Great Room. Two upstairs bedrooms, one with an 11-ft. vaulted ceiling, share a bath.

Plan AX-94317

Bedrooms: 3	Baths: 2½
Living Area:	
Upper floor	525 sq. ft.
Main floor	1,720 sq. ft.
Total Living Area:	**2,245 sq. ft.**
Standard basement	1,720 sq. ft.
Garage	502 sq. ft.
Storage/utility	51 sq. ft.
Exterior Wall Framing:	2x4

Foundation Options:

Standard basement

Crawlspace

Slab

(All plans can be built with your choice of foundation and framing. A generic conversion diagram is available. See order form.)

BLUEPRINT PRICE CODE: C

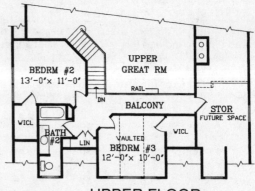

UPPER FLOOR

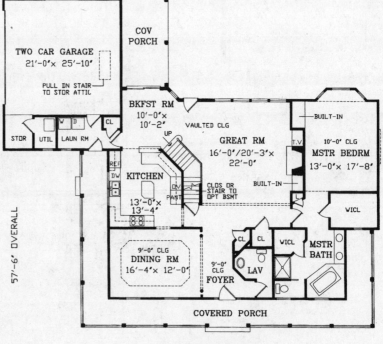

MAIN FLOOR

TO ORDER THIS BLUEPRINT, CALL TOLL-FREE 1-800-820-1283   Plan AX-94317   **PRICES AND DETAILS ON PAGES 12-15**

Grand Colonial Home

- This grand Colonial home boasts a porch entry framed by bay windows and gable towers.
- The two-story foyer flows to the dining room on the left and adjoins the bayed living room on the right, with its warm fireplace and flanking windows.
- At the rear, the family room features a 17-ft. ceiling, a media wall, a bar and terrace access through French doors.
- Connected to the family room is a high-tech kitchen with an island work area, a pantry, a work desk and a circular dinette.
- A private terrace, a romantic fireplace, a huge walk-in closet and a lavish bath with a whirlpool tub are featured in the main-floor master suite.
- Three bedrooms and two full baths share the upper floor.

Plan AHP-9120

Bedrooms: 4	Baths: 3
Living Area:	
Upper floor	776 sq. ft.
Main floor	1,551 sq. ft.
Total Living Area:	**2,327 sq. ft.**
Standard basement	1,580 sq. ft.
Garage	440 sq. ft.
Exterior Wall Framing:	2x4 or 2x6

Foundation Options:

Standard basement

Crawlspace

Slab

(All plans can be built with your choice of foundation and framing. A generic conversion diagram is available. See order form.)

BLUEPRINT PRICE CODE: C

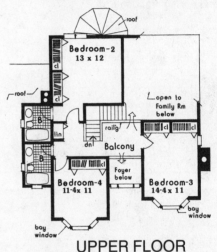

UPPER FLOOR

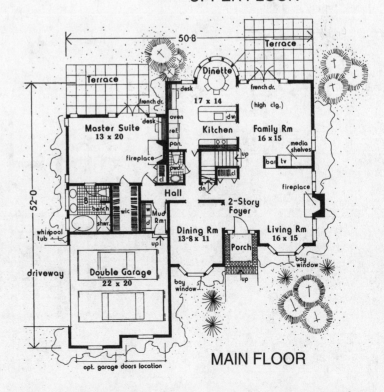

MAIN FLOOR

One More Time!

- The character and excitement of our most popular plan in recent years, E-3000, have been recaptured in this smaller version of the design.
- The appealing facade is distinguished by a covered front porch and accented with decorative columns, triple dormers and rail-topped corner windows.
- Off the foyer, a central gallery leads to the spacious family room, where a corner fireplace and a 17-ft. vaulted ceiling are highlights. Columns in the gallery introduce the kitchen and the dining areas.
- The kitchen showcases a walk-in pantry, a built-in desk and a long snack bar that serves the eating nook and the dining room.
- The stunning main-floor master suite offers a quiet sitting area and a private angled bath with dual vanities, a corner garden tub and a separate shower.
- A lovely curved stairway leads to a balcony that overlooks the family room and the foyer. Two large bedrooms, a split bath and easily accessible attics are also found upstairs.

Plan E-2307-A

Bedrooms: 3	Baths: 2½
Living Area:	
Upper floor	595 sq. ft.
Main floor	1,765 sq. ft.
Total Living Area:	**2,360 sq. ft.**
Standard basement	1,765 sq. ft.
Garage	484 sq. ft.
Storage	44 sq. ft.
Exterior Wall Framing:	2x6

Foundation Options:

Standard basement
Crawlspace
Slab

(All plans can be built with your choice of foundation and framing. A generic conversion diagram is available. See order form.)

BLUEPRINT PRICE CODE: C

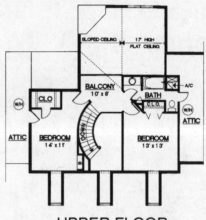

UPPER FLOOR

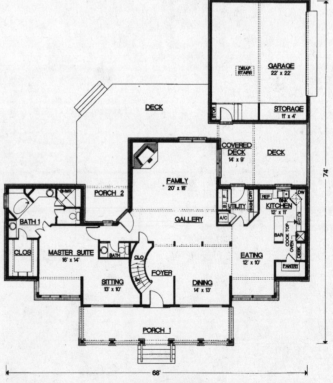

MAIN FLOOR

TO ORDER THIS BLUEPRINT, CALL TOLL-FREE 1-800-820-1283   Plan E-2307-A   *PRICES AND DETAILS ON PAGES 12-15*

Arched Accents

- Elegant arches add drama to the covered porch of this lovely home.
- Interior arches flank the two-story-high foyer, offering eye-catching entrances to the formal dining and living rooms.
- A dramatic window-framed fireplace and a 17-ft. ceiling enhance the spacious family room. A columned archway leads into the island kitchen, which offers a convenient serving bar.
- The adjoining breakfast area features a pantry closet, open shelves and a French door to the backyard. A half-bath and a laundry room are close by.
- The ceilings in all main-floor rooms are 9 ft. high unless otherwise specified.
- Upstairs, a balcony overlooks the family room and the foyer. The master suite flaunts a 10-ft. tray ceiling, a beautiful window showpiece and a private bath with a 13-ft. vaulted ceiling and a garden tub. The bedroom may be extended to include a sitting area.
- Boasting its own dressing vanity, the rear-facing bedroom offers private access to a compartmentalized bath that also serves the two remaining bedrooms.

Plan FB-2368

Bedrooms: 4	Baths: 2½
Living Area:	
Upper floor	1,168 sq. ft.
Main floor	1,200 sq. ft.
Total Living Area:	**2,368 sq. ft.**
Daylight basement	1,200 sq. ft.
Garage	504 sq. ft.
Exterior Wall Framing:	2x4

Foundation Options:
Daylight basement
Slab
(All plans can be built with your choice of foundation and framing. A generic conversion diagram is available. See order form.)

BLUEPRINT PRICE CODE: **C**

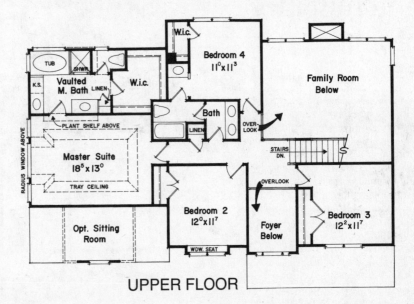

UPPER FLOOR

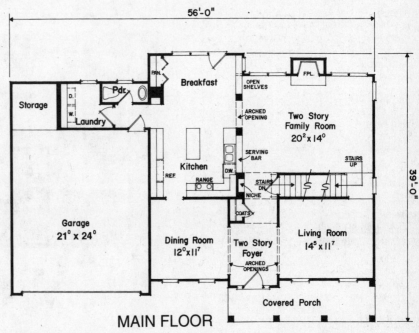

MAIN FLOOR

TO ORDER THIS BLUEPRINT,
CALL TOLL-FREE 1-800-820-1283

Plan FB-2368

PRICES AND DETAILS
ON PAGES 12-15

137

Contemporary Colonial

- A Palladian window and a half-round window above the entry door give this Colonial a new look. Inside, the design maximizes space while creating an open, airy atmosphere.
- The two-story-high foyer flows between the formal areas at the front of the home. Straight ahead, the exciting family room features a built-in wet bar and a fireplace framed by French doors.
- A bay window brightens the adjoining breakfast nook and kitchen. An angled counter looks to the nook and the family room, keeping the cook in touch with the family activities.
- The four bedrooms on the upper floor include a luxurious master suite with an 11-ft. vaulted ceiling and a skylighted bathroom. The upper-floor laundry also makes this a great family home.
- The basement plan (not shown) has room for an optional den or bedroom, a recreation room with a fireplace, a storage room and a utility area.

Plan CH-320-A

Bedrooms: 4+	Baths: 3
Living Area:	
Upper floor	1,164 sq. ft.
Main floor	1,293 sq. ft.
Total Living Area:	**2,457 sq. ft.**
Basement	1,293 sq. ft.
Garage	462 sq. ft.
Exterior Wall Framing:	2x4

Foundation Options:

Daylight basement

Standard basement

Crawlspace

(All plans can be built with your choice of foundation and framing. A generic conversion diagram is available. See order form.)

BLUEPRINT PRICE CODE: **C**

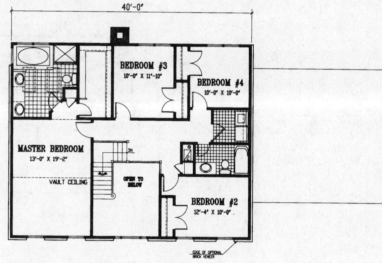

UPPER FLOOR

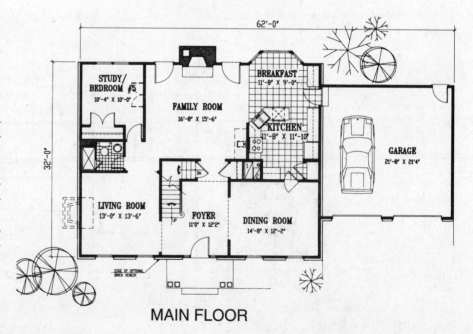

MAIN FLOOR

Picture-Perfect

- Those tall, cold glasses of summertime lemonade will taste even better when enjoyed on the shady front porch of this picture-perfect home.
- Inside, the two-story, sidelighted foyer unfolds to the formal living areas and the Great Room beyond.
- Fireplaces grace the living room and the Great Room, which are separated by French pocket doors. A TV nook borders the fireplace in the Great Room, letting the kids catch their favorite show while Mom and Dad fix dinner in the kitchen. Two sets of French doors swing wide to reveal a backyard deck.
- A glassy dinette with an 8-ft. ceiling makes breakfasts cozy and comfortable.
- Restful nights will be the norm in the master suite, which boasts a 14-ft. cathedral ceiling. Next to the walk-in closet, the private bath has a whirlpool tub in a fabulous boxed-out window.
- Unless otherwise noted, all main-floor rooms are topped by 9-ft. ceilings.
- At day's end, guests and children may retire to the upper floor, where four big bedrooms and a full bath await them.

Plan AHP-9512

Bedrooms: 5	Baths: 2½
Living Area:	
Upper floor	928 sq. ft.
Main floor	1,571 sq. ft.
Total Living Area:	**2,499 sq. ft.**
Standard basement	1,571 sq. ft.
Garage and storage	420 sq. ft.
Exterior Wall Framing:	2x4 or 2x6

Foundation Options:

Standard basement
Crawlspace
Slab

(All plans can be built with your choice of foundation and framing. A generic conversion diagram is available. See order form.)

BLUEPRINT PRICE CODE: C

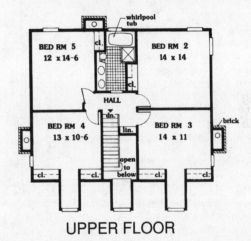

UPPER FLOOR

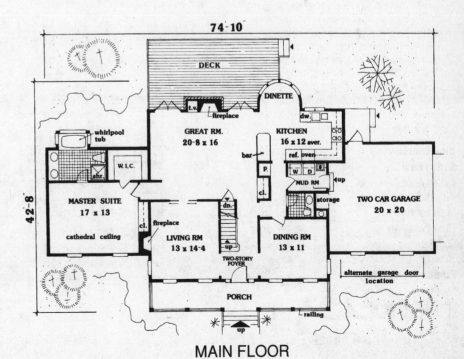

MAIN FLOOR

Transom Treats

- This home is so attractive that guests will walk right up for a visit. Terrific transom windows, louvered vents and brick accents lend charm and appeal.
- Stately brick columns support the arch of the front porch, while the glass-framed entry and half-round transom create a Palladian look.
- Off the two-story entry, double doors introduce the versatile den, home office or extra bedroom.
- A 14-ft. vaulted ceiling presides over the living room. Columns set off the adjacent dining room, where a 10-ft. tray ceiling adds to the ambience.
- The gourmet island kitchen offers a handy pantry. The attached breakfast bay hosts a useful menu desk and easy access to an inviting backyard deck.
- A fireplace warms the expansive family room, which also accesses the deck.
- Upstairs, the master bedroom boasts an 11½-ft. vaulted ceiling and two walk-in closets. The luxurious private bath shows off a garden tub and a dual-sink vanity with a makeup area.

Plan B-94021

Bedrooms: 3+	Baths: 2½
Living Area:	
Upper floor	946 sq. ft.
Main floor	1,463 sq. ft.
Total Living Area:	**2,409 sq. ft.**
Standard basement	1,463 sq. ft.
Garage	420 sq. ft.
Exterior Wall Framing:	2x6

Foundation Options:

Standard basement

(All plans can be built with your choice of foundation and framing. A generic conversion diagram is available. See order form.)

BLUEPRINT PRICE CODE: C

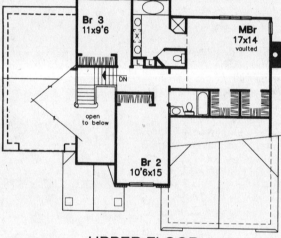

UPPER FLOOR

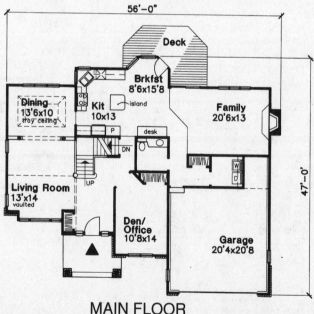

MAIN FLOOR

TO ORDER THIS BLUEPRINT, CALL TOLL-FREE 1-800-820-1283

Plan B-94021

PRICES AND DETAILS ON PAGES 12-15

Fantastic Facade, Stunning Spaces

- Matching dormers and a generous covered front porch give this home its fantastic facade. Inside, the open living spaces are just as stunning.
- A two-story foyer bisects the formal living areas. The living room offers three bright windows, an inviting fireplace and sliding French doors to the Great Room. The formal dining room overlooks the front porch and has easy access to the kitchen.
- The Great Room is truly grand, featuring a fireplace and a TV center flanked by French doors that lead to a large deck.
- A circular dinette connects the Great Room to the kitchen, which is handy to a mudroom and a powder room.
- The main-floor master suite boasts a 14-ft. cathedral ceiling, a walk-in closet and a private bath with a whirlpool tub.
- Upstairs, four large bedrooms share another whirlpool bath. One bedroom offers a 12-ft. sloped ceiling.

Plan AHP-9397

Bedrooms: 5	Baths: 2½
Living Area:	
Upper floor	928 sq. ft.
Main floor	1,545 sq. ft.
Total Living Area:	**2,473 sq. ft.**
Standard basement	1,165 sq. ft.
Garage and storage	432 sq. ft.
Exterior Wall Framing:	2x4 or 2x6

Foundation Options:

Standard basement

Crawlspace

Slab

(All plans can be built with your choice of foundation and framing. A generic conversion diagram is available. See order form.)

BLUEPRINT PRICE CODE:	C

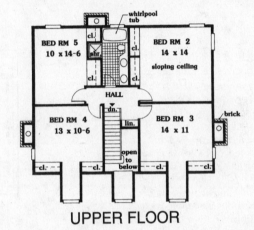

UPPER FLOOR

MAIN FLOOR

TO ORDER THIS BLUEPRINT,
CALL TOLL-FREE 1-800-820-1283

Plan AHP-9397

PRICES AND DETAILS
ON PAGES 12-15

141

Space and Elegance

- This two-story combines elegant European exterior touches with a thoroughly modern American interior.
- The living and dining rooms are separately defined, yet can be used as one unit for entertaining large groups.
- A huge country kitchen with a work island includes an ample area for informal dining.
- Note the convenient utility and half-bath area in the garage entryway.
- Upstairs, a deluxe master suite includes a private bath and large closet.
- Three larger-than-average secondary bedrooms share another full bath.

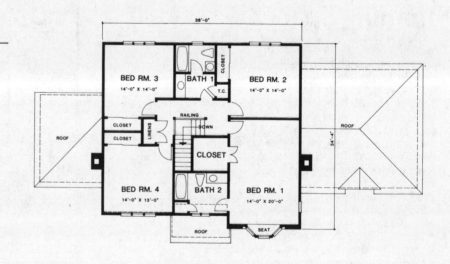

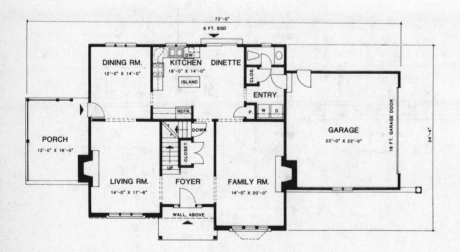

Plan A-2102-DS

Bedrooms: 4	Baths: 2½

Space:

Upper floor:	1,244 sq. ft.
Main floor:	1,224 sq. ft.
Total living area:	**2,468 sq. ft.**
Basement:	approx. 1,224 sq. ft.
Garage:	484 sq. ft.

Exterior Wall Framing: 2x4

Foundation options:
Standard basement only.
(Foundation & framing conversion diagram available — see order form.)

Blueprint Price Code: C

TO ORDER THIS BLUEPRINT, CALL TOLL-FREE 1-800-820-1283

Plan A-2102-DS

PRICES AND DETAILS ON PAGES 12-15

Country Classic

- Dormers and a huge covered porch make this home a country classic.
- The two-story foyer unfolds nicely into the open living areas, where light pours in from large front-facing windows.
- Just off the dining room, the gourmet kitchen boasts a handy serving bar and an attractive angled counter.
- The adjacent breakfast nook provides the perfect place to relax in the morning sun, or step out to a covered backyard porch through a French door.
- Expanded by an 18-ft. vaulted ceiling, the large family room features a high plant shelf and a fireplace flanked by bright windows with radius transoms.
- The master suite boasts a 9-ft., 8-in. tray ceiling, a walk-in closet and a private bath with a spa tub, a separate shower and a dual-sink vanity with knee space.
- Upstairs, railed balconies overlook the foyer and the family room below.
- Three remaining bedrooms share a full bath. For more space, a bonus room can be built above the garage.

Plan FB-5084-BALT

Bedrooms: 4+	Baths: 2½
Living Area:	
Upper floor	863 sq. ft.
Main floor	1,651 sq. ft.
Total Living Area:	**2,514 sq. ft.**
Optional bonus room	376 sq. ft.
Daylight basement	1,651 sq. ft.
Garage and storage	510 sq. ft.
Exterior Wall Framing:	2x4

Foundation Options:

Daylight basement

Slab

(All plans can be built with your choice of foundation and framing. A generic conversion diagram is available. See order form.)

BLUEPRINT PRICE CODE: D

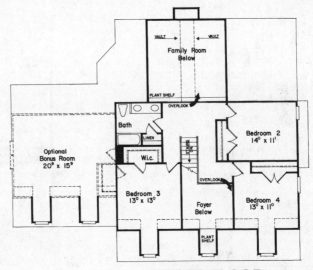

UPPER FLOOR

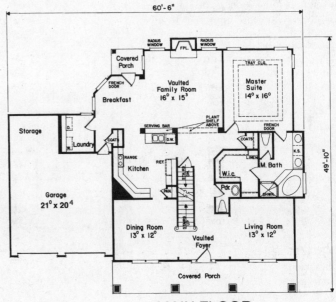

MAIN FLOOR

TO ORDER THIS BLUEPRINT,
CALL TOLL-FREE 1-800-820-1283

Plan FB-5084-BALT

PRICES AND DETAILS
ON PAGES 12-15

143

Formal Meets Informal

- The charming, columned front porch of this appealing home leads visitors into a two-story-high foyer with a beautiful turned staircase.
- The gracious formal living room shares a 15-ft. cathedral ceiling and a dramatic see-through fireplace with the adjoining family room.
- A railing separates the family room from the spacious breakfast area and the island kitchen. A unique butler's pantry joins the kitchen to the dining room, which is enhanced by a tray ceiling.
- A convenient laundry room is located between the kitchen and the entrance to the garage .
- All four bedrooms are located on the upper level. The master suite boasts an 11-ft. cathedral ceiling, a walk-in closet and a large, luxurious bath.

Plan OH-132

Bedrooms: 4	Baths: 2½
Living Area:	
Upper floor	1,118 sq. ft.
Main floor	1,396 sq. ft.
Total Living Area:	**2,514 sq. ft.**
Standard basement	1,396 sq. ft.
Garage	413 sq. ft.
Storage/workshop	107 sq. ft.
Exterior Wall Framing:	2x4

Foundation Options:

Standard basement

(All plans can be built with your choice of foundation and framing. A generic conversion diagram is available. See order form.)

BLUEPRINT PRICE CODE: D

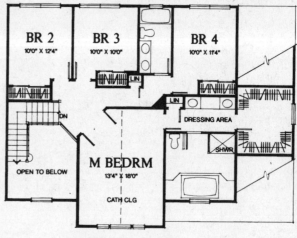

UPPER FLOOR

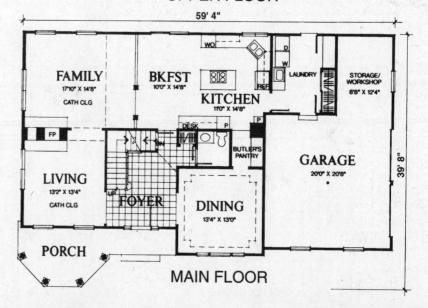

MAIN FLOOR

Plan OH-132 **PRICES AND DETAILS**
ON PAGES 12-15

Street Appeal Times Three

- Three optional elevations are offered to frame this attractive contemporary two-story. Please specify your elevation preference when ordering.
- The beautiful vaulted entryway opens to formal living areas and to a study or extra bedroom with vaulted ceiling, window-wall and French doors.
- The roomy kitchen adjoins a breakfast nook and family room, for uninterrupted family activities; the fireplace and the rear deck can both be seen from the kitchen.
- The spectacular master suite features a volume ceiling, generous closet space, dual vanities and a separate tub and shower.

ELEVATION A

ELEVATION B

ELEVATION C

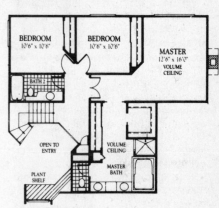

UPPER FLOOR

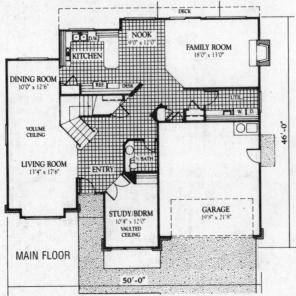

MAIN FLOOR

Plan R-2152

Bedrooms: 3-4	Baths: 2½
Living Area:	
Upper floor:	955 sq. ft.
Main floor	1,470 sq. ft.
Total Living Area:	**2,425 sq. ft.**
Garage	426 sq. ft.
Exterior Wall Framing:	2x6

Foundation Options:
Crawlspace
(Typical foundation & framing conversion diagram available—see order form.)

BLUEPRINT PRICE CODE: C

TO ORDER THIS BLUEPRINT,
CALL TOLL-FREE 1-800-820-1283

Plan R-2152

PRICES AND DETAILS
ON PAGES 12-15

145

Stately Colonial

- This stately Colonial features a covered front entry and a secondary entry near the garage and the utility room.
- The main foyer opens to a comfortable den with elegant double doors.
- The formal living areas adjoin to the left of the foyer and culminate in a lovely bay window overlooking the backyard.
- The open island kitchen has a great central location, easily accessed from each of the living areas. Informal dining can be extended to the outdoors through sliding doors in the dinette.
- A half-wall introduces the big family room, which boasts a high 16-ft., 9-in. vaulted ceiling, an inviting fireplace and optional built-in cabinets.
- The upper floor is shared by four bedrooms, including a spacious master bedroom with a large walk-in closet, a dressing area for two and a private bath. An alternate bath layout is included in the blueprints.
- A bonus room may be added above the garage for additional space.

Plan A-2283-DS

Bedrooms: 4+	Baths: 2½
Living Area:	
Upper floor	1,137 sq. ft.
Main floor	1,413 sq. ft.
Total Living Area:	**2,550 sq. ft.**
Optional bonus room	280 sq. ft.
Standard basement	1,413 sq. ft.
Garage	484 sq. ft.
Exterior Wall Framing:	2x6

Foundation Options:

Standard basement

(All plans can be built with your choice of foundation and framing. A generic conversion diagram is available. See order form.)

BLUEPRINT PRICE CODE: D

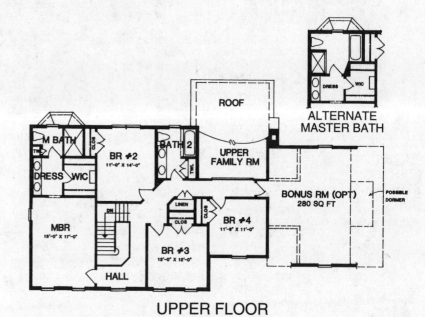

ALTERNATE MASTER BATH

UPPER FLOOR

MAIN FLOOR

Plan A-2283-DS

PRICES AND DETAILS ON PAGES 12-15

Classic Country-Style

- Almost completely surrounded by an expansive porch, this classic plan exudes warmth and grace.
- The foyer is liberal in size and leads guests to a formal dining room to the left or the large living room to the right.
- The open country kitchen includes a sunny, bay-windowed breakfast nook. A utility area, a full bath and garage access are nearby.
- Upstairs, the master suite is impressive, with its large sleeping area, walk-in closet and magnificent garden bath.
- Three secondary bedrooms share a full bath with a dual-sink vanity.
- Also note the stairs leading up to an attic, which is useful for storage space.

Plan J-86134

Bedrooms: 4	Baths: 3
Living Area:	
Upper floor	1,195 sq. ft.
Main floor	1,370 sq. ft.
Total Living Area:	**2,565 sq. ft.**
Standard basement	1,370 sq. ft.
Garage	576 sq. ft.
Exterior Wall Framing:	2x4

Foundation Options:

Standard basement

Crawlspace

Slab

(All plans can be built with your choice of foundation and framing. A generic conversion diagram is available. See order form.)

BLUEPRINT PRICE CODE: D

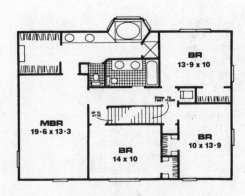

UPPER FLOOR

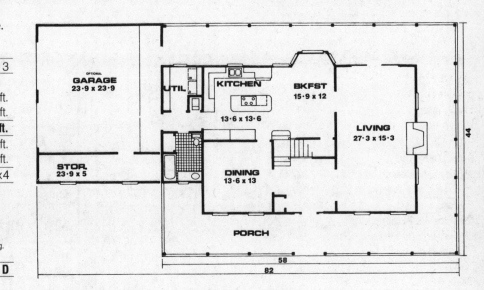

MAIN FLOOR

TO ORDER THIS BLUEPRINT,
CALL TOLL-FREE 1-800-820-1283

Plan J-86134

PRICES AND DETAILS
ON PAGES 12-15

147

Elegant Interior

- An inviting covered porch welcomes guests into the elegant interior of this spectacular country home.
- Just past the entrance, the formal dining room boasts a stepped ceiling and a nearby server with a sink.
- The adjoining island kitchen has an eating bar that serves the breakfast room, which is enhanced by a 12-ft. cathedral ceiling and a bayed area of 8- and 9-ft.-high windows. Sliding glass doors lead to a covered side porch.
- Brightened by a row of 8-ft.-high windows and a glass door to the backyard, the spacious Great Room features a stepped ceiling, a built-in media center and a corner fireplace.
- The master bedroom has a tray ceiling and a cozy sitting area. The skylighted master bath boasts a whirlpool tub, a separate shower and a walk-in closet.
- A second main-floor bedroom, or optional study, offers private access to a compartmentalized bath. Two more bedrooms share a third bath on the upper floor. Generous storage space is also included.

Plan AX-3305-B

Bedrooms: 3+	Baths: 3
Living Area:	
Upper floor	550 sq. ft.
Main floor	2,017 sq. ft.
Total Living Area:	**2,567 sq. ft.**
Upper-floor storage	377 sq. ft.
Standard basement	2,017 sq. ft.
Garage	415 sq. ft.
Exterior Wall Framing:	2x4

Foundation Options:

Standard basement
Crawlspace
Slab

(All plans can be built with your choice of foundation and framing. A generic conversion diagram is available. See order form.)

BLUEPRINT PRICE CODE: **D**

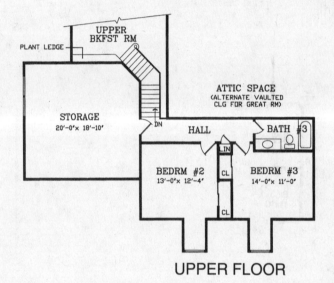

UPPER FLOOR

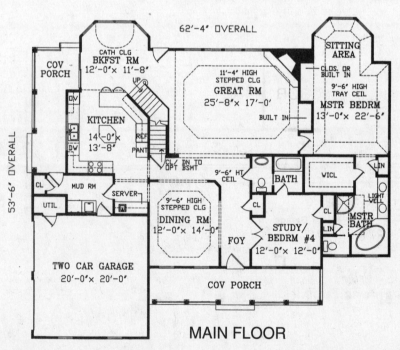

MAIN FLOOR

Plan AX-3305-B

Trendy Transitional Design

- This striking transitional design offers a combination of staggered hip and gable rooflines, arched transoms, brick trim and a three-car garage with decorative facade.
- The dramatic vaulted entry focuses on circular walls and a curved staircase.
- To the right, a large, vaulted living room with fireplace combines with a formal dining room for a spacious setting. The two rooms are separated by a decorative plant shelf and columns.
- Open to the walk-through kitchen are a gazebo breakfast area and a vaulted family room with corner window and second fireplace.
- The main-floor guest room can be used as a den or library.
- The upper-level master bedroom is separated from the three other bedrooms. A private master bath and octagonal sitting area are featured.

UPPER FLOOR

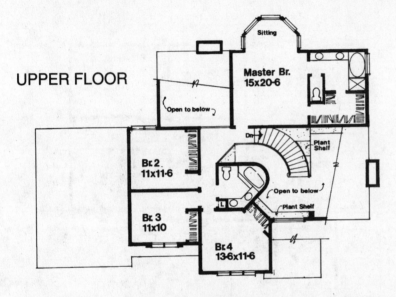

MAIN FLOOR

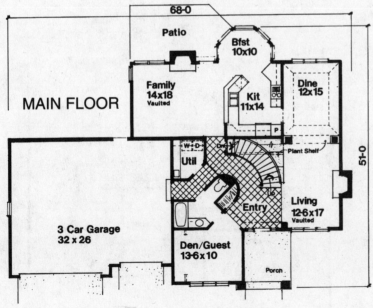

Plan AG-9104

Bedrooms: 4-5	Baths: 3
Living Area:	
Upper floor:	1,128 sq. ft.
Main floor	1,456 sq. ft.
Total Living Area:	**2,584 sq. ft.**
Standard basement	1,456 sq. ft.
Garage	832 sq. ft.
Exterior Wall Framing:	2x6

Foundation Options:

Standard basement
(Typical foundation & framing conversion diagram available—see order form.)

BLUEPRINT PRICE CODE:	D

REAR VIEW

Eye-Catching Executive Home

- This eye-catching executive home boasts a two-story bay window and unique transoms above both the front door and the garage doors.
- An equally dramatic interior is prefaced by a two-story-high foyer, which leads into the bayed living room and the adjoining dining room.
- The gourmet kitchen features an island cooktop, a sunny double sink and plenty of counter space.
- The bright breakfast area and the sunken family room each have sliding glass doors to the optional deck. A half-wall separates the two rooms and a fireplace warms the entire area.
- Upstairs, a balcony hall overlooks the foyer. The dazzling master suite has a 10-ft.-high tray ceiling in the sleeping area, a sloped ceiling in the skylighted master bath and a cathedral ceiling in the intimate sitting room.
- Three more spacious bedrooms, one with a bay window and a 10-ft. vaulted ceiling, share a second full bath.

Plan AX-2319

Bedrooms: 4	Baths: 2½
Living Area:	
Upper floor	1,501 sq. ft.
Main floor	1,366 sq. ft.
Total Living Area:	**2,867 sq. ft.**
Standard basement	1,366 sq. ft.
Garage	460 sq. ft.
Exterior Wall Framing:	2x6

Foundation Options:

Standard basement

Slab

(All plans can be built with your choice of foundation and framing. A generic conversion diagram is available. See order form.)

BLUEPRINT PRICE CODE: **D**

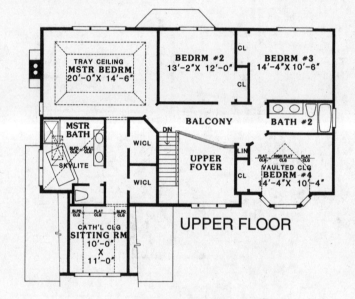

UPPER FLOOR

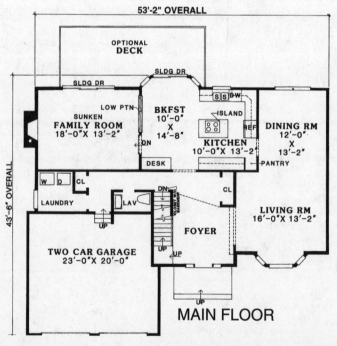

MAIN FLOOR

Plan AX-2319

PRICES AND DETAILS ON PAGES 12-15

Fine Details

- Elegant window treatments, eye-catching gables and a finely detailed stucco facade give this home a distinctive look.
- The spacious interior begins with an 18-ft.-high foyer and a dramatic two-way stairway with open railings.
- Decorative columns introduce the formal living room. Straight ahead, the spacious family room features a focal-point fireplace framed by windows.
- A French door between the family room and the breakfast room provides easy access to the backyard. The gourmet kitchen is highlighted by an angled serving bar/snack counter.
- Upstairs, the luxurious master bedroom features a 10-ft. tray ceiling and an intimate sitting room with a two-sided fireplace. Double doors open to the opulent master bath, which includes a huge walk-in closet and a 13½-ft.-high bathing area with an oval tub.
- Three more bedrooms share a compartmentalized bath. A balcony overlook with a beautiful plant shelf is open to the foyer below.

Plan FB-2600

Bedrooms: 4	Baths: 2½
Living Area:	
Upper floor	1,348 sq. ft.
Main floor	1,252 sq. ft.
Total Living Area:	**2,600 sq. ft.**
Daylight basement	1,252 sq. ft.
Garage and storage	484 sq. ft.
Exterior Wall Framing:	2x4

Foundation Options:

Daylight basement

Crawlspace

(All plans can be built with your choice of foundation and framing. A generic conversion diagram is available. See order form.)

BLUEPRINT PRICE CODE:	D

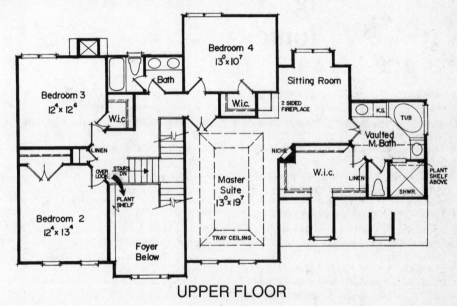

UPPER FLOOR

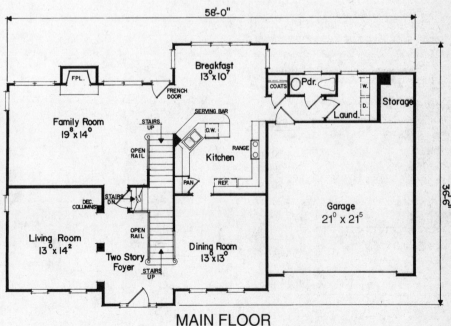

MAIN FLOOR

Two-Story Palace

- Decorative brick borders, a columned porch and dramatic arched windows give a classy look to this magnificent two-story palace.
- The open, sidelighted entry is flanked by the formal dining and living rooms, both of which feature elegant paned-glass windows. A coat closet and a powder room are just steps away.
- The spacious family room is warmed by a fireplace and brightened by a beautiful arched window set into a high-ceilinged area.
- The well-planned kitchen, highlighted by an island worktop and a windowed sink, is centrally located to provide easy service to both the dining room and the bayed morning room. The morning room offers access to a large, inviting backyard deck.
- A bright and heartwarming sun room also overlooks the deck, and is a perfect spot to read or just relax.
- A handy laundry/utility area is located at the entrance to the two-car garage.
- Windows surround the main-floor master suite, which boasts a luxurious bath with a garden tub, a separate shower and a dual-sink vanity. Three walk-in closets provide plenty of space for wardrobe storage.
- Ceilings in all main-floor rooms are 9 ft. high for added spaciousness.
- Upstairs, three good-sized bedrooms share a compartmentalized bath. A large and convenient attic area offers additional storage possibilities.

Plan DD-2689	
Bedrooms: 4	**Baths:** 2½
Living Area:	
Upper floor	755 sq. ft.
Main floor	1,934 sq. ft.
Total Living Area:	**2,689 sq. ft.**
Standard basement	1,934 sq. ft.
Garage	436 sq. ft.
Exterior Wall Framing:	2x4

Foundation Options:

Standard basement

Crawlspace

Slab

(All plans can be built with your choice of foundation and framing. A generic conversion diagram is available. See order form.)

BLUEPRINT PRICE CODE:	D

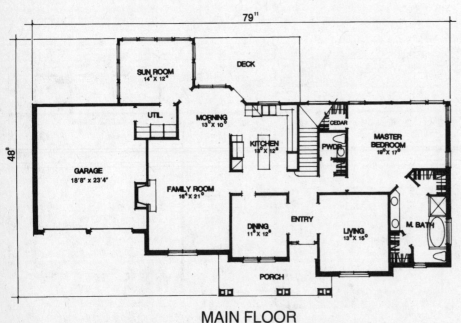

MAIN FLOOR

UPPER FLOOR

Plan DD-2689

PRICES AND DETAILS ON PAGES 12-15

Graceful Estate

- A wraparound covered porch and a bright stucco exterior add style and grace to this beautiful country home.
- The inviting foyer boasts an impressive 18-ft.-high ceiling and is highlighted by overhead plant shelves. The other main-floor rooms have 9-ft. ceilings.
- Off the foyer, the living room is set off from the formal dining room by two elegant columns.
- The adjacent island kitchen offers a pantry, a corner windowed sink and a sunny breakfast area with a French door to the backyard.

- The adjoining family room features a wet bar and a handsome window-flanked fireplace that adds warmth.
- Upstairs, beyond a dramatic railed balcony, the secluded master suite boasts a stylish 9-ft., 8-in. tray ceiling. A separate sitting room makes the suite an elegant adult retreat.
- A 14-ft. vaulted ceiling, overhead plant shelves and a garden tub add luxury to the master bath, which has a dual-sink vanity with knee space.
- Two more bedrooms include private access to a split bath. A fourth bedroom with a 9-ft. ceiling and a walk-in closet is also serviced by the hall bath.

Plan FB-5343-MONT

Bedrooms: 4	Baths: 2½
Living Area:	
Upper floor	1,399 sq. ft.
Main floor	1,281 sq. ft.
Total Living Area:	**2,680 sq. ft.**
Daylight basement	1,281 sq. ft.
Garage and storage	473 sq. ft.
Exterior Wall Framing:	2x4

Foundation Options:
Daylight basement
(All plans can be built with your choice of foundation and framing. A generic conversion diagram is available. See order form.)

BLUEPRINT PRICE CODE:	D

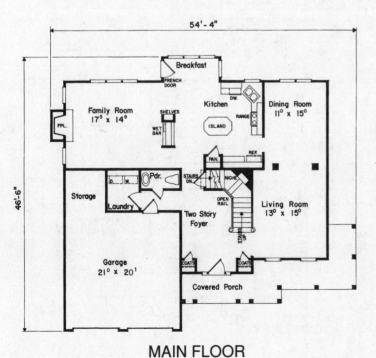

MAIN FLOOR

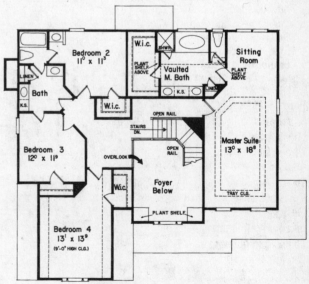

UPPER FLOOR

Fantastic
Front Entry

- A fantastic arched window presides over the 18-ft.-high entry of this two-story, giving guests a bright welcome.
- The spacious living room is separated from the dining room by a pair of boxed columns with built-in shelves.
- The kitchen offers a walk-in pantry, a serving bar and a sunny breakfast room with a French door to the backyard.
- A boxed column accents the entry to the 18-ft. vaulted family room, which boasts a dramatic window bank and an inviting fireplace.
- The main-floor den is easily converted into an extra bedroom or guest room.
- The master suite has a 10-ft. tray ceiling, a huge walk-in closet and decorative plant shelves. The 15½-ft. vaulted bath features an oval tub and two vanities, one with knee space.
- Three additional bedrooms share another full bath near the second stairway to the main floor.

Plan FB-2680

Bedrooms: 4+	Baths: 3
Living Area:	
Upper floor	1,256 sq. ft.
Main floor	1,424 sq. ft.
Total Living Area:	**2,680 sq. ft.**
Daylight basement	1,424 sq. ft.
Garage	496 sq. ft.
Exterior Wall Framing:	2x4

Foundation Options:

Daylight basement
(All plans can be built with your choice of foundation and framing. A generic conversion diagram is available. See order form.)

BLUEPRINT PRICE CODE:	D

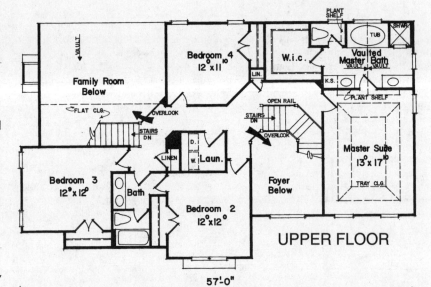

UPPER FLOOR

57'-0"

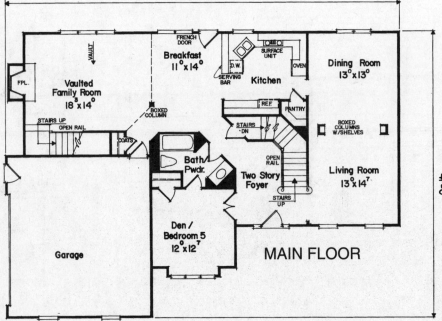

MAIN FLOOR

41'-0"

TO ORDER THIS BLUEPRINT, CALL TOLL-FREE 1-800-820-1283   Plan FB-2680   **PRICES AND DETAILS ON PAGES 12-15**

French Farmhouse

- An optional game room or fifth bedroom is offered in this classic French-styled farmhouse. The upper level also features a balcony that overlooks the Great Room.
- Bay windows are found throughout the main level, including the formal dining room, versatile studio, the nook and the secluded master suite and bath.
- At the center of the home, the Great Room has a vaulted ceiling, massive corner fireplace and access to the rear porch.
- A convenient utility room houses extra freezer, storage space and washer/dryer.

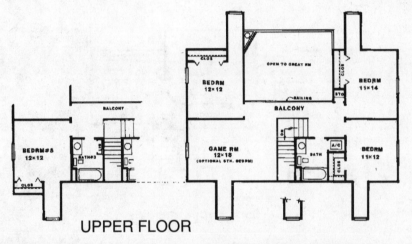

UPPER FLOOR

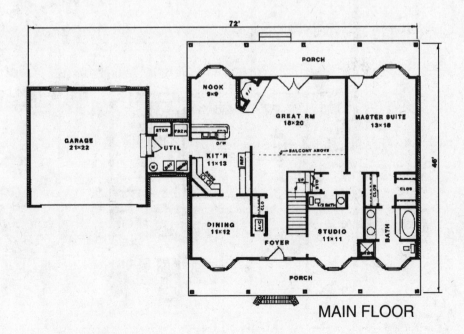

MAIN FLOOR

Plan VL-2716

Bedrooms: 4-5	Baths: 2 ½-3 ½
Space:	
Upper floor	1,127 sq. ft.
Main floor	1,589 sq. ft.
Total Living Area	**2,716 sq. ft.**
Garage	469 sq. ft.
Exterior Wall Framing	2x4

Foundation options:
Crawlspace
Slab
(Foundation & framing conversion diagram available—see order form.)

Blueprint Price Code	**D**

TO ORDER THIS BLUEPRINT,
CALL TOLL-FREE 1-800-820-1283

Plan VL-2716

PRICES AND DETAILS
ON PAGES 12-15

155

Elegant Fun

- The noble facade of this elegant two-story conceals a playful and entertaining interior floor plan.
- From the 17-ft.-high entry, wood columns enhance the view of the living room and the backyard porch beyond. Built-in bookshelves flank a fireplace, while a 19-ft. ceiling slopes overhead.
- A stepped ceiling and a boxed-out window grace the master suite. The master bath enjoys a marble tub, a separate shower and dual vanities.
- Wide-open spaces highlight the kitchen, with its angled desk and convenient snack bar. The formal dining room is nearby. The breakfast nook has a boxed-out window and a built-in hutch.
- Three bedrooms share a split bath on the upper floor. At the other end of the unique balcony bridge, a bonus room awaits use as a fantastic game room or media room.
- Unless otherwise specified, all main-floor rooms have 10-ft. ceilings. The upper-floor ceilings are 8 ft. high.

Plan RD-2556

Bedrooms: 4+	Baths: 2½
Living Area:	
Upper floor	794 sq. ft.
Main floor	1,762 sq. ft.
Bonus room	218 sq. ft.
Total Living Area:	**2,774 sq. ft.**
Standard basement	1,700 sq. ft.
Garage and storage	499 sq. ft.
Exterior Wall Framing:	**2x4**

Foundation Options:

Standard basement

Crawlspace

Slab

(All plans can be built with your choice of foundation and framing. A generic conversion diagram is available. See order form.)

BLUEPRINT PRICE CODE: D

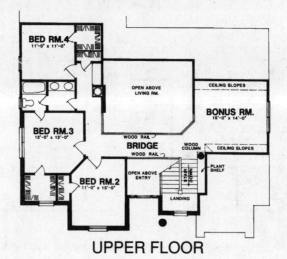

UPPER FLOOR

MAIN FLOOR

Plan RD-2556

PRICES AND DETAILS
ON PAGES 12-15

New Look of Old

- Country and Victorian features are given a new look in this outstanding three-bedroom home.
- Turret-like bay windows, a covered front porch and oval leaded-glass windows capture the best of the past. Inside, the floor plan makes the most of today's amenities and efficiencies.
- The sunken family room offers French doors opening to the backyard and a fireplace that also can be enjoyed from the kitchen and dinette. The dinette is separated from the family room by a railing and is brightened by three windows. A boxed-out window illuminates the step-saving kitchen.
- The formal living room offers a stunning bay window, while the formal dining room has a large picture window overlooking the front porch.
- Upstairs, the balcony stairway is open to the foyer below. Each of the three bedrooms has a beautiful bay window and ample closet space. The master suite includes a private bath with a step-up whirlpool tub, a great vanity, and a separate shower/toilet compartment.

UPPER FLOOR

Plan PI-87-466	
Bedrooms: 3	**Baths: 2½**
Living Area:	
Upper floor	1,240 sq. ft.
Main floor	1,450 sq. ft.
Total Living Area:	**2,690 sq. ft.**
Basement	1,412 sq. ft.
Garage	576 sq. ft.
Exterior Wall Framing:	**2x6**

Foundation Options:
Daylight basement
Standard basement
(Typical foundation & framing conversion diagram available—see order form.)

BLUEPRINT PRICE CODE:	**D**

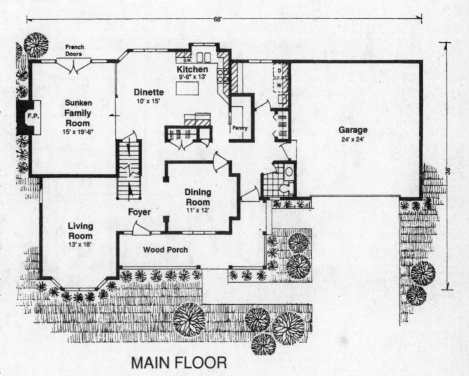

MAIN FLOOR

TO ORDER THIS BLUEPRINT,
CALL TOLL-FREE 1-800-820-1283

Plan PI-87-466

PRICES AND DETAILS
ON PAGES 12-15

157

A Family Tradition

- This traditional design has clean, sharp styling, with family-sized areas for formal and casual gatherings.
- The sidelighted foyer is graced with a beautiful open staircase and a wide coat closet. Flanking the foyer are the spacious formal living areas.
- The everyday living areas include an island kitchen, a bayed dinette and a large family room with a fireplace.
- Just off the entrance from the garage, double doors open to the quiet study, which boasts built-in bookshelves.
- A powder room and a deluxe laundry room with cabinets are convenient to the active areas of the home.
- Upstairs, the master suite features a roomy split bath and a large walk-in closet. Three more bedrooms share another split bath.

Plan A-118-DS

Bedrooms: 4+	Baths: 2½
Living Area:	
Upper floor	1,344 sq. ft.
Main floor	1,556 sq. ft.
Total Living Area:	**2,900 sq. ft.**
Standard basement	1,556 sq. ft.
Garage	576 sq. ft.
Exterior Wall Framing:	2x4

Foundation Options:

Standard basement

(All plans can be built with your choice of foundation and framing. A generic conversion diagram is available. See order form.)

BLUEPRINT PRICE CODE: D

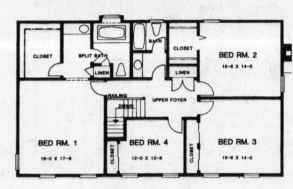

UPPER FLOOR

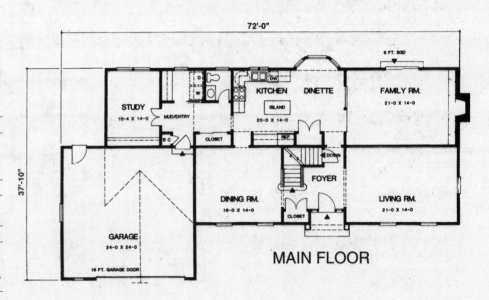

MAIN FLOOR

TO ORDER THIS BLUEPRINT, CALL TOLL-FREE 1-800-820-1283   Plan A-118-DS   *PRICES AND DETAILS ON PAGES 12-15*

Sprawling French Country

- A hip roof and gable accents give this sprawling home a country, French look.
- To the left of the entry, the formal dining room is illuminated with a tall arched window arrangement.
- The spectacular living room stretches from the entry of the home to the rear. A vaulted ceiling in this expansive space rises to 19 ft., and windows at both ends offer light and a nice breeze.
- Angled walls add interest to the roomy informal areas, which overlook the covered lanai. The island kitchen opens to the adjoining morning room and the sunny family room.
- The spacious main-floor master suite is highlighted by a 13-ft. vaulted ceiling and a bayed sitting area. The master bath features dual walk-in closets, a large spa tub and a separate shower.
- Three extra bedrooms and two more baths share the upper level.

Plan DD-2889

Bedrooms: 4	Baths: 3½
Living Area:	
Upper floor	819 sq. ft.
Main floor	2,111 sq. ft.
Total Living Area:	**2,930 sq. ft.**
Standard basement	2,111 sq. ft.
Garage	622 sq. ft.
Exterior Wall Framing:	2x4

Foundation Options:
Standard basement
Crawlspace
Slab

(All plans can be built with your choice of foundation and framing. A generic conversion diagram is available. See order form.)

BLUEPRINT PRICE CODE:	D

UPPER FLOOR

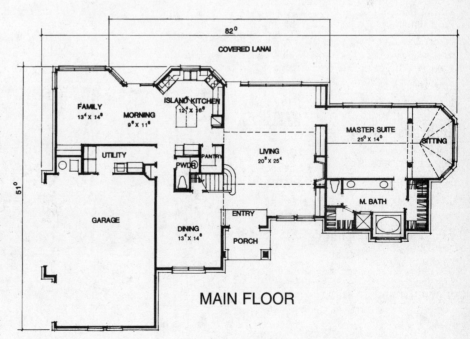

MAIN FLOOR

TO ORDER THIS BLUEPRINT,
CALL TOLL-FREE 1-800-820-1283

Plan DD-2889

PRICES AND DETAILS
ON PAGES 12-15

159

Verandas Add Extra Charm

- Porches, columns and dormers give this home a charming facade.
- The interior is equally appealing, with its beautiful two-story foyer and practical room arrangement.
- The central living room has a fireplace and access to a covered porch.
- A great island kitchen is conveniently situated between the two dining areas.
- A multipurpose room and an office are perfect for hobbies and projects.
- The secluded master suite offers a private study with a sloped ceiling. The master bath is large and symmetrical.
- Three bedrooms upstairs share a compartmentalized bath.

Plan E-2900

Bedrooms: 4	Baths: 2½
Living Area:	
Upper floor	903 sq. ft.
Main floor	2,029 sq. ft.
Total Living Area:	**2,932 sq. ft.**
Standard basement	2,029 sq. ft.
Garage and storage	470 sq. ft.
Exterior Wall Framing:	2x6

Foundation Options:
Standard basement
Crawlspace
Slab
(Typical foundation & framing conversion diagram available—see order form.)

BLUEPRINT PRICE CODE: D

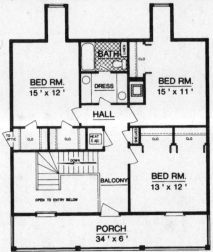

UPPER FLOOR

MAIN FLOOR

Plan E-2900
PRICES AND DETAILS ON PAGES 12-15

Affordable Victorian

- This compact Victorian design incorporates four bedrooms and three full baths into an attractive, affordable home that's only 30 ft. wide.
- In from the covered front porch, the spacious parlor includes a fireplace, and the formal dining room has a beautiful bay window.
- The galley-style kitchen offers efficient service to the breakfast nook. A laundry closet and a pantry are nearby.
- The main-floor bedroom makes a great office or guest bedroom, with a convenient full bath nearby.
- Upstairs, the master suite features an adjoining sitting room with a 14-ft. cathedral ceiling. The luxurious master bath includes a dual-sink vanity and a whirlpool tub with a shower. Two more large bedrooms share another full bath.
- An attached two-car garage off the kitchen is available upon request.

Plan C-8347-A

Bedrooms: 3+	Baths: 3
Living Area:	
Upper floor	783 sq. ft.
Main floor	954 sq. ft.
Total Living Area:	**1,737 sq. ft.**
Exterior Wall Framing:	2x4

Foundation Options:

Crawlspace
Slab
(All plans can be built with your choice of foundation and framing. A generic conversion diagram is available. See order form.)

BLUEPRINT PRICE CODE: B

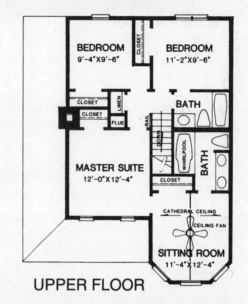

UPPER FLOOR

MAIN FLOOR

Open, Flowing Floor Plan

- Open, flowing rooms punctuated with wonderful windows enhance this spacious four-bedroom home.
- The two-story-high foyer is brightened by an arched window above. To the left lies the living room, which flows into the family room. An inviting fireplace and windows overlooking a rear terrace highlight the family room.
- The centrally located kitchen serves both the formal dining room and the dinette, with a view of the family room beyond. Sliding glass doors in the dinette open to a lovely terrace.
- Upstairs, the master suite features an arched window and a walk-in closet with a dressing area. The private master bath includes a dual-sink vanity, a skylighted whirlpool tub and a separate shower.
- The three remaining bedrooms share another skylighted bath.

Plan AHP-9020

Bedrooms: 4	Baths: 2½
Living Area:	
Upper floor	1,021 sq. ft.
Main floor	1,125 sq. ft.
Total Living Area:	**2,146 sq. ft.**
Standard basement	1,032 sq. ft.
Garage	480 sq. ft.
Exterior Wall Framing:	2x6

Foundation Options:

Standard basement
Crawlspace
Slab

(All plans can be built with your choice of foundation and framing. A generic conversion diagram is available. See order form.)

BLUEPRINT PRICE CODE: C

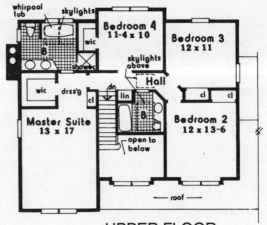

UPPER FLOOR

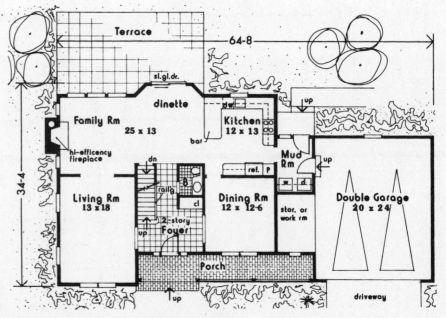

MAIN FLOOR

Fantastic Floor Plan!

- Featured on "Hometime," the popular PBS television program, this unique design combines a dynamic exterior with a fantastic floor plan.
- The barrel-vaulted entry leads into the vaulted foyer, which is outlined by elegant columns. To the left, the living room features a 13-ft. vaulted ceiling, a curved wall and corner windows. To the right, the formal dining room is enhanced by a tray ceiling.
- Overlooking a large backyard deck, the island kitchen includes a corner pantry and a built-in desk. The breakfast room shares a columned snack bar with the family room, which has a fireplace and a 17-ft., 8-in. vaulted ceiling.
- The master suite boasts a 15-ft. vaulted ceiling and private access to a romantic courtyard. The sunken master bath features an enticing spa tub and a separate shower, both encased by a curved glass-block wall.
- The two upstairs bedrooms have private access to a large full bath.

Plan B-88015

Bedrooms: 3	Baths: 2½
Living Area:	
Upper floor	534 sq. ft.
Main floor	1,689 sq. ft.
Total Living Area:	**2,223 sq. ft.**
Standard basement	1,689 sq. ft.
Garage	455 sq. ft.
Exterior Wall Framing:	2x4

Foundation Options:

Standard basement

(All plans can be built with your choice of foundation and framing. A generic conversion diagram is available. See order form.)

BLUEPRINT PRICE CODE: C

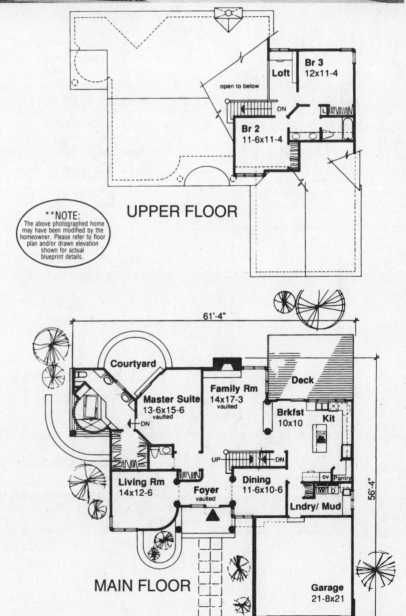

NOTE: The above photographed home may have been modified by the homeowner. Please refer to floor plan and/or drawn elevation shown for actual blueprint details.

UPPER FLOOR

Br 3 12x11-4

Loft

open to below

DN

Br 2 11-6x11-4

MAIN FLOOR

61'-4"

Courtyard

Master Suite 13-6x15-6 vaulted

Family Rm 14x17-3 vaulted

Deck

Brkfst 10x10

Kit

DN

Living Rm 14x12-6

Foyer vaulted

UP

DN

Dining 11-6x10-6

Pantry

ov

Lndry/ Mud

56'-4"

Garage 21-8x21

Gracious Traditional

- This traditional home is perfect for a corner lot, with a quaint facade and an attached garage around back.
- Tall windows, elegant dormers and a covered front porch welcome guests to the front entry and into the foyer.
- Just off the foyer, the formal dining room boasts a built-in hutch and views to the front porch.
- The expansive, skylighted Great Room features a wet bar, a 16-ft. vaulted

ceiling, a stunning fireplace and access to the screened back porch.
- The kitchen includes a large pantry and an eating bar to the bayed breakfast nook. A large utility room with garage access is nearby.
- The master bedroom offers a walk-in closet and a bath with a large corner tub and his-and-hers vanities.
- Two additional bedrooms have big walk-in closets, built-in desks and easy access to another full bath.
- Upstairs, a loft overlooks the Great Room and is perfect as an extra bedroom or a recreation area.

Plan C-8920	
Bedrooms: 3+	**Baths:** 3
Living Area:	
Upper floor	305 sq. ft.
Main floor	1,996 sq. ft.
Total Living Area:	**2,301 sq. ft.**
Daylight basement	1,996 sq. ft.
Garage	469 sq. ft.
Exterior Wall Framing:	2x4
Foundation Options:	
Daylight basement	
Crawlspace	

(All plans can be built with your choice of foundation and framing. A generic conversion diagram is available. See order form.)

BLUEPRINT PRICE CODE:	C

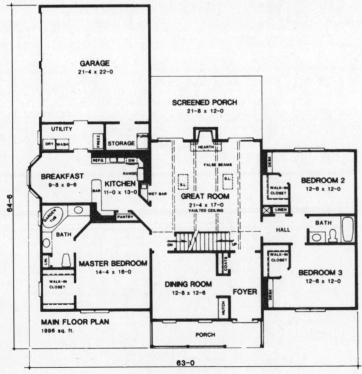

MAIN FLOOR

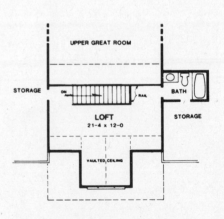

UPPER FLOOR

Plan C-8920

PRICES AND DETAILS ON PAGES 12-15

Classic Victorian

- This classic exterior is built around an interior that offers all the amenities desired by today's families.
- In from the covered front porch, the entry features a curved stairway and a glass-block wall to the dining room.
- A step down from the entry, the Great Room boasts a dramatic 24½-ft. cathedral ceiling and provides ample space for large family gatherings.
- The formal dining room is available for special occasions, while the 13-ft.-high breakfast nook serves everyday needs.
- The adjoining island kitchen offers plenty of counter space and opens to a handy utility room and a powder room.
- The deluxe main-floor master suite features a 14½-ft. cathedral ceiling and an opulent private bath with a garden spa tub and a separate shower.
- Upstairs, two secondary bedrooms share a full bath and a balcony overlooking the Great Room below.
- Plans for a two-car garage are available upon request.

Plan DW-2112

Bedrooms: 3	Baths: 2½
Living Area:	
Upper floor	514 sq. ft.
Main floor	1,598 sq. ft.
Total Living Area:	**2,112 sq. ft.**
Standard basement	1,598 sq. ft.
Exterior Wall Framing:	**2x4**

Foundation Options:

Standard basement
Crawlspace
Slab

(All plans can be built with your choice of foundation and framing. A generic conversion diagram is available. See order form.)

BLUEPRINT PRICE CODE:	**C**

UPPER FLOOR

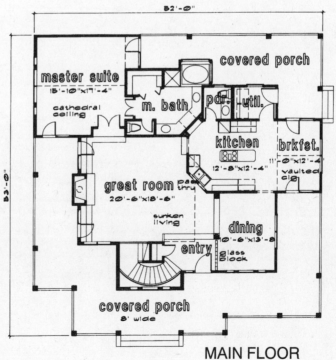

MAIN FLOOR

TO ORDER THIS BLUEPRINT,
CALL TOLL-FREE 1-800-820-1283

Plan DW-2112

PRICES AND DETAILS
ON PAGES 12-15

165

You Asked for It!

- Our most popular plan in recent years, E-3000, has now been downsized for affordability, without sacrificing character or excitement.
- Exterior appeal is created with a covered front porch with decorative columns, triple dormers and rail-topped bay windows.
- The floor plan has combined the separate living and family rooms available in E-3000 into one spacious family room with corner fireplace, which flows into the dining room through a columned gallery.
- The kitchen serves the breakfast room over an angled snack bar, and features a huge pantry.
- The stunning main-floor master suite offers a private sitting area, a walk-in closet and a dramatic, angled bath.
- There are two large bedrooms upstairs accessible via a curved staircase with bridge balcony.

Plan E-2307

Bedrooms: 3	Baths: 2½
Living Area:	
Upper floor	595 sq. ft.
Main floor	1,765 sq. ft.
Total Living Area:	**2,360 sq. ft.**
Standard basement	1,765 sq. ft.
Garage	484 sq. ft.
Storage	44 sq. ft.
Exterior Wall Framing:	2x6

Foundation Options:
Standard basement
Crawlspace
Slab

(All plans can be built with your choice of foundation and framing. A generic conversion diagram is available. See order form.)

BLUEPRINT PRICE CODE: C

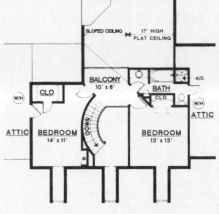

UPPER FLOOR

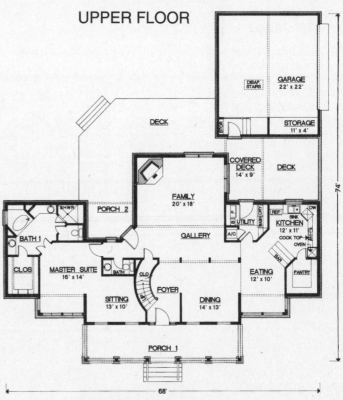

MAIN FLOOR

      Plan E-2307   PRICES AND DETAILS ON PAGES 12-15

Old-Fashioned Charm

- A trio of dormers add old-fashioned charm to this modern design.
- Both the living room and the dining room offer 12-ft.-high vaulted ceilings and flow together to create a sense of even more spaciousness.
- The open kitchen/nook/family room features a sunny alcove, a walk-in pantry and a woodstove.
- A first-floor den and a walk-through utility room are other big bonuses.
- Upstairs, the master suite includes a walk-in closet and a deluxe bath with a spa tub and a separate shower and water closet.
- Two more bedrooms, each with a window seat, and a bonus room complete this stylish design.

Plan CDG-2004

Bedrooms: 3+	Baths: 2½
Living Area:	
Upper floor	928 sq. ft.
Main floor	1,317 sq. ft.
Bonus area	192 sq. ft.
Total Living Area:	**2,437 sq. ft.**
Partial daylight basement	780 sq. ft.
Garage	537 sq. ft.
Exterior Wall Framing:	2x6

Foundation Options:

Partial daylight basement

Crawlspace

(All plans can be built with your choice of foundation and framing. A generic conversion diagram is available. See order form.)

BLUEPRINT PRICE CODE:	C

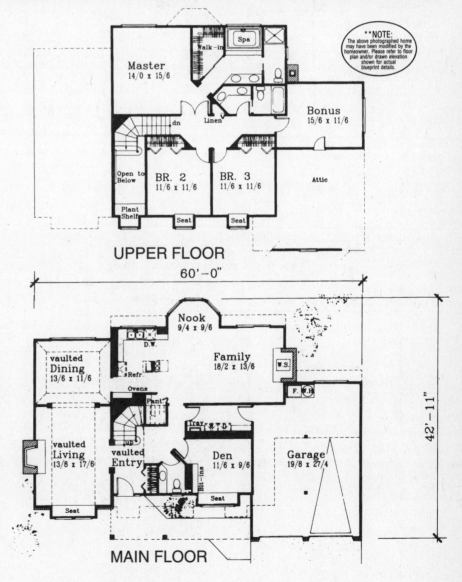

UPPER FLOOR

MAIN FLOOR

TO ORDER THIS BLUEPRINT,
CALL TOLL-FREE 1-800-820-1283

Plan CDG-2004

PRICES AND DETAILS
ON PAGES 12-15

167

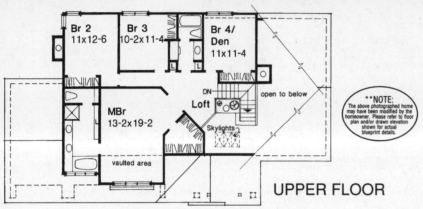

UPPER FLOOR

NOTE:
The above photographed home may have been modified by the homeowner. Please refer to floor plan and/or drawn elevation shown for actual blueprint details.

Two-Story for Today

- The charm and character of yesterday are re-created in this two-story design for today. The quaint exterior is highlighted by half-round windows, planter boxes and a covered front porch.

- The dramatic skylighted entry preludes a formal, sunken living room with a stunning corner fireplace and an adjoining formal dining room with a built-in hutch. Both rooms are also enhanced by vaulted ceilings.

- A large kitchen with a built-in desk and a pantry opens to a sunny breakfast room and a large, sunken family room at the rear of the home. The family room features an exciting fireplace wall and French doors that open to the rear deck.

- The upstairs loft leads to a luxurious master bedroom with a vaulted ceiling, angled walk-in closet and private bath. Two to three additional bedrooms and a second bath are also included.

Plan B-159-86

Bedrooms: 3-4	Baths: 2½
Living Area:	
Upper floor	1,155 sq. ft.
Main floor	1,290 sq. ft.
Total Living Area:	**2,445 sq. ft.**
Standard basement	1,290 sq. ft.
Garage	683 sq. ft.
Exterior Wall Framing:	2x4

Foundation Options:
Standard basement
(Typical foundation & framing conversion diagram available—see order form.)

BLUEPRINT PRICE CODE:	C

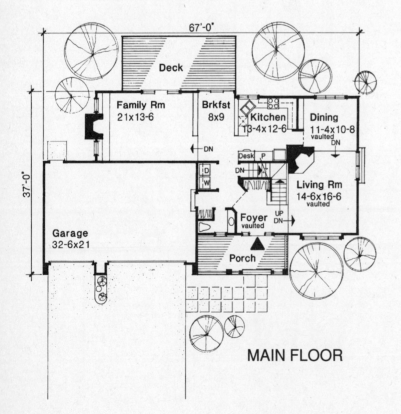

MAIN FLOOR

Plan B-159-86

PRICES AND DETAILS
ON PAGES 12-15

Tasteful Style

- Traditional lines and a contemporary floor plan combine to make this home a perfect choice for the '90s.
- The two-story-high entry introduces the formal living room, which is warmed by a fireplace and brightened by a round-top window arrangement. The living room's ceiling rises to 13 ft., 9 inches.
- A handy pocket door separates the formal dining room from the kitchen for special occasions. The U-shaped kitchen features an eating bar, a work desk and a bayed nook with access to an outdoor patio.
- The spacious family room includes a second fireplace and outdoor views.
- Ceilings in all main-floor rooms are at least 9 ft. high for added spaciousness.
- Upstairs, the master suite features a 12-ft. vaulted ceiling, two walk-in closets and a compartmentalized bath with a luxurious tub in a window bay.
- Two additional bedrooms share a split bath. A versatile bonus room could serve as an extra bedroom or as a sunny area for hobbies or paperwork.

Plan S-8389

Bedrooms: 3+	Baths: 2½
Living Area:	
Upper floor	932 sq. ft.
Main floor	1,290 sq. ft.
Bonus room	228 sq. ft.
Total Living Area:	**2,450 sq. ft.**
Standard basement	1,290 sq. ft.
Garage	429 sq. ft.
Exterior Wall Framing:	2x6

Foundation Options:

Standard basement

Crawlspace

Slab

(All plans can be built with your choice of foundation and framing. A generic conversion diagram is available. See order form.)

BLUEPRINT PRICE CODE: C

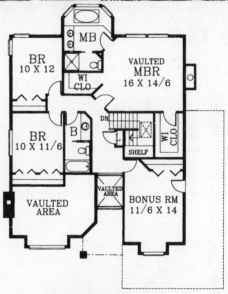

UPPER FLOOR

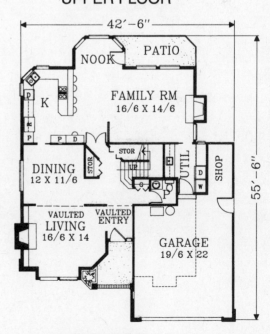

MAIN FLOOR

Panoramic Porch

- A gracious, ornately rounded front porch and a two-story turreted bay lend Victorian charm to this home.
- A two-story foyer with round-top transom windows and a plant ledge above greets guests at the entry.
- The living room enjoys a 13-ft.-high ceiling and a panoramic view overlooking the front porch and yard.
- The formal dining room and den each feature a bay window for added style.
- The sunny kitchen incorporates an angled island cooktop with a eating bar to the bayed breakfast room.
- A step down, the family room offers a corner fireplace that may be enjoyed throughout the casual living spaces.
- The upper floor is highlighted by a stunning master suite, which flaunts an octagonal sitting area with a 10-ft. tray ceiling and turreted bay. The master bath offers a corner spa tub and a separate shower. Two additional bedrooms share another full bath.

Plan AX-90307

Bedrooms: 3+	Baths: 3
Living Area:	
Upper floor	956 sq. ft.
Main floor	1,499 sq. ft.
Total Living Area:	**2,455 sq. ft.**
Standard basement	1,499 sq. ft.
Garage	410 sq. ft.
Exterior Wall Framing:	2x4

Foundation Options:
Standard basement
Slab
(All plans can be built with your choice of foundation and framing. A generic conversion diagram is available. See order form.)

BLUEPRINT PRICE CODE: C

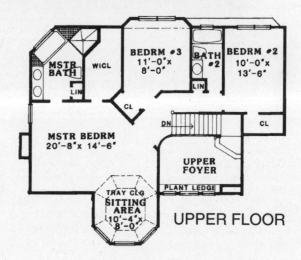

UPPER FLOOR

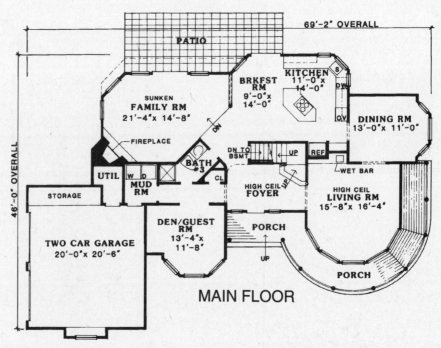

MAIN FLOOR

TO ORDER THIS BLUEPRINT, CALL TOLL-FREE 1-800-820-1283

Plan AX-90307

PRICES AND DETAILS ON PAGES 12-15

Privacy and Luxury

- This home's large roof planes and privacy fences enclose a thoroughly modern, open floor plan.
- A beautiful courtyard greets guests on their way to the secluded entrance. Inside, a two-story-high entry area leads directly into the living and dining rooms, which boast an 11-ft. vaulted ceiling, plus floor-to-ceiling windows and a fireplace with a stone hearth.
- The angular kitchen features a snack bar to the adjoining family room and a passive-solar sun room that offers natural brightness.
- A 14½-ft. vaulted ceiling presides over the family room. Sliding glass doors access a backyard patio with a sun deck and a hot tub.
- The luxurious master suite opens to both the front courtyard and the backyard hot tub area. The 11-ft.-high vaulted bath includes a dual-sink vanity, a raised garden tub, a separate shower and a corner walk-in closet.
- Two secondary bedrooms and another bath share the upper floor, which boasts commanding views of main-floor areas.

Plans P-7663-3A & -3D

Bedrooms: 3+	Baths: 3
Living Area:	
Upper floor	569 sq. ft.
Main floor	2,039 sq. ft.
Total Living Area:	**2,608 sq. ft.**
Daylight basement	2,039 sq. ft.
Garage	799 sq. ft.
Exterior Wall Framing:	2x4
Foundation Options:	**Plan #**
Daylight basement	P-7663-3D
Crawlspace	P-7663-3A

(All plans can be built with your choice of foundation and framing. A generic conversion diagram is available. See order form.)

BLUEPRINT PRICE CODE: **D**

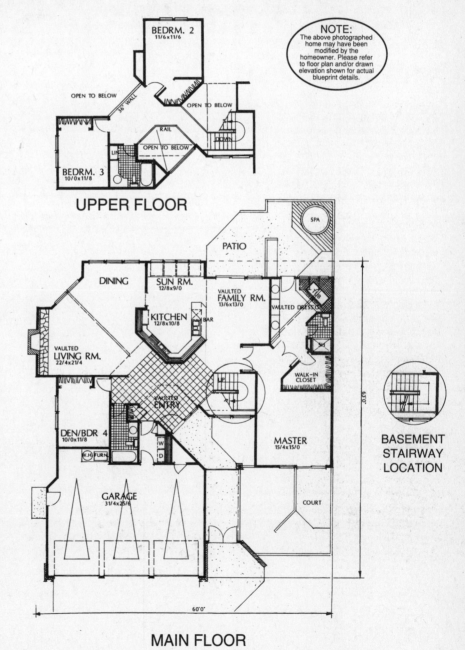

BEDRM. 2
11/6 x 11/6

OPEN TO BELOW

OPEN TO BELOW

RAIL

DOWN

OPEN TO BELOW

BEDRM. 3
10/0 x 11/8

UPPER FLOOR

NOTE:
The above photographed home may have been modified by the homeowner. Please refer to floor plan and/or drawn elevation shown for actual blueprint details.

SPA

PATIO

DINING

SUN RM.
12/8 x 9/0

VAULTED FAMILY RM.
13/6 x 13/0

VAULTED DRESS.

KITCHEN
12/8 x 10/8

BAR

VAULTED LIVING RM.
22/4 x 21/4

WALK-IN CLOSET

VAULTED ENTRY

UP

DEN/BDR 4
10/0 x 11/8

MASTER
15/4 x 15/0

W.H FURN

GARAGE
31/4 x 25/6

COURT

60'0"

MAIN FLOOR

BASEMENT STAIRWAY LOCATION

TO ORDER THIS BLUEPRINT,
CALL TOLL-FREE 1-800-820-1283

Plans P-7663-3A & -3D

PRICES AND DETAILS
ON PAGES 12-15

171

Dynamic Design

- Angled walls, vaulted ceilings and lots of glass set the tempo for this dynamic home.
- The covered front entry opens to a raised foyer and a beautiful staircase with a bayed landing.
- One step down, a spectacular see-through fireplace with a raised hearth and built-in wood storage is visible from both the bayed dining room and the stunning Great Room.
- The Great Room also showcases an 18-ft.-high vaulted ceiling, wraparound windows and access to a deck or patio.
- The adjoining nook has a door to the deck and is served by the kitchen's snack bar. The kitchen is enhanced by a 9-ft. ceiling, corner windows and a pass-through to the dining room.
- Upstairs, the master suite offers a 10-ft.-high coved ceiling, a splendid bath, a large walk-in closet and a private deck.

Plan S-41587

Bedrooms: 3+	Baths: 3
Living Area:	
Upper floor	1,001 sq. ft.
Main floor	1,550 sq. ft.
Total Living Area:	**2,551 sq. ft.**
Basement	1,550 sq. ft.
Garage (three-car)	773 sq. ft.
Exterior Wall Framing:	2x6

Foundation Options:

Daylight basement

Standard basement

Crawlspace

Slab

(All plans can be built with your choice of foundation and framing. A generic conversion diagram is available. See order form.)

BLUEPRINT PRICE CODE: D

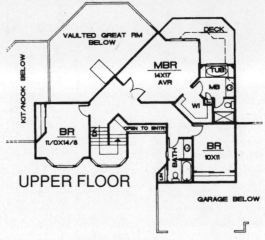

UPPER FLOOR

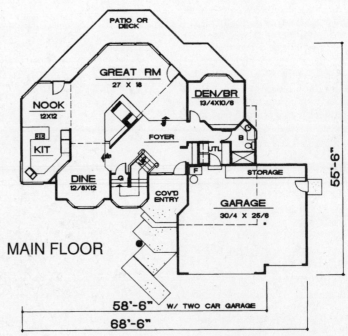

MAIN FLOOR

Plan S-41587

Large-Scale Living

- Eye-catching windows and an appealing wraparound porch highlight the exterior of this outstanding home.
- Inside, high ceilings and large-scale living spaces prevail, beginning with the foyer, which has an 18-ft. ceiling.
- The spacious living room flows into the formal dining room, which opens to the porch and to an optional rear deck.
- The island kitchen extends to a bright breakfast room with deck access. The family room offers an 18-ft. vaulted ceiling and a corner fireplace.
- Unless otherwise noted, every main-floor room boasts a 9-ft. ceiling.
- Upstairs, the lushs master bedroom boasts an 11-ft. vaulted ceiling and two walk-in closets. The skylighted master bath features a spa tub, a separate shower and a dual-sink vanity.
- Three more bedrooms are reached by a balcony, which overlooks the family room. In one bedroom, the ceiling jumps to 10 ft. at the beautiful window.

Plan AX-93309

Bedrooms: 4	Baths: 2½
Living Area:	
Upper floor	1,180 sq. ft.
Main floor	1,290 sq. ft.
Total Living Area:	**2,470 sq. ft.**
Basement	1,290 sq. ft.
Garage and storage	421 sq. ft.
Exterior Wall Framing:	2x4

Foundation Options:

Daylight basement
Standard basement
Slab

(All plans can be built with your choice of foundation and framing. A generic conversion diagram is available. See order form.)

BLUEPRINT PRICE CODE: C

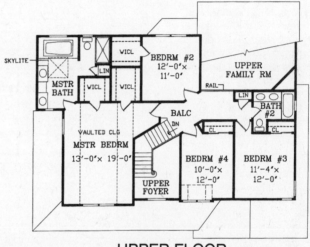

UPPER FLOOR

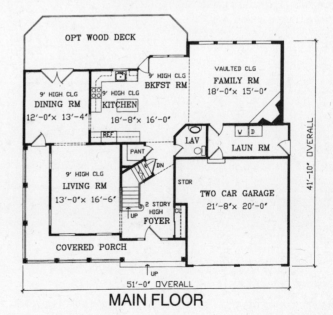

MAIN FLOOR

Innovative Floor Plan

- The wide, covered front porch, arched windows and symmetrical lines of this traditional home conceal the modern, innovative floor plan found within.
- A two-story-high foyer guides guests to the front-oriented formal areas, which have views to the front porch.
- The hotspot of the home is the Great Room, with one of the home's three fireplaces and a media wall. Flanking doors open to a large backyard deck.
- The island kitchen and glassed-in eating nook overlook the deck and access a handy mudroom. High 9-ft. ceilings add to the aura of warmth and hospitality found on the main floor of this home.
- Another of the fireplaces is offered in the master suite. This private oasis also boasts a 13-ft.-high cathedral ceiling and a delicious bath with a garden tub.
- Upstairs, one bedroom has a sloped ceiling and a private bath. Three more bedrooms share another full bath.

Plan AHP-9360

Bedrooms: 5	Baths: 3½
Living Area:	
Upper floor	970 sq. ft.
Main floor	1,735 sq. ft.
Total Living Area:	**2,705 sq. ft.**
Standard basement	1,550 sq. ft.
Garage and utility area	443 sq. ft.
Exterior Wall Framing:	2x6

Foundation Options:

Standard basement
Crawlspace
Slab

(All plans can be built with your choice of foundation and framing. A generic conversion diagram is available. See order form.)

BLUEPRINT PRICE CODE:	D

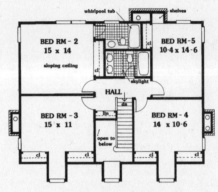

UPPER FLOOR

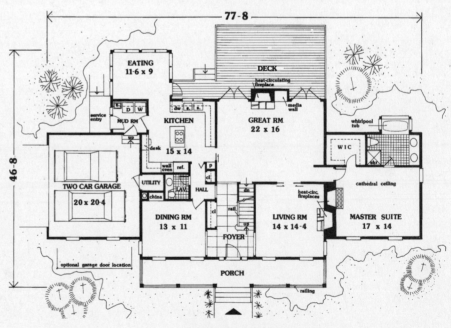

MAIN FLOOR

Take the Plunge!

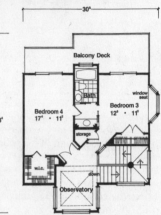

UPPER FLOOR

- From the elegant portico to the striking rooflines, this home's facade is magnificent. But the rear area is equally fine, with its spa, waterfall and pool.
- Double doors lead from the entry into a columned foyer where a 12-ft.-high ceiling extends into the central living room beyond. A sunken wet bar juts into the pool area, allowing guests to swim up to the bar for refreshments.
- The dining room boasts window walls and a tiered pedestal ceiling. The island kitchen easily services both the formal and the informal areas of the home.
- A large breakfast room flows into a warm family room with a fireplace and sliding glass doors to the patio and pool.
- The stunning master suite offers an opulent bath, patio access and views of the pool through a curved window wall.
- A railed staircase leads to the upper floor, where there are two bedrooms, a continental bath and a shared balcony deck overlooking the pool area.
- The observatory features high windows to accommodate an amateur stargazer's telescope. This room could also be used as an activity area for hobbies or games

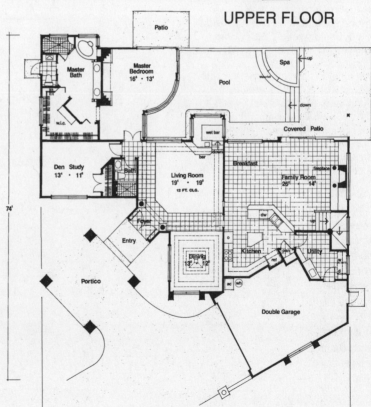

MAIN FLOOR

Plan HDS-99-154

Bedrooms: 3+	Baths: 3
Living Area:	
Upper floor	675 sq. ft.
Main floor	2,212 sq. ft.
Total Living Area:	**2,887 sq. ft.**
Garage	479 sq. ft.
Exterior Wall Framing:	2x4

Foundation Options:

Slab

(All plans can be built with your choice of foundation and framing. A generic conversion diagram is available. See order form.)

BLUEPRINT PRICE CODE: **D.**

Dramatic Rear Views

- Columned front and rear porches offer country styling to this elegant two-story.
- The formal dining room and living room flank the two-story-high foyer.
- A dramatic array of windows stretches along the informal, rear-oriented living areas, where the central family room features a 17-ft.-high vaulted ceiling and a striking fireplace.
- The modern kitchen features an angled snack counter, a walk-in pantry and a work island, in addition to the bayed morning room.
- The exciting and secluded master suite has a sunny bayed sitting area with its own fireplace. Large walk-in closets lead to a luxurious private bath with angled dual vanities, a garden spa tub and a separate shower.
- The centrally located stairway leads to three extra bedrooms and two full baths on the upper floor.

Plan DD-2912

Bedrooms: 4	Baths: 3½
Living Area:	
Upper floor	916 sq. ft.
Main floor	2,046 sq. ft.
Total Living Area:	**2,962 sq. ft.**
Standard basement	1,811 sq. ft.
Garage	513 sq. ft.
Exterior Wall Framing:	2x4

Foundation Options:

Standard basement
Crawlspace
Slab

(All plans can be built with your choice of foundation and framing. A generic conversion diagram is available. See order form.)

BLUEPRINT PRICE CODE: D

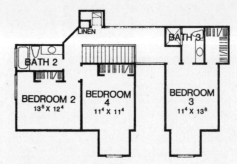

UPPER FLOOR

MAIN FLOOR

Spacious and Stately

- This popular home design boasts a classic Creole exterior and a symmetrical layout, with 9-ft.-high ceilings on the main floor.
- French doors lead from the formal living and dining rooms to the large family room. The central fireplace is flanked by French doors that open to a covered rear porch and an open-air deck.
- The kitchen is reached easily from the family room, the dining room and the rear entrance. An island cooktop and a window-framed eating area are other features found here.
- The real seller, though, is the main-floor master suite with its spectacular bath. Among its many extras are a built-in vanity, a spa tub and a 16-ft. sloped ceiling with a skylight.
- Three upstairs bedrooms, each with double closets and private bath access, make this the perfect family-sized home.

Plan E-3000

Bedrooms: 4	Baths: 3½
Living Area:	
Upper floor	1,027 sq. ft.
Main floor	2,008 sq. ft.
Total Living Area:	**3,035 sq. ft.**
Standard basement	2,008 sq. ft.
Garage	484 sq. ft.
Storage	96 sq. ft.
Exterior Wall Framing:	2x6

Foundation Options:

Standard basement
Crawlspace
Slab

(All plans can be built with your choice of foundation and framing. A generic conversion diagram is available. See order form.)

BLUEPRINT PRICE CODE: E

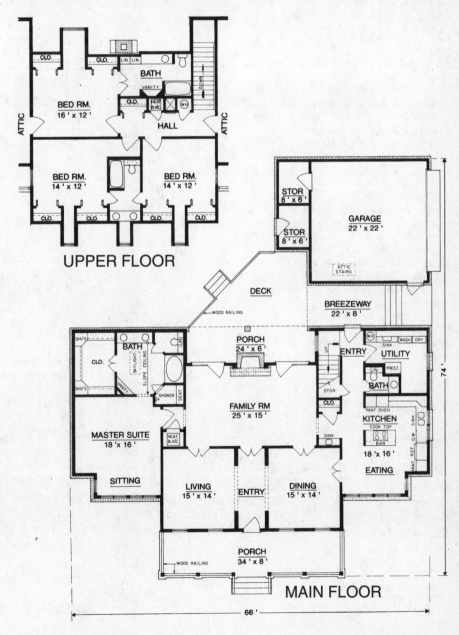

UPPER FLOOR

MAIN FLOOR

TO ORDER THIS BLUEPRINT,
CALL TOLL-FREE 1-800-820-1283

Plan E-3000

PRICES AND DETAILS
ON PAGES 12-15

177

Stately and Roomy

- The exquisite exterior of this two-story home opens to a very roomy interior.
- The magnificent two-story-high foyer shows off a curved, open-railed stairway to the upper floor and opens to a study on the right and the formal living areas on the left.
- The spacious living room flows into a formal dining room that overlooks the outdoors through a lovely bay window.
- A large work island and snack counter sit at the center of the open kitchen and breakfast room. An oversized pantry closet, a powder room and a laundry room are all close at hand.
- Adjoining the breakfast room is the large sunken family room, featuring a 12-ft.-high vaulted ceiling, a cozy fireplace and outdoor access.
- The upper floor includes a stunning master bedroom with an 11-ft. vaulted ceiling and a luxurious private bath.
- Three additional bedrooms share a second full bath.

Plan CH-280-A

Bedrooms: 4+	Baths: 2½
Living Area:	
Upper floor	1,262 sq. ft.
Main floor	1,797 sq. ft.
Total Living Area:	**3,059 sq. ft.**
Basement	1,797 sq. ft.
Garage	462 sq. ft.
Exterior Wall Framing:	2x4

Foundation Options:

Daylight basement

Standard basement

Crawlspace

(All plans can be built with your choice of foundation and framing. A generic conversion diagram is available. See order form.)

BLUEPRINT PRICE CODE: E

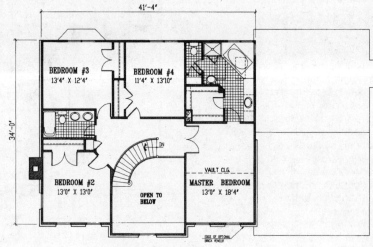

UPPER FLOOR

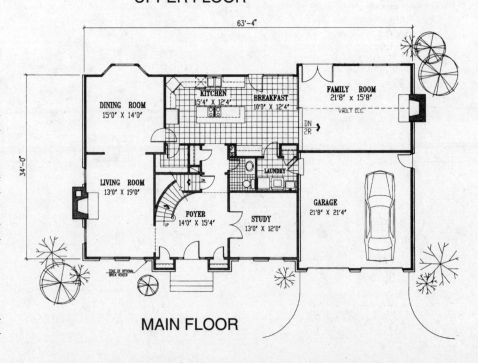

MAIN FLOOR

   Plan CH-280-A

Large and Luxurious

- This two-story home offers large, luxurious living areas with a variety of options to complement any lifestyle.
- The two-story-high foyer shows off an angled stairway and flows to the elegant formal living spaces on the right.
- The gourmet kitchen boasts a sunny sink, a walk-in pantry and an island cooktop with a serving bar. The adjoining breakfast nook has French doors opening to the backyard.
- Highlighting the main floor is a huge sunken family room, which is expanded by a 17-ft. vaulted ceiling and hosts a handy wet bar and a handsome fireplace. An open rail views to the breakfast room and kitchen beyond.
- Completing the main floor is a den or guest bedroom with private access to a full bath, making a great guest suite.
- Upstairs, the master suite boasts a 10-ft. tray ceiling in the sleeping area and a 15-ft. vaulted ceiling in the garden bath.
- Each of the three remaining bedrooms has private access to a bath.

Plan FB-3071

Bedrooms: 4+	Baths: 4
Living Area:	
Upper floor	1,419 sq. ft.
Main floor	1,652 sq. ft.
Total Living Area:	**3,071 sq. ft.**
Daylight basement	1,652 sq. ft.
Garage	456 sq. ft.
Exterior Wall Framing:	2x4

Foundation Options:

Daylight basement

(All plans can be built with your choice of foundation and framing. A generic conversion diagram is available. See order form.)

BLUEPRINT PRICE CODE:	E

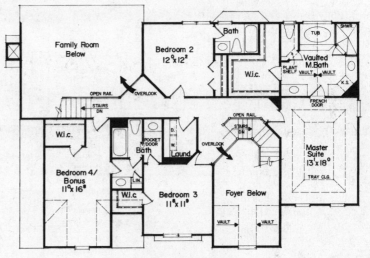

UPPER FLOOR

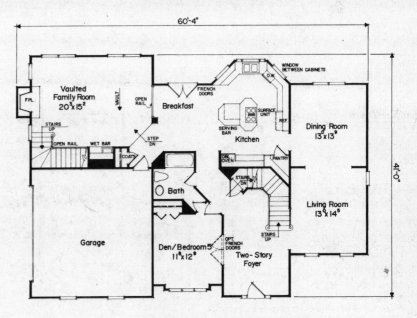

MAIN FLOOR

TO ORDER THIS BLUEPRINT,
CALL TOLL-FREE 1-800-820-1283

Plan FB-3071

PRICES AND DETAILS
ON PAGES 12-15

179

Tall Two-Story

- This gorgeous two-story is introduced by a barrel-vaulted entry and supporting columns. Inside, a spectacular curved staircase leads to a balcony overlook.
- Off the two-story-high foyer, a library with a 16-ft.-high vaulted ceiling is perfect for reading or study.
- A formal dining room opposite the library opens to the fabulous island kitchen. The kitchen offers an angled serving bar to the bayed breakfast area and adjoining living room.
- The spacious living room, with an 18-ft. vaulted ceiling, opens to a backyard patio. A fireplace flanked by built-in shelving warms the whole family area.
- The master bedroom boasts a 10-ft. gambrel ceiling, a sunny bay window and patio access. The spacious master bath offers his-and-hers walk-in closets, an oval tub and a separate shower.
- A second stairway near the utility room leads to the upper floor, where there are three more bedrooms, two baths and a bonus room above the garage. The bonus room could be finished as a game room, a media center or a hobby area.

Plan DD-3125

Bedrooms: 4+	Baths: 3½
Living Area:	
Upper floor	982 sq. ft.
Main floor	2,147 sq. ft.
Total Living Area:	**3,129 sq. ft.**
Unfinished Bonus	196 sq. ft.
Standard basement	1,996 sq. ft.
Garage	771 sq. ft.
Exterior Wall Framing:	2x4

Foundation Options:

Standard basement

Crawlspace

Slab

(All plans can be built with your choice of foundation and framing. A generic conversion diagram is available. See order form.)

BLUEPRINT PRICE CODE: E

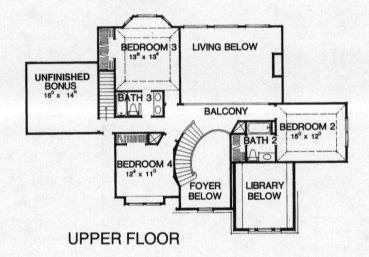

UPPER FLOOR

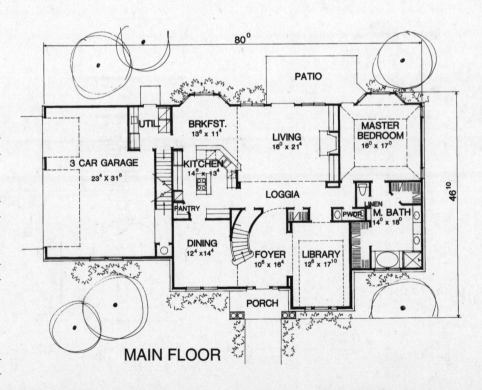

MAIN FLOOR

 TO ORDER THIS BLUEPRINT, CALL TOLL-FREE 1-800-820-1283

Plan DD-3125

PRICES AND DETAILS ON PAGES 12-15

Victorian Farmhouse

- Fish-scale shingles and horizontal siding team up with the detailed front porch to create a look of yesterday. Brickwork enriches the sides and rear of the home.
- The main level features 10-ft.-high ceilings throughout the central living space. The front-oriented formal areas merge with the family room via three sets of French doors.

- The island kitchen and skylighted eating area have 16-ft. sloped ceilings.
- A breezeway off the deck connects the house to a roomy workshop. A two-car garage is located under the workshop and a large utility room is just inside the rear entrance.
- The main-floor master suite offers an opulent skylighted bath with a garden vanity, a spa tub, a separate shower and an 18-ft.-high sloped ceiling.
- The upper floor offers three more bedrooms, two full baths and a balcony that looks to the backyard.

Plan E-3103	
Bedrooms: 4	**Baths:** 3½
Living Area:	
Upper floor	1,113 sq. ft.
Main floor	2,040 sq. ft.
Total Living Area:	**3,153 sq. ft.**
Daylight basement	2,040 sq. ft.
Tuck-under garage and storage	580 sq. ft.
Workshop and storage	580 sq. ft.
Exterior Wall Framing:	2x6
Foundation Options:	
Daylight basement	
Crawlspace	
Slab	

(All plans can be built with your choice of foundation and framing. A generic conversion diagram is available. See order form.)

BLUEPRINT PRICE CODE: E

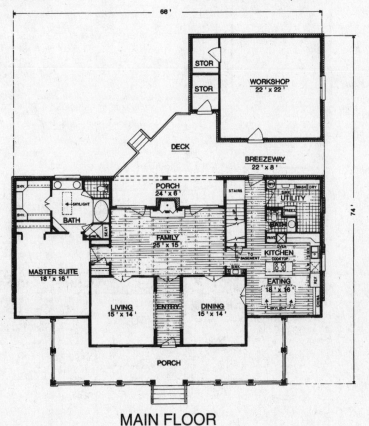

MAIN FLOOR

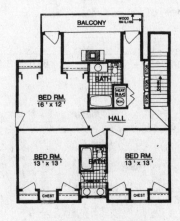

UPPER FLOOR

TO ORDER THIS BLUEPRINT,
CALL TOLL-FREE 1-800-820-1283

Plan E-3103

PRICES AND DETAILS
ON PAGES 12-15

181

Extravagant Arches

- The extravagant porch and window arches, an elegant upper balcony and a tiled roof give this home a striking Mediterranean look.
- Inside, formal living areas flank the long foyer, each adorned with entry columns and arched window treatments.
- The central family room offers a warm fireplace and a spectacular view of the patio and the optional pool.
- A large island kitchen is equipped with a walk-in pantry and generous counter space. A snack counter separates the kitchen from the bayed morning room, which also overlooks the patio.
- At the opposite end of the home is the spacious master suite, which features a bayed sitting area, a private bath, two walk-in closets and an exercise room.
- Upstairs are three more bedrooms, each with a private dressing area or bath. An exciting game room is also included!

Plan DD-3045

Bedrooms: 4	Baths: 3½
Living Area:	
Upper floor	1,202 sq. ft.
Main floor	1,952 sq. ft.
Total Living Area:	**3,154 sq. ft.**
Standard basement	1,728 sq. ft.
Garage	480 sq. ft.
Exterior Wall Framing:	2x4

Foundation Options:
Standard basement
Crawlspace
Slab
(Typical foundation & framing conversion diagram available—see order form.)

BLUEPRINT PRICE CODE: E

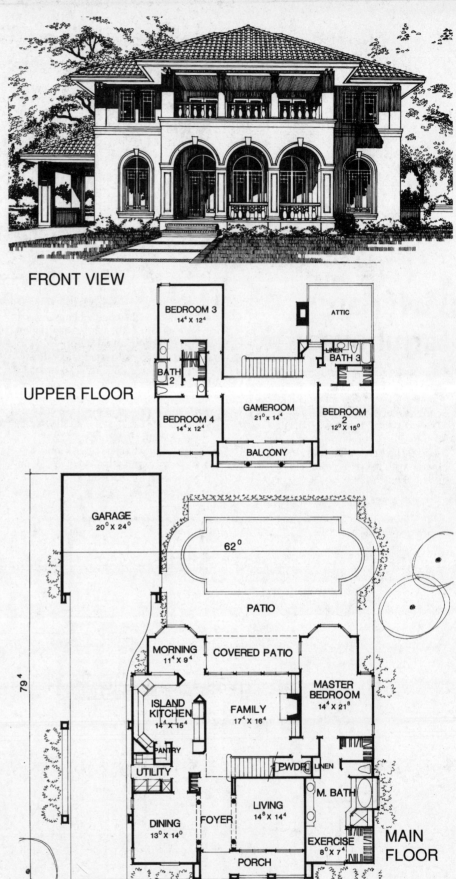

FRONT VIEW

UPPER FLOOR

MAIN FLOOR

REAR VIEW

  Plan DD-3045 *PRICES AND DETAILS ON PAGES 12-15*

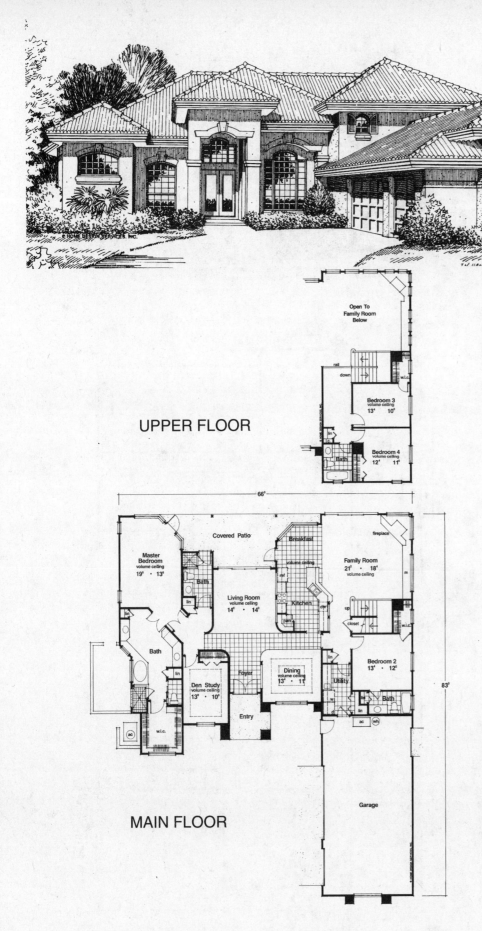

UPPER FLOOR

MAIN FLOOR

Innovative Use of Space

- This fascinating design is recognized for its innovative use of space.
- The central formal spaces separate the master suite and the den or study from the informal spaces. The rear window wall in the living room allows a view of the outdoors from the oversized foyer.
- The unique arrangement of the master suite lets traffic flow easily from the bedroom to the dressing areas, to the garden tub and to a walk-in closet that you could get lost in.
- The spacious two-story family room, kitchen and breakfast room open to one another, forming a large family activity area with corner fireplace, snack counter and surrounding windows.
- A second main-floor bedroom, two upper-floor bedrooms and three extra baths complete the floor plan.

Plan HDS-99-166	
Bedrooms: 4-5	**Baths: 4**
Living Area:	
Upper floor	540 sq. ft.
Main floor	2,624 sq. ft.
Total Living Area:	**3,164 sq. ft.**
Garage	770 sq. ft.
Exterior Wall Framing:	2x4
Foundation Options:	
Slab	
(Typical foundation & framing conversion diagram available—see order form.)	
BLUEPRINT PRICE CODE:	E

TO ORDER THIS BLUEPRINT,
CALL TOLL-FREE 1-800-820-1283

Plan HDS-99-166

*PRICES AND DETAILS
ON PAGES 12-15*

183

Ornate Design

- This exciting home is distinguished by an ornate facade with symmetrical windows and a columned entry.
- A beautiful arched window highlights the two-story-high foyer, with its open-railed stairway and high plant shelf. The foyer separates the two formal rooms and flows back to the family room.
- With an 18-ft. ceiling, the family room is brightened by corner windows and warmed by a central fireplace.
- Columns introduce the sunny breakfast area and the gourmet kitchen, which features an angled island/serving bar and a butler's pantry near the dining room. A laundry room and a second stairway to the upper floor are nearby.
- Ceilings in all main-floor rooms are 9 ft. high unless otherwise specified.
- Upstairs, a dramatic balcony overlooks the family room and the foyer.
- The master suite boasts a 10-ft. tray ceiling, a sitting room and an opulent garden bath with a 12-ft. vaulted ceiling. Three more bedrooms, each with a walk-in closet and private bath access, complete the upper floor.

Plan FB-5347-HAST

Bedrooms: 4+	Baths: 4
Living Area:	
Upper floor	1,554 sq. ft.
Main floor	1,665 sq. ft.
Total Living Area:	**3,219 sq. ft.**
Daylight basement	1,665 sq. ft.
Garage	462 sq. ft.
Exterior Wall Framing:	2x4

Foundation Options:

Daylight basement

Crawlspace

(All plans can be built with your choice of foundation and framing. A generic conversion diagram is available. See order form.)

BLUEPRINT PRICE CODE: E

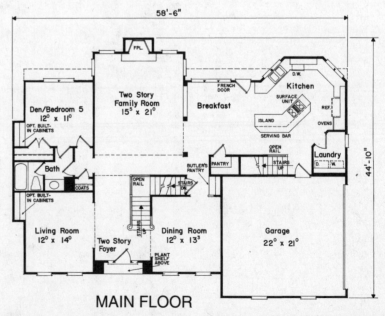

UPPER FLOOR

MAIN FLOOR

Plan FB-5347-HAST

Deluxe Master Suite

- This traditional home has an enticing style all its own, with a deluxe main-floor master suite.
- In from the covered porch, the front entry flows into the main living areas.
- Straight ahead, the family room features a handsome fireplace flanked by doors to a screened back porch.
- The kitchen easily services the formal dining room and offers a snack bar to the bayed breakfast nook. A nice utility room with a pantry and a half-bath is just off the nook and the garage entry.
- The secluded master suite boasts a 9-ft. tray ceiling and a luxurious bath with a garden tub, a separate shower and two vanities, one with knee space.
- Upstairs, each of the two additional bedrooms has a walk-in closet and a private bath. The optional bonus room can be finished as a large game room, a bedroom or an office.

Plan C-8915

Bedrooms: 3+	Baths: 3½
Living Area:	
Upper floor	832 sq. ft.
Main floor	1,927 sq. ft.
Bonus room	624 sq. ft.
Total Living Area:	**3,383 sq. ft.**
Daylight basement	1,674 sq. ft.
Garage	484 sq. ft.
Exterior Wall Framing:	2x4

Foundation Options:

Daylight basement

Crawlspace

(All plans can be built with your choice of foundation and framing. A generic conversion diagram is available. See order form.)

BLUEPRINT PRICE CODE: **E**

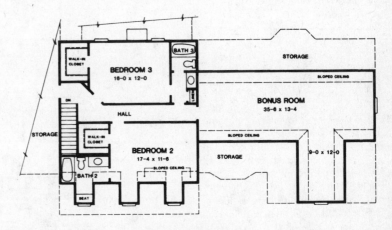

UPPER FLOOR

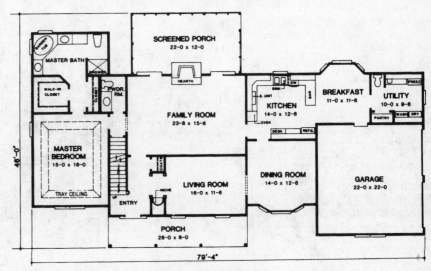

MAIN FLOOR

TO ORDER THIS BLUEPRINT,
CALL TOLL-FREE 1-800-820-1283

Plan C-8915

PRICES AND DETAILS
ON PAGES 12-15

185

Soaring Gables

- Majestic arched windows and soaring gables adorn the exterior of this incredible brick home.
- Inside, the two-story entry provides breathtaking views into the open Great Room, which showcases a wet bar and a handsome fireplace flanked by picture windows and high arched transoms.
- Lovely columns define the sun-drenched dining room, which includes hutch space and a lovely bay window.
- The spacious kitchen features access to the upper floor, plus a columned island that serves the breakfast nook and adjoining hearth room.
- French doors open to the luxurious master suite. Amenities here include two huge walk-in closets and a glamorous whirlpool bath.
- A curved stairway climbs gracefully to the upper floor, which overlooks the entry below.
- Three bedrooms are housed on this level, one of which boasts a private balcony and bi-fold doors that look out over the breakfast nook.

Plan CC-3505-M

Bedrooms: 4+	Baths: 3½
Living Area:	
Upper floor	1,013 sq. ft.
Main floor	2,492 sq. ft.
Total Living Area:	**3,505 sq. ft.**
Standard basement	2,492 sq. ft.
Garage	769 sq. ft.
Exterior Wall Framing:	2x4

Foundation Options:

Standard basement
(All plans can be built with your choice of foundation and framing. A generic conversion diagram is available. See order form.)

BLUEPRINT PRICE CODE:	F

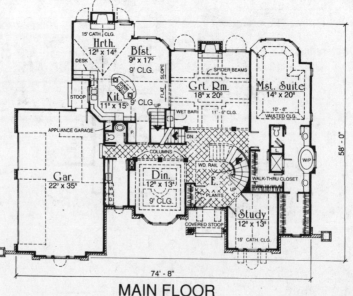

REAR VIEW

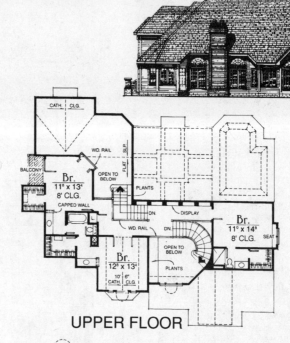

UPPER FLOOR

MAIN FLOOR

Master Suite Showpiece

- The traditional exterior of this upscale home features arched windows accented by decorative keystones.
- Arches also embellish the entrance to the formal dining room, while elegant French doors in the formal living room open to a delightful porch.
- The heartbeat of the home is the vaulted family room, the octagonal breakfast nook and the gourmet kitchen. This open area hosts many built-ins, including bookshelves, a wet bar, a plant ledge and a serving bar.
- Two separate stairways lead to the upper floor, where a balcony hall overlooks the family room and the foyer.
- The real showpiece is the marvelous master suite, featuring a two-sided fireplace, built-in bookshelves and a vaulted sitting room. The plush bath adjoins a huge walk-in closet.
- The two corner bedrooms have private access to a full bath, while the central bedroom enjoys a bath of its own.

Plan FB-5051-MART

Bedrooms: 4+	Baths: 4
Living Area:	
Upper floor	1,677 sq. ft.
Main floor	1,851 sq. ft.
Total Living Area:	**3,528 sq. ft.**
Daylight basement	1,851 sq. ft.
Garage	455 sq. ft.
Exterior Wall Framing:	2x4

Foundation Options:
Daylight basement
(Typical foundation & framing conversion diagram available—see order form.)

BLUEPRINT PRICE CODE:	F

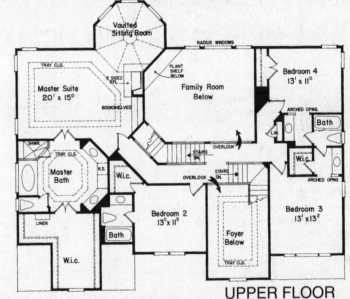

UPPER FLOOR

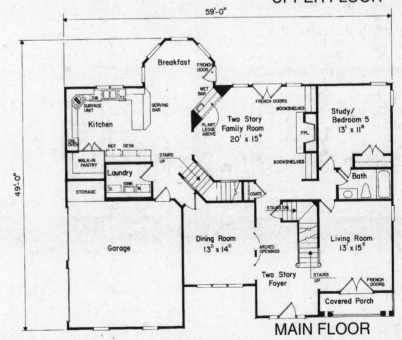

MAIN FLOOR

TO ORDER THIS BLUEPRINT,
CALL TOLL-FREE 1-800-820-1283

Plan FB-5051-MART

PRICES AND DETAILS
ON PAGES 12-15

187

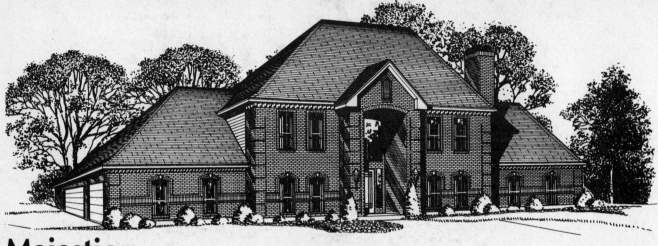

Majestic Estate Home

- A classic brick exterior and a spacious, luxurious interior are the defining features of this two-story home.
- The grand entry welcomes you into an impressive two-story foyer with a dramatic, curving staircase.
- The main floor was designed with entertainment in mind. The formal dining room has its own serving buffet, while the formal living room features a handsome fireplace.
- The roomy island kitchen is nestled between an oversized breakfast room and a spacious family room with a built-in entertainment center. The gourmet kitchen boasts a walk-in pantry and a handy snack counter.
- Luxury abounds throughout the master suite, from the bayed sitting area and the high ceiling to the luxurious garden bath and the private study.
- The upper floor offers three additional bedrooms, two full baths, an exciting exercise room and room for future expansion.

Plan KY-3626

Bedrooms: 4+	Baths: 3½
Living Area:	
Upper floor	1,147 sq. ft.
Main floor	2,479 sq. ft.
Total Living Area:	**3,626 sq. ft.**
Garage	714 sq. ft.
Exterior Wall Framing:	2x4

Foundation Options:

Slab

(Typical foundation & framing conversion diagram available—see order form.)

BLUEPRINT PRICE CODE: F

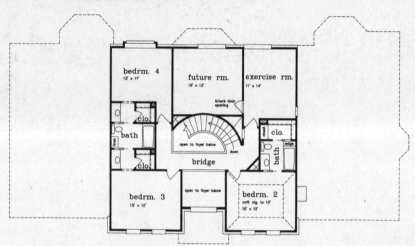

UPPER FLOOR

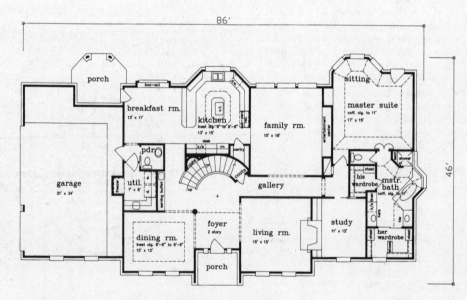

MAIN FLOOR

Plan KY-3626

Elegant Arches

- Gracious arched windows and an entry portico create rhythm and style for this home's brick-clad exterior.
- An elegant curved staircase lends interest to the raised, two-story foyer.
- Two steps down to the left of the foyer lies the living room, with its dramatic 14-ft. cathedral ceiling. Lovely columns define the adjoining dining room. A cozy fireplace warms the entire area.
- The island kitchen overlooks the bayed breakfast room and offers a handy pass-through to the adjoining family room.
- The two-story-high family room boasts a second fireplace and a wall of windows topped by large transoms.
- The quiet master bedroom features a bay window and an 11-ft. sloped ceiling. The master bath shows off a garden tub and a separate shower.
- A sizable deck is accessible from both the breakfast room and the master suite.
- Three more bedrooms and two baths share the upper floor. A balcony bridge overlooks the foyer and family room.

Plan DD-3639

Bedrooms: 4+	Baths: 3½
Living Area:	
Upper floor	868 sq. ft.
Main floor	2,771 sq. ft.
Total Living Area:	**3,639 sq. ft.**
Standard basement	2,771 sq. ft.
Garage	790 sq. ft.
Exterior Wall Framing:	2x4

Foundation Options:

Standard basement

Crawlspace

Slab

(All plans can be built with your choice of foundation and framing. A generic conversion diagram is available. See order form.)

BLUEPRINT PRICE CODE: F

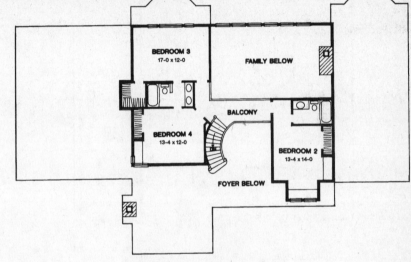

UPPER FLOOR

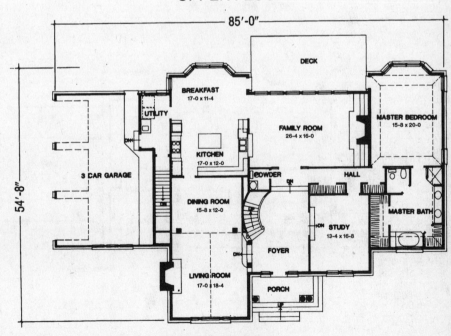

MAIN FLOOR

Prairie-Style Country Rambler

- A colonnaded, covered front porch, fieldstone and lap siding, prairie-style windows and a standing-seam metal roof create a prairie country appeal.
- The floor plan is very symmetrically organized, with a central formal living/dining area flanked by two-story wings to the right and left. A main and upper floor gallery, accessed by an interesting stair tower, overlook the formal living/dining rooms with covered rear porch beyond.
- The right wing houses the family room with fireplace and bay windowed breakfast room, with an island kitchen in-between.
- The left wing includes a guest bedroom and bath as well as a stunning master suite. The master bedroom features a private stairway leading up to a secluded studio. There is also a lavish master bath and two walk-in closets.
- There are three additional bedrooms and two baths upstairs.

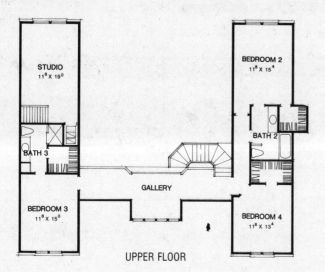

UPPER FLOOR

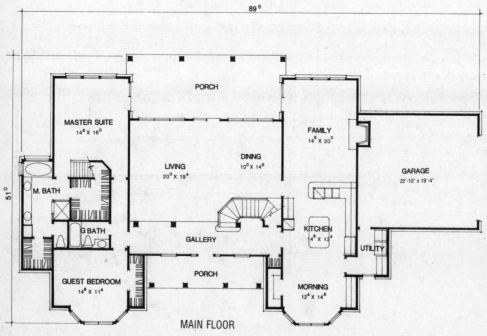

MAIN FLOOR

Plan DD-3623

Bedrooms: 4-5	Baths: 4

Space:

Upper floor:	1,273 sq. ft.
Main floor:	2,393 sq. ft.

Total living area:	**3,666 sq. ft.**
Basement:	1,420 sq. ft.
Garage:	441 sq. ft.

Exterior Wall Framing:	**2x4**

Ceiling Heights:

Upper floor:	8'
Main floor:	9'

Foundation options:
Daylight basement.
Slab.
(Foundation & framing conversion diagram available — see order form.)

Blueprint Price Code:	F

Plan DD-3623

PRICES AND DETAILS ON PAGES 12-15

Grand Entry

- Four regal columns and dramatic window arrangements accent this Mediterranean home's grand entry.
- Inside, the dining room boasts an arched inset to show off fine furniture, while niches on either side nicely display family treasures.
- The dining room, a quiet den and the bright living room all feature 12-ft. ceilings and French doors that open to covered outdoor areas.
- The home's casual living areas include the family room, the bayed breakfast nook and the kitchen, which has an

island cooktop, a serving bar and a pass-through to a summer kitchen on the covered backyard patio.
- A pleasant sitting area and French doors to the patio make the main-floor master suite an inviting refuge. A luxurious tub, a separate shower and two vanities highlight the master bath.
- Unless otherwise mentioned, each of the above-mentioned rooms boasts a striking 10-ft. ceiling.
- A secluded guest room and a full bath nearby complete the floor.
- The upper floor houses two large bedrooms and two baths. A sunken bonus room offers a handy wet bar.

Plan HDS-99-218	
Bedrooms: 4+	**Baths:** 4½
Living Area:	
Upper floor	796 sq. ft.
Main floor	2,761 sq. ft.
Bonus room	284 sq. ft.
Total Living Area:	**3,841 sq. ft.**
Garage and storage	863 sq. ft.

Exterior Wall Framing:
2x4 and 8-in. concrete block

Foundation Options:
Slab
(All plans can be built with your choice of foundation and framing. A generic conversion diagram is available. See order form.)

BLUEPRINT PRICE CODE:	F

MAIN FLOOR

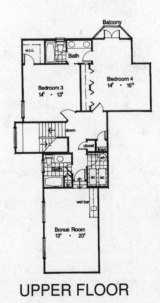

UPPER FLOOR

TO ORDER THIS BLUEPRINT,
CALL TOLL-FREE 1-800-820-1283

Plan HDS-99-218

PRICES AND DETAILS
ON PAGES 12-15
191

Elegance Perfected

- The grand style of this luxurious home brings elegance and grace to perfection.
- The contemporary architecture exudes an aura of grandeur, drawing the eye to its stately 2½-story entry portico.
- The interior is equally stunning with open, flowing spaces, high ceilings and decorative, room-defining columns.
- The formal zone is impressive, with a vast foyer and a sunken living room highlighted by dramatic window walls and a 20½-ft. ceiling. Round columns set off a stunning octagonal dining room with a 19-ft., 4-in. ceiling. A curved wet bar completes the effect!
- The informal areas consist of an island kitchen, a breakfast nook, a large family room and an octagonal media room. Activities can be extended to the covered back patio through doors in the breakfast nook and the family room.
- The fabulous master suite shows off a romantic fireplace, a 12-ft. ceiling, an enormous walk-in closet and a garden bath with a circular shower!
- Two more main-floor bedrooms, an upper-floor bedroom and loft area, plus two more baths complete the plan.

Plan HDS-90-819

Bedrooms: 4+	Baths: 3½
Living Area:	
Upper floor	765 sq. ft.
Main floor	3,770 sq. ft.
Total Living Area:	**4,535 sq. ft.**
Garage	750 sq. ft.
Exterior Wall Framing:	2x4

Foundation Options:

Slab

(All plans can be built with your choice of foundation and framing. A generic conversion diagram is available. See order form.)

BLUEPRINT PRICE CODE:	H

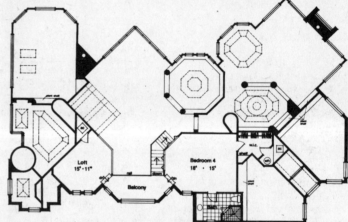

UPPER FLOOR

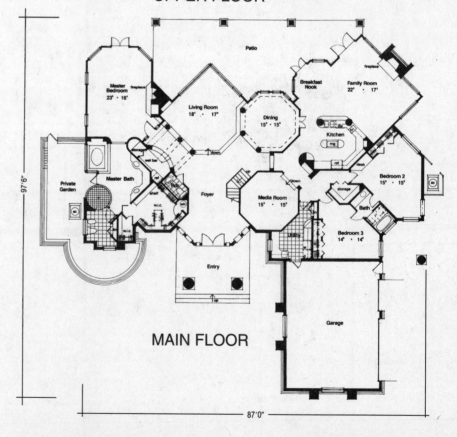

MAIN FLOOR

TO ORDER THIS BLUEPRINT, CALL TOLL-FREE 1-800-820-1283

Plan HDS-90-819

PRICES AND DETAILS ON PAGES 12-15

Estate Living

- This grand estate is as big and beautiful on the inside as it is on the outside.
- The formal dining room and parlor, each with a tall window, flank the entry's graceful curved staircase.
- The sunken family room is topped by a two-story-high ceiling and wrapped in floor-to-ceiling windows. A patio door opens to the covered porch, which features a nifty built-in barbecue.
- The island kitchen and the bright breakfast area also overlook the porch, with access through the deluxe utility room.

- The master suite has it all, including a romantic fireplace framed by bookshelves. The opulent bath offers a raised spa tub, a separate shower, his-and-hers walk-in closets and a dual-sink vanity. The neighboring bedroom, which also has a private bath, would make an ideal nursery.
- The upper floor hosts a balcony hall that provides a breathtaking view of the family room below. Each of the two bedrooms here has its own bath.
- The main floor is expanded by 10-ft. ceilings, while 9-ft. ceilings grace the upper floor.

Plan DD-4300-B	
Bedrooms: 4	**Baths:** 4½
Living Area:	
Upper floor	868 sq. ft.
Main floor	3,416 sq. ft.
Total Living Area:	**4,284 sq. ft.**
Standard basement	3,416 sq. ft.
Garage and storage	633 sq. ft.
Exterior Wall Framing:	2x4 or 2x6
Foundation Options:	
Standard basement	
Crawlspace	
Slab	

(All plans can be built with your choice of foundation and framing. A generic conversion diagram is available. See order form.)

BLUEPRINT PRICE CODE: G

MAIN FLOOR

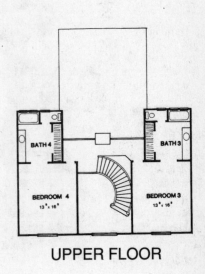

UPPER FLOOR

Design Leaves Out Nothing

- This design has it all, from the elegant detailing of the exterior to the exciting, luxurious spaces of the interior.

- High ceilings, large, open rooms and lots of glass are found throughout the home. Nearly all of the main living areas, as well as the master suite, overlook the veranda.

- Unusual features include a built-in ale bar in the formal dining room, an art niche in the Grand Room and a TV niche in the Gathering Room. The Gathering Room also features a fireplace framed by window seats, a wall of windows facing the backyard and a half-wall open to the morning room. The cooktop-island kitchen is conveniently accessible from all of the living areas.

- The delicious master suite includes a raised lounge, a three-sided fireplace and French doors that open to the veranda. The spiral stairs nearby lead to the "evening deck" above. The master bath boasts two walk-in closets, a sunken shower and a Roman tub.

- The upper floor hosts two complete suites and a loft, plus a vaulted bonus room reached via a separate stairway.

Plan EOF-61

Bedrooms: 3+	**Baths:** 4½

Living Area:	
Upper floor	877 sq. ft.
Main floor	3,094 sq. ft.
Bonus room	280 sq. ft.
Total Living Area:	**4,251 sq. ft.**
Garage	774 sq. ft.
Exterior Wall Framing:	2x6

Foundation Options:

Slab

(All plans can be built with your choice of foundation and framing. A generic conversion diagram is available. See order form.)

BLUEPRINT PRICE CODE: G

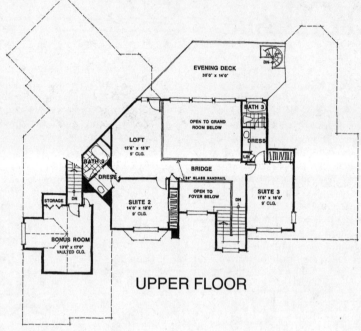

UPPER FLOOR

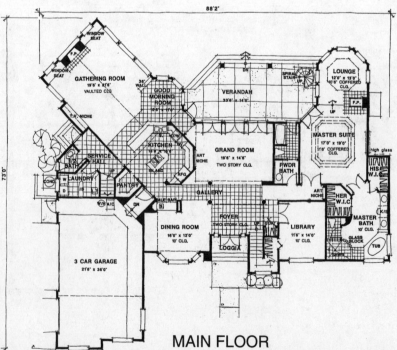

MAIN FLOOR

TO ORDER THIS BLUEPRINT, CALL TOLL-FREE 1-800-820-1283

Plan EOF-61

PRICES AND DETAILS ON PAGES 12-15

Let in the Sun!

- A sun-drenched "Florida room" with three sets of French doors to a skylighted patio gives this home exotic appeal.
- The foyer is open to the formal dining room and the Gathering Room, which is warmed by a handsome fireplace flanked by media shelves. French doors lead to the "Florida room" and the patio.
- Secluded from the rest of the home, the sprawling master bedroom enjoys a quiet sitting area with a wet bar and media shelves.
- The master bath includes an exercise area, a raised soaking tub, a separate shower and two large walk-in closets.

- Adjacent to the master bedroom, a serene study offers private access to a full bath.
- Efficiency and elegance blend in the open kitchen, which features a work island and a pass-through to the patio. A serving counter faces the bayed breakfast nook, with easy patio access just steps away.
- Two nearby bedrooms boast private access to a split bath.
- A guest room pampers visitors with gorgeous outdoor views, a handy wet bar and private bath access.
- An upper-floor bonus suite would be perfect for a "boomerang child," with its deck, kitchen and personal bath.

Plan HDS-99-221

Bedrooms: 4+	Baths: 5

Living Area:	
Main floor	4,290 sq. ft.
Bonus suite	652 sq. ft.

Total Living Area:	**4,942 sq. ft.**
Garage	921 sq. ft.

Exterior Wall Framing:
2x4 and 8-in. concrete block

Foundation Options:
Slab
(All plans can be built with your choice of foundation and framing. A generic conversion diagram is available. See order form.)

BLUEPRINT PRICE CODE: H

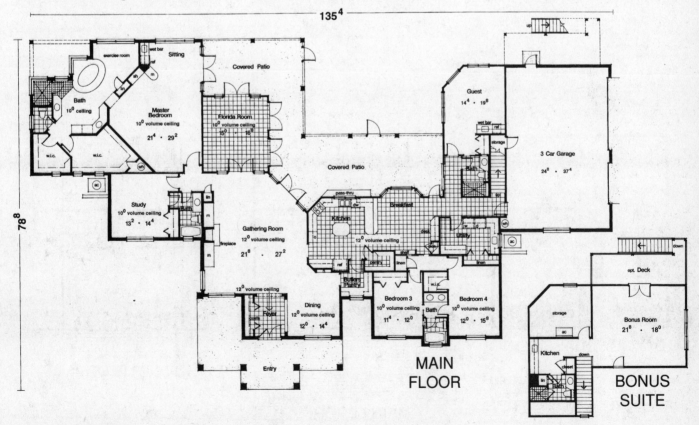

Super Chalet

- The charming Alpine detailing of the exterior and the open, flexible layout of the interior make this one of our most popular plans.
- In from the large front deck, the living room wraps around a central fireplace or woodstove, providing a warm and expansive multipurpose living space. Sliding glass doors open to the deck for outdoor entertaining.
- The adjoining dining room is easily serviced from the galley-style kitchen. A convenient full bath serves a nearby bedroom and the remainder of the main floor.
- Two upper-floor bedrooms have 12-ft.-high sloped ceilings, extra closet space and access to another full bath. The larger bedroom offers sliding glass doors to a lofty deck.
- The blueprints recommend finishing the interior walls with solid lumber paneling for a rich, rustic look.
- In addition to a large general-use area and a shop, the optional daylight basement has space for a car or a boat.

Plans H-26-1 & -1A

Bedrooms: 3	Baths: 2
Living Area:	
Upper floor	476 sq. ft.
Main floor	728 sq. ft.
Daylight basement	410 sq. ft.
Total Living Area:	**1,204/1,614 sq. ft.**
Tuck-under garage	318 sq. ft.
Exterior Wall Framing:	2x4

Foundation Options:	Plan #
Daylight basement	H-26-1
Crawlspace	H-26-1A

(All plans can be built with your choice of foundation and framing. A generic conversion diagram is available. See order form.)

BLUEPRINT PRICE CODE:	A/B

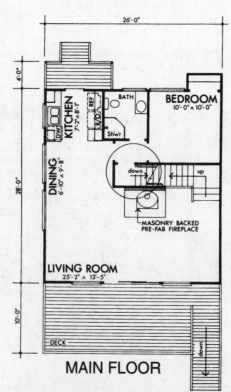

MAIN FLOOR

STORAGE

DAYLIGHT BASEMENT

STAIRWAY AREA IN CRAWLSPACE VERSION

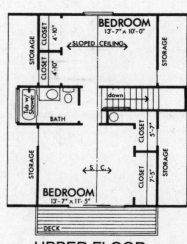

UPPER FLOOR

TO ORDER THIS BLUEPRINT, CALL TOLL-FREE 1-800-820-1283

Plans H-26-1 & -1A

PRICES AND DETAILS ON PAGES 12-15

Panoramic Prow View

- This glass-filled prow gable design is almost as spectacular as the panoramic view from inside.
- French doors open from the front deck to the dining room. A stunning window wall illuminates the adjoining living room, which flaunts a 20-ft.-high cathedral ceiling.

- The open, corner kitchen is perfectly angled to service the dining room and the family room, while offering views of the front and rear decks.
- A handy utility/laundry room opens to the rear deck. Two bedrooms share a full bath, to complete the main floor.
- A dramatic, open-railed stairway leads up to the secluded master bedroom, which boasts a dressing room and a private bath with a dual-sink vanity and a separate tub and shower.

Plan NW-196	
Bedrooms: 3	**Baths:** 2
Living Area:	
Upper floor	394 sq. ft.
Main floor	1,317 sq. ft.
Total Living Area:	**1,711 sq. ft.**
Exterior Wall Framing:	2x6
Foundation Options:	

Crawlspace
(All plans can be built with your choice of foundation and framing. A generic conversion diagram is available. See order form.)

| **BLUEPRINT PRICE CODE:** | **B** |

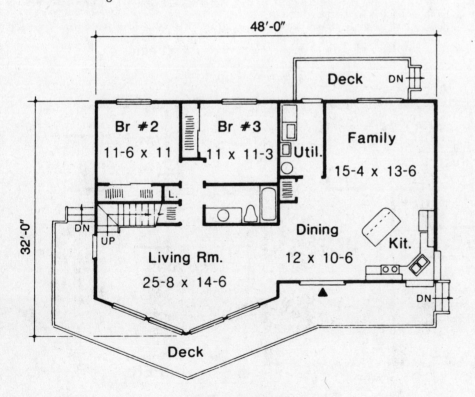

MAIN FLOOR

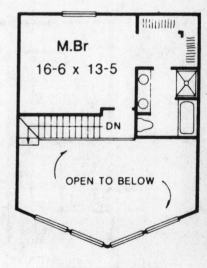

UPPER FLOOR

*TO ORDER THIS BLUEPRINT,
CALL TOLL-FREE 1-800-820-1283*

Plan NW-196

*PRICES AND DETAILS
ON PAGES 12-15*

197

Family-Style Leisure Living

- This handsome ranch-style home features a floor plan that is great for family living and entertaining.
- In from the quaint covered porch, the spacious formal areas flow together for a dramatic impact. The living room is enhanced by a fireplace and a sloped ceiling. A patio door in the dining room extends activities to the outdoors.
- The efficient U-shaped kitchen opens to the dining room and offers a pantry, a

window above the sink and abundant counter space.
- A good-sized utility room with convenient laundry facilities opens to the carport. This area also includes a large storage room and disappearing stairs to even more storage space.
- Three bedrooms and two baths occupy the sleeping wing. The master suite features a large walk-in closet and a private bath.
- The two remaining bedrooms are well proportioned and share a hall bath. Storage space is well accounted for here as well, with two linen closets and a coat closet in the bedroom hall.

Plan E-1308	
Bedrooms: 3	**Baths: 2**
Living Area:	
Main floor	1,375 sq. ft.
Total Living Area:	**1,375 sq. ft.**
Carport	430 sq. ft.
Storage	95 sq. ft.
Exterior Wall Framing:	2x4
Foundation Options:	
Crawlspace	
Slab	

(All plans can be built with your choice of foundation and framing. A generic conversion diagram is available. See order form.)

BLUEPRINT PRICE CODE: **A**

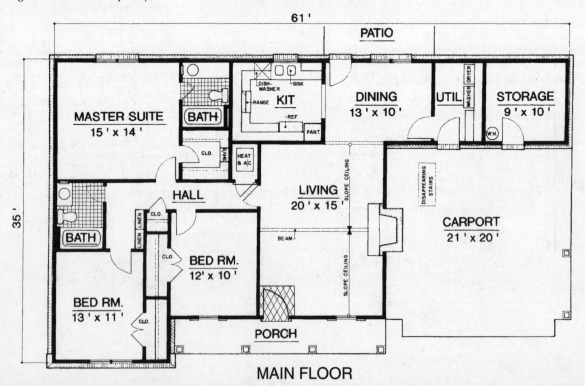

MAIN FLOOR

Plan E-1308

PRICES AND DETAILS ON PAGES 12-15

Stylish Exterior, Open Floor Plan

- With its simple yet stylish exterior, this modest-sized design is suitable for country or urban settings.
- A covered front porch and a gabled roof extension accent the facade while providing plenty of sheltered space for outdoor relaxation.
- Inside, the open floor plan puts available space to efficient use.
- The living room, which offers an inviting fireplace, is expanded by a cathedral ceiling. The adjoining dining area is open to the island kitchen, and all three rooms combine to create one huge gathering place.
- The master suite features a private bath and a large walk-in closet.
- Two more good-sized bedrooms share a second full bath.
- A convenient utility area leads to the carport, which incorporates extra storage space.

Plan J-86155

Bedrooms: 3	Baths: 2
Living Area:	
Main floor	1,385 sq. ft.
Total Living Area:	**1,385 sq. ft.**
Standard basement	1,385 sq. ft.
Carport	380 sq. ft.
Exterior Wall Framing:	2x4

Foundation Options:

Standard basement

Crawlspace

Slab

(All plans can be built with your choice of foundation and framing. A generic conversion diagram is available. See order form.)

BLUEPRINT PRICE CODE: A

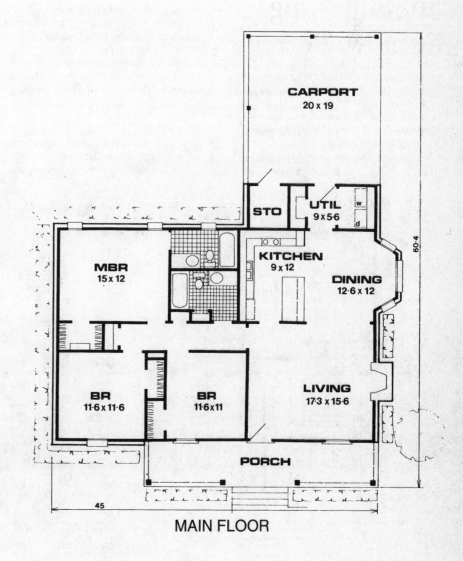

MAIN FLOOR

TO ORDER THIS BLUEPRINT,
CALL TOLL-FREE 1-800-820-1283

Plan J-86155

PRICES AND DETAILS
ON PAGES 12-15
199

Inviting Country Porch

- A columned porch with double doors invites you into the rustic living areas of this ranch-style home.
- Inside, the entry allows views back to the expansive, central living room and the backyard beyond.
- The living room boasts an exposed-beam ceiling and a massive fireplace with a wide stone hearth, a wood box and built-in bookshelves. A sunny patio offers additional entertaining space.
- The dining room and the efficient kitchen combine for easy meal service, with a serving bar separating the two.
- The main hallway leads to the sleeping wing, which offers a large master bedroom with a walk-in closet and a private bath.
- Two additional bedrooms share another full bath, and a laundry closet is accessible to the entire bedroom wing.

Plan E-1304

Bedrooms: 3	**Baths:** 2

Living Area:	
Main floor	1,395 sq. ft.
Total Living Area:	**1,395 sq. ft.**
Garage & storage	481 sq. ft.
Exterior Wall Framing:	2x4

Foundation Options:
Crawlspace
Slab
(All plans can be built with your choice of foundation and framing. A generic conversion diagram is available. See order form.)

BLUEPRINT PRICE CODE: A

MAIN FLOOR

TO ORDER THIS BLUEPRINT, CALL TOLL-FREE 1-800-820-1283

Plan E-1304

PRICES AND DETAILS ON PAGES 12-15

Cottage Suits Small Lot

- Designed to fit on a sloping or small lot, this compact country-style cottage has the amenities of a much larger home.
- The large front porch opens to the home's surprising two-story-high foyer, which views into the living room.
- The spacious living room is warmed by a handsome fireplace that is centered between built-in bookshelves.
- Enhanced by a sunny bay that opens to a backyard deck, the dining room offers a comfortable eating area that is easily served by the island kitchen.
- The secluded main-floor master bedroom includes a roomy walk-in closet. The spectacular master bath showcases a corner garden tub, a designer shower, a built-in bench and a dual-sink vanity.
- Upstairs, a railed balcony overlooks the foyer. Two secondary bedrooms with walk-in closets share a central bath.

Plan C-8870

Bedrooms: 3	Baths: 2
Living Area:	
Upper floor	664 sq. ft.
Main floor	1,100 sq. ft.
Total Living Area:	**1,764 sq. ft.**
Daylight basement/garage	1,100 sq. ft.
Exterior Wall Framing:	2x4

Foundation Options:

Daylight basement
(All plans can be built with your choice of foundation and framing. A generic conversion diagram is available. See order form.)

BLUEPRINT PRICE CODE:	**B**

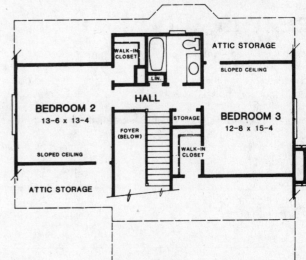

UPPER FLOOR

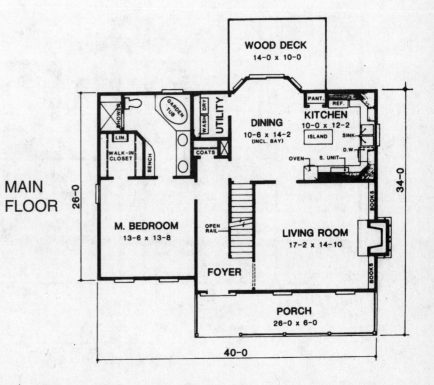

MAIN FLOOR

26-0

34-0

40-0

Breezy Beauty

- A nostalgic covered front porch, a backyard deck and a sprawling screened porch combine to make this beautiful one-story home a breezy delight.
- The front entry opens into the Great Room, which is crowned by a soaring 12-ft.-high cathedral ceiling. A handsome fireplace is flanked by built-in bookshelves and cabinets.
- The large, bayed dining room offers a 9-ft. tray ceiling and deck access through French doors.

- The adjoining kitchen boasts plenty of counter space and a handy built-in recipe desk.
- From the kitchen, a side door leads to the screened porch. A wood floor and deck access highlight this cheery room.
- A quiet hall leads past a convenient utility room to the sleeping quarters.
- The secluded master bedroom is enhanced by a spacious walk-in closet. The private master bath includes a lovely garden tub, a separate shower and dual vanities.
- Two more bedrooms with walk-in closets share a hall bath.

Plan C-8905

Bedrooms: 3	Baths: 2
Living Area:	
Main floor	1,811 sq. ft.
Total Living Area:	**1,811 sq. ft.**
Screened porch	240 sq. ft.
Daylight basement	1,811 sq. ft.
Garage	484 sq. ft.
Exterior Wall Framing:	2x4

Foundation Options:

Daylight basement
Crawlspace
(All plans can be built with your choice of foundation and framing. A generic conversion diagram is available. See order form.)

BLUEPRINT PRICE CODE: B

MAIN FLOOR

DECK
28-0 x 12-0

BATH

GARDEN TUB

SHOWER

WALK-IN CLOSET

BEDROOM 2
11-0 x 13-6

CLOSET

WALK-IN CLOSET

DINING
12-0 x 13-6
TRAY CEILING

DRY WASH

UTILITY

DW
SINK
S UNIT
REFG
OVEN

KITCHEN
10-0 x 13-6
DESK

PANTRY

SCR. PORCH
12-0 x 20-0

GARAGE
22-0 x 22-0

BOOKS

MASTER BEDROOM
12-0 x 18-0

BATH

LINEN

HALL

DESK

COATS

CATHEDRAL CEILING W/ FALSE BEAMS

HEARTH

BOOKS

BEDROOM 3
12-0 x 11-4

GREAT ROOM
19-0 x 17-6

WALK-IN CLOSET

PORCH
25-0 x 6-0

50-0
38-4
89-6

Indoor/Outdoor Delights

- A curved porch in the front and a garden sun room in the back make this home an indoor/outdoor delight.
- Inside, a roomy kitchen is open to a five-sided, glassed-in dining room that views out to the porch.
- The living room features a fireplace along a glass wall that adjoins the gloriously sunny garden room.

- Wrapped in windows, the garden room accesses the backyard as well as a large storage area in the unobtrusive, side-entry garage.
- The master suite is no less luxurious, featuring a a sumptuous master bath with a garden spa tub, a corner shower and a walk-in closet.
- Each of the two remaining bedrooms has a boxed-out window and a walk-in closet. A full bath with a corner shower and a dual-sink vanity is close by.
- A stairway leads to the attic, which provides more potential living space.

Plan DD-1852	
Bedrooms: 3	Baths: 2
Living Area:	
Main floor	1,852 sq. ft.
Total Living Area:	**1,852 sq. ft.**
Standard basement	1,852 sq. ft.
Garage	528 sq. ft.
Exterior Wall Framing:	2x4

Foundation Options:
Standard basement
Crawlspace
Slab
(All plans can be built with your choice of foundation and framing. A generic conversion diagram is available. See order form.)

BLUEPRINT PRICE CODE:	B

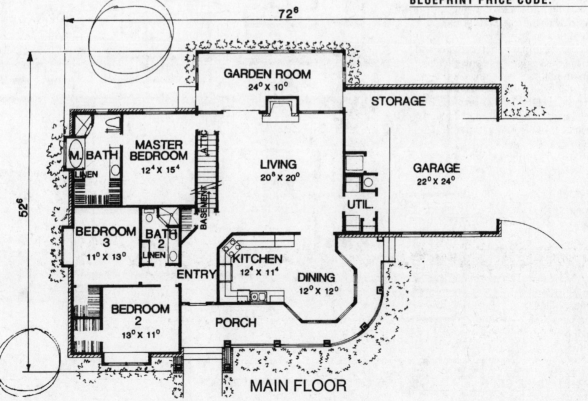

MAIN FLOOR

Distinguished Durability

- Sturdy tapered columns with brick pedestals give this unique home a feeling of durability and security.
- Off the foyer, the spacious living room is brightened by the incoming light of the double dormers above. The high 14-ft. ceiling and the glass-framed fireplace add further ambience. An atrium door opens to the wraparound porch.
- Decorative wood columns and an 11-ft. ceiling enhance the dining room.
- The neat kitchen shares serving counters with the breakfast nook and the living room, for easy service to both locations. A central cooktop island and a built-in desk are other conveniences.
- The main bath has twin sinks and is easily accessible from the secondary bedrooms and the living areas.
- An oval garden tub, an isolated toilet and dual sinks are featured in the master bath. The master suite also boasts a 13-ft. vaulted ceiling, a huge walk-in closet and a private porch.

Plan DW-1883

Bedrooms: 3	Baths: 2
Living Area:	
Main floor	1,883 sq. ft.
Total Living Area:	**1,883 sq. ft.**
Standard basement	1,883 sq. ft.
Exterior Wall Framing:	2x4

Foundation Options:
Standard basement
Crawlspace
Slab
(All plans can be built with your choice of foundation and framing. A generic conversion diagram is available. See order form.)

BLUEPRINT PRICE CODE:	B

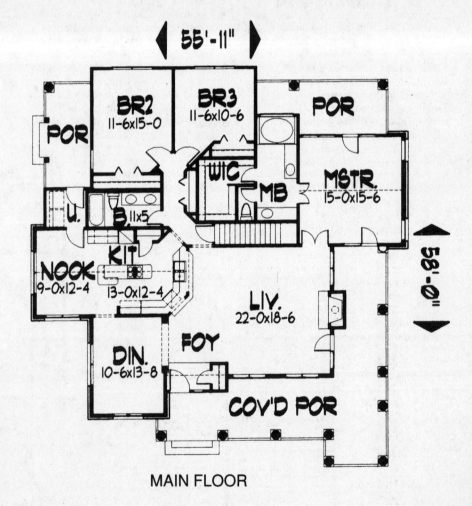

MAIN FLOOR

Plan DW-1883

PRICES AND DETAILS ON PAGES 12-15

Octagonal Home Has Lofty Views

- There's no better way to avoid the ordinary than to build an octagonal home and escape from conventional square corners and rigid rooms.
- The roomy main floor of this exciting home offers plenty of space for full-time family living or for comfortable second-home recreation.
- The two-story entry hall leads to the bedrooms on the right and to the Great Room around to the left.
- Warmed by a woodstove, the Great Room offers a relaxing retreat that includes a 12-ft. ceiling and a panoramic view of the outdoors.
- At the core of the main floor are two baths, one of which boasts a spa tub and private access from the adjoining master bedroom.
- A roomy kitchen and a handy utility room are also featured.
- The upper floor, surrounded by windows and topped by a 12-ft. ceiling, is designed as a recreation room, with a woodstove and a wet bar.
- The optional daylight basement adds a fourth bedroom, another bath, a garage and a large storage area.

Plans P-532-3A & -3D

Bedrooms: 3+	Baths: 2-3
Living Area:	
Upper floor	355 sq. ft.
Main floor	1,567 sq. ft.
Daylight basement	430 sq. ft.
Total Living Area:	**1,922/2,352 sq. ft.**
Opt. tuck-under garage/storage	1,137 sq. ft.
Exterior Wall Framing:	2x6
Foundation Options:	**Plan #**
Daylight basement	P-532-3D
Crawlspace	P-532-3A

(All plans can be built with your choice of foundation and framing. A generic conversion diagram is available. See order form.)

BLUEPRINT PRICE CODE:	**B/C**

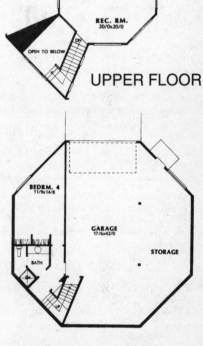

UPPER FLOOR

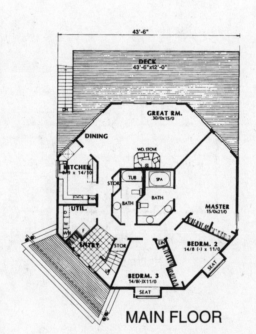

MAIN FLOOR   **DAYLIGHT BASEMENT**

REAR VIEW

Country Living

- A covered porch, half-round transom windows and three dormers give this home its warm, nostalgic appeal. Shuttered windows and a louvered vent beautify the side-entry, two-car garage.

- Designed for the ultimate in country living, the floor plan starts off with a dynamic Great Room that flows to a bayed dining area. A nice fireplace adds warmth, while a French door provides access to a backyard covered porch. A powder room is just steps away.

- A 12-ft., 4-in. vaulted ceiling presides over the large country kitchen, which offers a bayed nook, an oversized breakfast bar and a convenient pass-through to the rear porch.

- The exquisite master suite boasts a tray ceiling, a bay window and an alcove for built-in shelves or extra closet space. Other amenities include a large walk-in closet and a compartmentalized bath.

- Upstairs, 9-ft. ceilings enhance two more bedrooms and a second full bath. Each bedroom boasts a cozy dormer window and two closets.

Plan AX-93311

Bedrooms: 3	Baths: 2½
Living Area:	
Upper floor	570 sq. ft.
Main floor	1,375 sq. ft.
Total Living Area:	**1,945 sq. ft.**
Standard basement	1,280 sq. ft.
Garage	450 sq. ft.
Exterior Wall Framing:	2x4

Foundation Options:

Standard basement
Crawlspace
Slab

(All plans can be built with your choice of foundation and framing. A generic conversion diagram is available. See order form.)

BLUEPRINT PRICE CODE: B

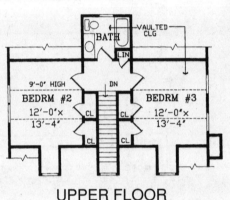

UPPER FLOOR

VIEW INTO GREAT ROOM

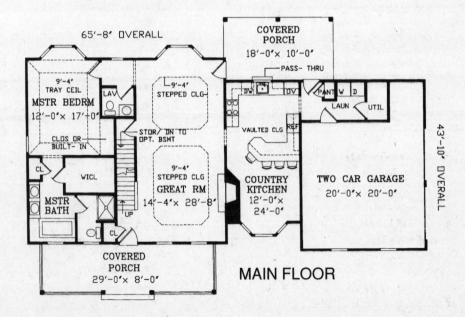

MAIN FLOOR

Plan AX-93311

PRICES AND DETAILS ON PAGES 12-15

Luxurious Country Home

- This country cottage hosts many luxuries, such as an expansive Great Room, good-sized sleeping areas and a large screened back porch.
- The rustic front porch opens into the Great Room, which offers a handsome fireplace and access to the large screened back porch.
- The bright kitchen features a huge work island, and unfolds to both the formal dining room and the breakfast bay. A handy laundry closet and access to the garage are also offered.
- The removed master suite has views of the front porch and offers a private bath with two walk-in closets, a dual-sink vanity, a spa tub and a separate shower.
- Upstairs are two oversized bedrooms, each with a dressing room that accesses a common bath.

Plan C-8535

Bedrooms: 3	Baths: 2½
Living Area:	
Upper floor	765 sq. ft.
Main floor	1,535 sq. ft.
Total Living Area:	**2,300 sq. ft.**
Daylight basement	1,535 sq. ft.
Garage	424 sq. ft.
Exterior Wall Framing:	2x4
Foundation Options:	

Daylight basement

(All plans can be built with your choice of foundation and framing. A generic conversion diagram is available. See order form.)

BLUEPRINT PRICE CODE: C

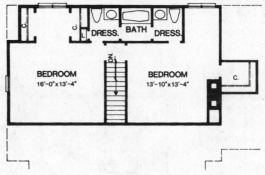

UPPER FLOOR

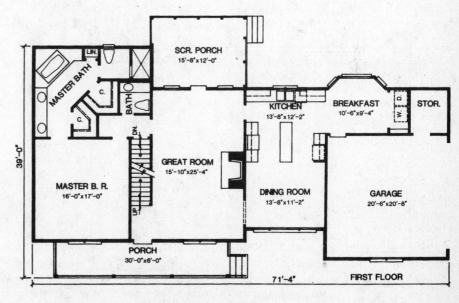

MAIN FLOOR

TO ORDER THIS BLUEPRINT,
CALL TOLL-FREE 1-800-820-1283

Plan C-8535

PRICES AND DETAILS
ON PAGES 12-15

207

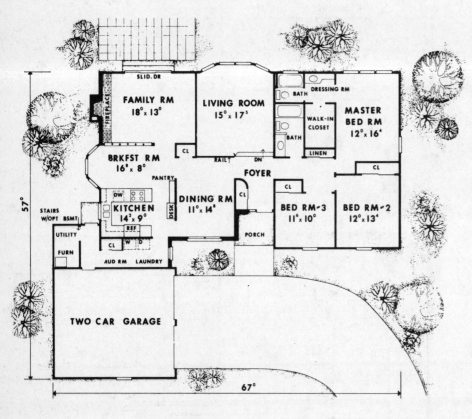

Country Classic

- A variety of siding materials blend together for a classic country exterior look.
- A dramatic sunken living room with bay window-wall is the view that greets arriving guests.
- A front-facing dining room completes the formal living area.
- The family room with fireplace is open to the kitchen and breakfast bay for informal family shared time.
- Three bedrooms and two full baths make up the sleeping wing of the home.

Plan AX-9762

Bedrooms: 3	Baths: 2
Space:	
Total living area:	2,003 sq. ft.
Basement:	2,003 sq. ft.
Garage:	485 sq. ft.
Exterior Wall Framing:	2x4

Foundation options:
Standard basement.
Slab.
(Foundation & framing conversion diagram available — see order form.)

Blueprint Price Code: C

TO ORDER THIS BLUEPRINT,
CALL TOLL-FREE 1-800-820-1283

Plan AX-9762

*PRICES AND DETAILS
ON PAGES 12-15*

Build It Yourself

- Everything you need for a leisure or retirement retreat is neatly packaged in this affordable, easy-to-build design.
- The basic rectangular shape features a unique wraparound deck, entirely covered by a projecting roofline.
- A central fireplace and a vaulted ceiling that rises to 10 ft. visually enhance the cozy living and dining rooms.
- The efficient kitchen offers convenient service to the adjoining dining room. In the crawlspace version, the kitchen also includes a snack bar.
- Two main-floor bedrooms share a large full bath.
- The daylight-basement option is suitable for building on a sloping lot and consists of an extra bedroom, a general-purpose area and a garage.

Plans H-833-7 & -7A

Bedrooms: 2+	Baths: 1
Living Area:	
Main floor	952 sq. ft.
Daylight basement	676 sq. ft.
Total Living Area:	**952/1,628 sq. ft.**
Tuck-under garage	276 sq. ft.
Exterior Wall Framing:	2x6
Foundation Options:	**Plan #**
Daylight basement	H-833-7
Crawlspace	H-833-7A

(All plans can be built with your choice of foundation and framing. A generic conversion diagram is available. See order form.)

BLUEPRINT PRICE CODE:	**A A/B**

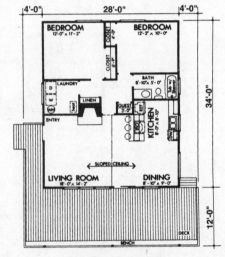

MAIN FLOOR
Crawlspace version

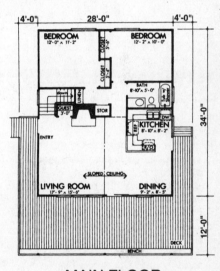

MAIN FLOOR
Basement version

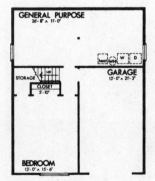

DAYLIGHT BASEMENT

TO ORDER THIS BLUEPRINT,
CALL TOLL-FREE 1-800-820-1283

Plans H-833-7 & -7A

PRICES AND DETAILS
ON PAGES 12-15

209

Covered Porch Invites Visitors

- This nice home welcomes visitors with its covered front porch and its wide-open living areas.
- Detailed columns, railings and shutters decorate the front porch that guides guests to the central entry.
- Just off the entry, the bright living room merges with the dining room. The side wall is lined with glass, including a glass door that opens to the yard.
- The angled kitchen features a serving counter facing the dining room. A handry laundry closet and access to a storage area and the garage is nearby.
- An angled hall leads to the bedroom wing. The master suite offers a private bath, a walk-in closet and a dressing area with a vanity. Two additional bedrooms and another full bath are located down the hall.

Plan E-1217

Bedrooms: 3	Baths: 2
Living Area:	
Main floor	1,266 sq. ft.
Total Living Area:	**1,266 sq. ft.**
Garage and storage	550 sq. ft.
Exterior Wall Framing:	2x6

Foundation Options:

Crawlspace

Slab

(All plans can be built with your choice of foundation and framing. A generic conversion diagram is available. See order form.)

BLUEPRINT PRICE CODE:	**A**

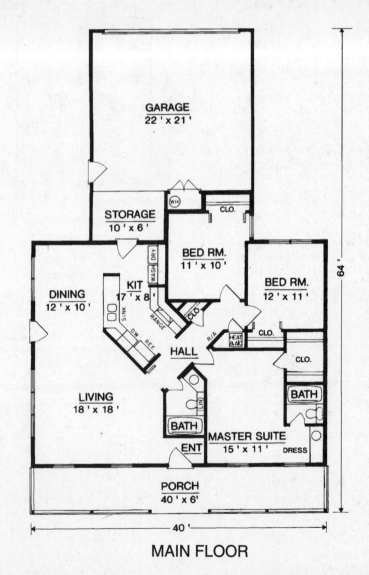

MAIN FLOOR

Plan E-1217

PRICES AND DETAILS ON PAGES 12-15

A Chalet for Today

- With its wraparound deck and soaring windows, this chalet-style home is ideal for recreational living and scenic sites.
- The living and dining rooms are combined to take advantage of the dramatic 23-ft. cathedral ceiling, the rugged stone fireplace and the view through the spectacular windows.
- A quaint balcony above adds to the warm country feeling of the living area, which extends to the expansive deck.

- The open kitchen features a bright corner sink and a nifty breakfast bar that adjoins the living area.
- The handy main-floor laundry area is close to two bedrooms and a full bath.
- A 17-ft. sloped ceiling crowns the quiet study, which is a feature rarely found in a home of this size and style.
- The master suite and a storage area encompass the upper floor. A 13-ft., 8-in. cathedral ceiling, a whirlpool bath and sweeping views from the balcony give this space an elegant feel.
- The basement option includes a tuck-under garage, additional storage space and a separate utility area.

Plan AHP-9340

Bedrooms: 3+	Baths: 2
Living Area:	
Upper floor	332 sq. ft.
Main floor	974 sq. ft.
Total Living Area:	**1,306 sq. ft.**
Basement	624 sq. ft.
Tuck-under garage	350 sq. ft.
Exterior Wall Framing:	2x4 or 2x6

Foundation Options:

Standard basement
Daylight basement
Crawlspace
Slab

(All plans can be built with your choice of foundation and framing. A generic conversion diagram is available. See order form.)

BLUEPRINT PRICE CODE:	A

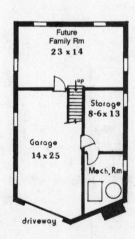

BASEMENT

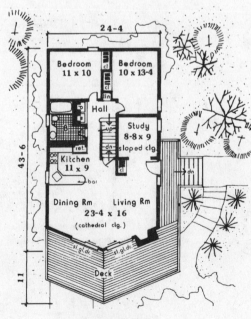

MAIN FLOOR

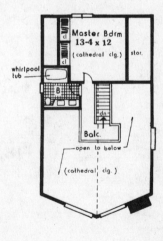

UPPER FLOOR

Lofty Cottage Retreat

- This generous cottage home offers wide-open living areas and a delightful balcony space.
- Off the recessed entry, the living room merges into the dining room for a spacious effect. A woodstove or fireplace adds an inviting ambience.
- The adjacent kitchen has a convenient raised service counter over the sink area and handy access to both the laundry closet and the back porch.
- The master suite offers a huge walk-in closet, a bayed sitting alcove and private access to the main bath, which features a soaking tub and a sit-down angled vanity.
- Upstairs, a large balcony bedroom overlooks the living areas below. This lofty space boasts a built-in desk and a bath with a shower.

Plan E-1002

Bedrooms: 1+	Baths: 2
Living Area:	
Upper floor	267 sq. ft.
Main floor	814 sq. ft.
Total Living Area:	**1,081 sq. ft.**
Standard basement	814 sq. ft.
Exterior Wall Framing:	2x4

Foundation Options:

Standard basement
Crawlspace
Slab
(All plans can be built with your choice of foundation and framing. A generic conversion diagram is available. See order form.)

BLUEPRINT PRICE CODE: A

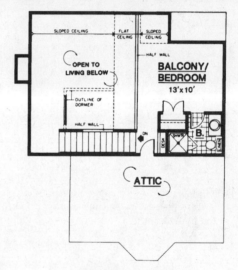

UPPER FLOOR

MAIN FLOOR

   TO ORDER THIS BLUEPRINT, CALL TOLL-FREE 1-800-820-1283   Plan E-1002   *PRICES AND DETAILS ON PAGES 12-15*

UPPER FLOOR

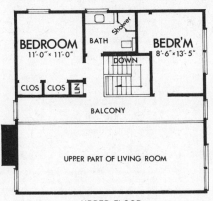

BEDROOM 11'-0" × 11'-0"

BATH

Shower

BEDR'M 8'-6" × 13'-5"

DOWN

CLOS CLOS LIN

BALCONY

UPPER PART OF LIVING ROOM

UPPER FLOOR

4'-0"   32'-0"   4'-0"

GARAGE 23'-3" × 11'-3"

12'-0"

CARPORT

FURNACE AND WATER HEATER IN PLAN WITHOUT BASEMENT ARE LOCATED IN CRAWLSPACE.

10'-0"

BEDROOM 11'-0" × 11'-0"

BATH

dry/wash

KITCHEN 13'-9" × 11'-0"

refr

dw

STORAGE OR STAIRS DOWN

UP

rge

CLOS CLOS LIN

Breakfast

30'-0"

Balcony rail above

LIVING ROOM 31'-3" × 15'-6"

10'-0"

DECK

MAIN FLOOR

Surprising Spaces via Beamed Ceilings

- Open and spacious floor plan allows for uninhibited movement.
- Bordering decks beckon you to the outdoors.
- Expansive living room features beamed ceiling open to second level and front window wall at an attractive angle.
- Large, versatile kitchen and breakfast bar make dining a pleasure and laundry an easy chore.
- Inviting balcony adjoins second level bedrooms.

Plans H-876-1 & -1A

Bedrooms: 3	Baths: 2
Space:	
Upper floor:	592 sq. ft.
Main floor:	960 sq. ft.
Total living area:	1,552 sq. ft.
Basement:	approx. 960 sq. ft.
Garage:	262 sq. ft.
Exterior Wall Framing:	2x4

Foundation options:
Standard basement (Plan H-876-1).
Crawlspace (Plan H-876-1A).
(Foundation & framing conversion diagram available — see order form.)

Blueprint Price Code: B

TO ORDER THIS BLUEPRINT,
CALL TOLL-FREE 1-800-820-1283

Plans H-876-1 & -1A

PRICES AND DETAILS
ON PAGES 12-15

213

Rustic Comfort

- Rustic charm highlights the exterior of this design, while the interior is filled with all the latest comforts.
- The wide, covered porch opens to a roomy entry, where two 7-ft.-high openings with decorative railings view into the dining room.
- Straight ahead lies the sunken living room, which features a 16-ft.-high vaulted ceiling with exposed beams. The fireplace is faced with floor-to-ceiling fieldstone, adding to the rustic look. A rear door opens to a large patio with twin plant areas.

- The large U-shaped kitchen has such nice extras as a china niche with glass shelves. Other bonuses include the adjacent sewing/hobby room, the oversized utility room and the storage area and built-in workbench in the side-entry garage.
- The secluded master suite hosts a sunken sleeping area with built-in bookshelves. One step up is a cozy sitting area that is outlined by brick columns and a railed room divider. Double doors open to the deluxe bath, which offers a niche with glass shelves.
- Double doors conceal two more bedrooms and a full bath.

Plan E-1607

Bedrooms: 3	**Baths: 2**
Living Area:	
Main floor	1,600 sq. ft.
Total Living Area:	**1,600 sq. ft.**
Standard basement	1,600 sq. ft.
Garage	484 sq. ft.
Storage	132 sq. ft.
Exterior Wall Framing:	2x6

Foundation Options:
Standard basement
Crawlspace
Slab
(All plans can be built with your choice of foundation and framing. A generic conversion diagram is available. See order form.)

BLUEPRINT PRICE CODE: B

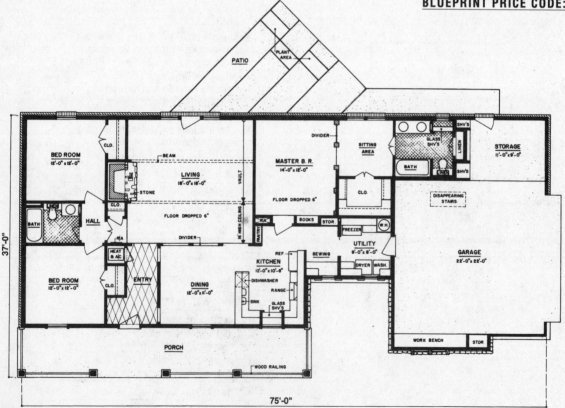

MAIN FLOOR

TO ORDER THIS BLUEPRINT, CALL TOLL-FREE 1-800-820-1283

Plan E-1607

PRICES AND DETAILS ON PAGES 12-15

Spacious Economy

- This economical country cottage features wide, angled spaces and 9-ft., 4-in. ceilings in both the Great Room and the master bedroom for roomy appeal and year-round comfort.
- The Great Room boasts a cozy fireplace with a raised hearth and a built-in niche for a TV, making this room perfect for winter gatherings. On warm nights, a homey covered porch at the rear can be accessed through sliding glass doors.
- Amenities in the luxurious master bedroom include a large walk-in closet, a private whirlpool bath and a dual-sink vanity.
- The nicely appointed kitchen offers nearby laundry facilities and porch access. A serving bar allows for casual dining and relaxed conversation.
- The optional daylight basement includes a tuck-under, two-car garage.

Plan AX-94322

Bedrooms: 3	Baths: 2½
Living Area:	
Upper floor	545 sq. ft.
Main floor	1,134 sq. ft.
Total Living Area:	**1,679 sq. ft.**
Daylight basement	618 sq. ft.
Standard basement	1,134 sq. ft.
Tuck-under garage	516 sq. ft.
Exterior Wall Framing:	2x4

Foundation Options:

Daylight basement
Standard basement
Crawlspace
Slab

(All plans can be built with your choice of foundation and framing. A generic conversion diagram is available. See order form.)

BLUEPRINT PRICE CODE: B

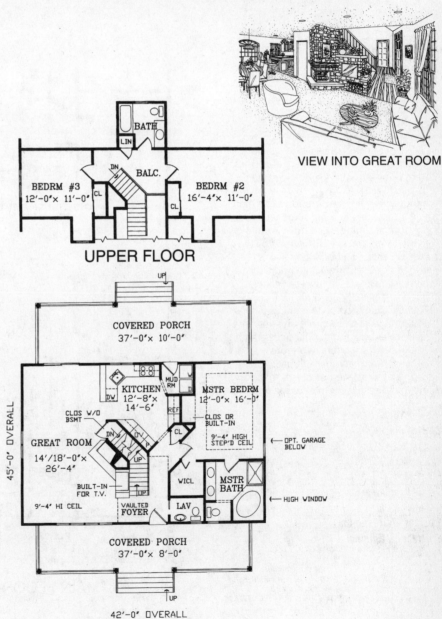

VIEW INTO GREAT ROOM

UPPER FLOOR

BATH
LIN
DN BALC.
BEDRM #3 12'-0"x 11'-0" CL
BEDRM #2 16'-4"x 11'-0" CL

MAIN FLOOR

UP
COVERED PORCH 37'-0"x 10'-0"
KITCHEN 12'-8"x 14'-6"
MUD RM
MSTR BEDRM 12'-0"x 16'-0"
DW
CLOS W/O BSMT
REF
CL
CLOS OR BUILT-IN
9'-4" HIGH STEP'D CEIL
← OPT. GARAGE BELOW
GREAT ROOM 14'/18'-0"x 26'-4"
DN
UP
WICL
MSTR BATH
← HIGH WINDOW
BUILT-IN FOR T.V.
9'-4" HI CEIL
VAULTED FOYER
LAV
UP
COVERED PORCH 37'-0"x 8'-0"
UP
45'-0" OVERALL
42'-0" OVERALL

Photo courtesy of Breland & Farmer Designers, Inc.

Stylish and Compact

- This country-style home has a classic exterior and a space-saving and compact interior.
- A quaint covered porch extends along the front of the home. The oval-glassed front door opens to the entry, which leads to the spacious living room with a handsome fireplace, windows at either end and access to a big screened porch.
- The formal dining room flows from the living room and is easily served by the convenient U-shaped kitchen.
- A nice-sized laundry room and a full bath are nearby. The two-car garage offers a super storage area.
- The deluxe master suite features a huge walk-in closet. A separate dressing area leads to an adjoining, dual-access bath.
- The upper floor offers two more bedrooms and another full bath. Each bedroom has generous closet space and independent access to attic space.

Plan E-1626

Bedrooms: 3	Baths: 2
Living Area:	
Upper floor	464 sq. ft.
Main floor	1,136 sq. ft.
Total Living Area:	**1,600 sq. ft.**
Garage	462 sq. ft.
Exterior Wall Framing:	2x6

Foundation Options:

Crawlspace

Slab

(All plans can be built with your choice of foundation and framing. A generic conversion diagram is available. See order form.)

BLUEPRINT PRICE CODE:	B

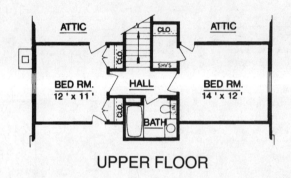

UPPER FLOOR

✱✱NOTE:
The above photographed home may have been modified by the homeowner. Please refer to floor plan and/or drawn elevation shown for actual blueprint details.

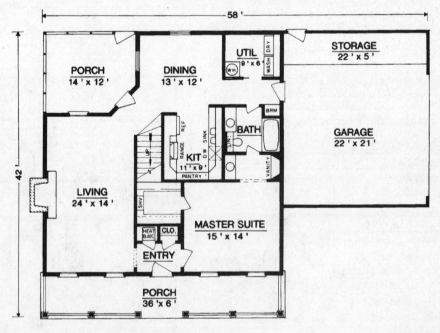

MAIN FLOOR

TO ORDER THIS BLUEPRINT, CALL TOLL-FREE 1-800-820-1283

Plan E-1626

PRICES AND DETAILS ON PAGES 12-15

Dynamic Design

- This dynamic five-sided design is perfect for scenic sites. The front (or street) side of the home is shielded by a two-car garage, while the back of the home hosts a glass-filled living area surrounded by a spectacular deck.
- The unique shape of the home allows for an unusually open and spacious interior design.
- The living/dining room is further expanded by a 20-ft.-high vaulted ceiling. The centrally located fireplace provides a focal point while distributing heat efficiently.
- The space-saving galley-style kitchen is connected to the living/dining area by a snack bar.
- A large main-floor bedroom has two closets and easy access to a full bath.
- The upper floor is highlighted by a breathtaking balcony overlook. Also, two bedrooms share a nice-sized bath.
- The optional daylight basement includes a huge recreation room.

Plans H-855-1 & -1A

Bedrooms: 3	Baths: 2
Living Area:	
Upper floor	625 sq. ft.
Main floor	1,108 sq. ft.
Daylight basement	1,108 sq. ft.
Total Living Area:	**1,733/2,841 sq. ft.**
Garage	346 sq. ft.
Exterior Wall Framing:	2x6
Foundation Options:	Plan #
Daylight basement	H-855-1
Crawlspace	H-855-1A

(All plans can be built with your choice of foundation and framing. A generic conversion diagram is available. See order form.)

BLUEPRINT PRICE CODE:	**B/D**

UPPER FLOOR

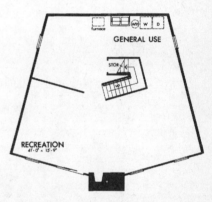

DAYLIGHT BASEMENT

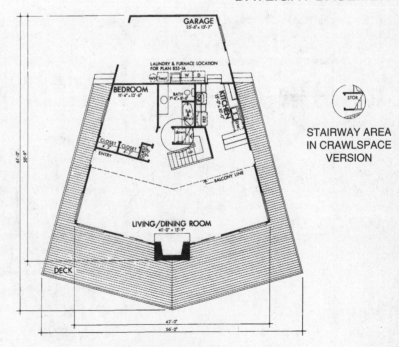

STAIRWAY AREA IN CRAWLSPACE VERSION

MAIN FLOOR

Classic Country-Style

- At the center of this rustic country-style home is an enormous living room with a flat beamed ceiling, a massive stone fireplace and access to a patio and a covered rear porch.
- The adjoining eating area and kitchen provide plenty of room for casual dining and meal preparation. The eating

area is visually enhanced by a 14-ft. sloped ceiling with false beams. The kitchen includes a snack bar, a pantry closet and a built-in spice cabinet.
- The formal dining room gets plenty of pizzazz from the stone-faced wall and arched planter facing the living room.
- The secluded master suite has it all, including a private bath, a separate dressing area and a large walk-in closet with built-in shelves.
- The two remaining bedrooms have big closets and easy access to a full bath.

Plan E-1808	
Bedrooms: 3	**Baths:** 2
Living Area:	
Main floor	1,800 sq. ft.
Total Living Area:	**1,800 sq. ft.**
Garage	605 sq. ft.
Exterior Wall Framing:	2x4

Foundation Options:

Crawlspace
Slab
(All plans can be built with your choice of foundation and framing. A generic conversion diagram is available. See order form.)

BLUEPRINT PRICE CODE:	B

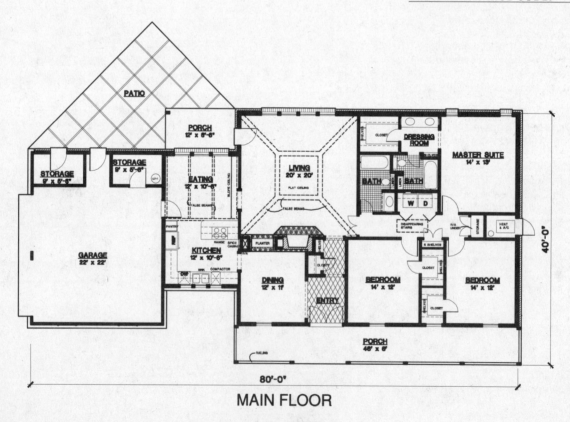

MAIN FLOOR

Plan E-1808

PRICES AND DETAILS
ON PAGES 12-15

Photo by Carren Strock

Proven Plan Features Passive Sun Room

- A passive sun room, energy-efficient wood stove, and a panorama of windows make this design highly economical.
- Open living/dining room features attractive balcony railing, stone hearth, and adjoining sun room with durable stone floor.
- Well-equipped kitchen is separated from dining area by a convenient breakfast bar.
- Second level sleeping areas border a hallway and balcony.
- Optional basement plan provides extra space for entertaining or work.

Plans H-855-3A & -3B

Bedrooms: 3	Baths: 2-3

Space:	
Upper floor:	586 sq. ft.
Main floor:	1,192 sq. ft.
Sun room:	132 sq. ft.
Total living area:	**1,910 sq. ft.**
Basement:	approx. 1,192 sq. ft.
Garage:	520 sq. ft.

Exterior Wall Framing:	2x6

Foundation options:
Daylight basement (Plan H-855-3B).
Crawlspace (Plan H-855-3A).
(Foundation & framing conversion diagram available — see order form.)

Blueprint Price Code:	
Without basement	B
With basement	E

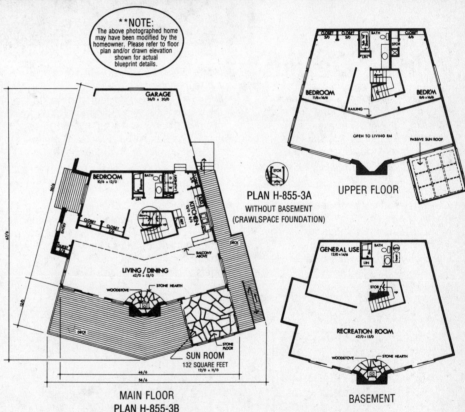

NOTE:
The above photographed home may have been modified by the homeowner. Please refer to floor plan and/or drawn elevation shown for actual blueprint details.

GARAGE
24/0 x 20/0

BEDROOM
10/6 x 12/0

KITCHEN

LIVING / DINING
42/0 x 15/0

WOODSTOVE   STONE HEARTH

BALCONY ABOVE

SUN ROOM
132 SQUARE FEET
12/0 x 11/0

MAIN FLOOR
PLAN H-855-3B
WITH DAYLIGHT BASEMENT

PLAN H-855-3A
WITHOUT BASEMENT
(CRAWLSPACE FOUNDATION)

BEDROOM
11/6 x 16/6

BEDR'M
8/6 x 16/6

OPEN TO LIVING RM

PASSIVE SUN ROOF

UPPER FLOOR

GENERAL USE
12/0 x 14/6

RECREATION ROOM
42/0 x 15/0

WOODSTOVE   STONE HEARTH

BASEMENT

TO ORDER THIS BLUEPRINT,
CALL TOLL-FREE 1-800-820-1283

Plans H-855-3A & -3B

PRICES AND DETAILS
ON PAGES 12-15

219

Photo by Bob Hallinen

Soaring Design

- Dramatic windows soar to the peak of this prowed chalet, offering unlimited views of outdoor scenery.
- The spacious living room flaunts a fabulous fireplace, a soaring 26-ft. vaulted ceiling, a striking window wall and sliding glass doors to a wonderful wraparound deck.
- An oversized window brightens a dining area on the left side of the living room. The sunny, L-shaped kitchen is spacious and easily accessible.
- The secluded main-floor bedroom has convenient access to a full bath, a linen closet, a good-sized laundry room and the rear entrance.
- A central, open-railed staircase leads to the upper floor, which contains two more bedrooms and a full bath.
- A skylighted balcony is the high point of this design, offering a railed overlook into the living room below and sweeping outdoor vistas through the wall of windows.
- The optional daylight basement provides another fireplace in a versatile recreation room. The extra-long, tuck-under garage includes plenty of room for hobbies, while the service room offers additional storage space.

Plans H-930-1 & -1A	
Bedrooms: 3	**Baths:** 2
Living Area:	
Upper floor	710 sq. ft.
Main floor	1,210 sq. ft.
Daylight basement	605 sq. ft.
Total Living Area:	**1,920/2,525 sq. ft.**
Tuck-under garage/shop	605 sq. ft.
Exterior Wall Framing:	2x6
Foundation Options:	**Plan #**
Daylight basement	H-930-1
Crawlspace	H-930-1A

(All plans can be built with your choice of foundation and framing. A generic conversion diagram is available. See order form.)

BLUEPRINT PRICE CODE:	**B/D**

DAYLIGHT BASEMENT

STAIRWAY AREA IN
CRAWLSPACE VERSION

MAIN FLOOR

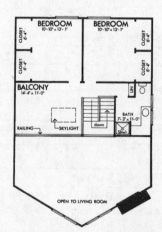

UPPER FLOOR

NOTE:
The above photographed home may have been modified by the homeowner. Please refer to floor plan and/or drawn elevation shown for actual blueprint details.

Plans H-930-1 & -1A

PRICES AND DETAILS
ON PAGES 12-15

PHOTO © 1990 EVERETT & SOULE

Unique Inside and Out

- This delightful design is as striking on the inside as it is on the outside.
- The focal point of the home is the huge Grand Room, which features a vaulted ceiling, plant shelves and lots of glass, including a clerestory window. French doors flanking the fireplace lead to the covered porch and the two adjoining sun decks.
- The centrally located kitchen offers easy access from any room in the house, and a full bath, a laundry area and the garage entrance are nearby.
- The two main-floor master suites are another unique design element of the home. Both of the suites showcase a volume ceiling, a sunny window seat, a walk-in closet, a private bath and French doors that open to a sun deck.
- Upstairs, two guest suites overlook the vaulted Grand Room below.

Plan EOF-13

Bedrooms: 4	**Baths:** 3

Living Area:

Upper floor	443 sq. ft.
Main floor	1,411 sq. ft.
Total Living Area:	**1,854 sq. ft.**
Garage	264 sq. ft.
Storage	50 sq. ft.
Exterior Wall Framing:	2x6

Foundation Options:

Crawlspace
(Typical foundation & framing conversion diagram available—see order form.)

BLUEPRINT PRICE CODE:	**B**

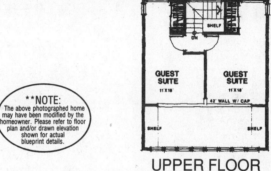

**NOTE:
The above photographed home may have been modified by the homeowner. Please refer to floor plan and/or drawn elevation shown for actual blueprint details.

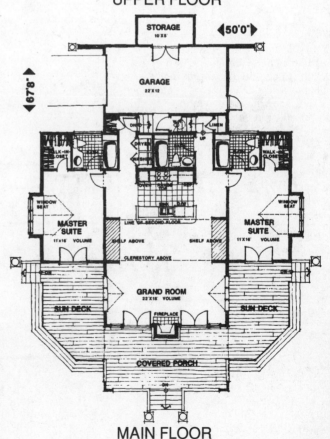

UPPER FLOOR

MAIN FLOOR

TO ORDER THIS BLUEPRINT, CALL TOLL-FREE 1-800-820-1283

Plan EOF-13

PRICES AND DETAILS ON PAGES 12-15

Country Kitchen

- A lovely front porch, dormers and shutters give this home a country-style exterior and complement its comfortable and informal interior.
- The roomy country kitchen connects with the sunny breakfast nook and the formal dining room.
- The central portion of the home consists of a large family room with a handsome fireplace and easy access to a backyard deck.
- The main-floor master suite, particularly impressive for a home of this size, features a majestic master bath with a corner garden tub, two walk-in closets and a dual-sink vanity with knee space.
- Upstairs, you will find two more good-sized bedrooms, a double bath and a large storage area.

Plan C-8645

Bedrooms: 3	Baths: 2½
Living Area:	
Upper floor	704 sq. ft.
Main floor	1,477 sq. ft.
Total Living Area:	**2,181 sq. ft.**
Standard basement	1,400 sq. ft.
Garage and storage	561 sq. ft.
Exterior Wall Framing:	2x4

Foundation Options:

Standard basement

Crawlspace

Slab

(All plans can be built with your choice of foundation and framing. A generic conversion diagram is available. See order form.)

BLUEPRINT PRICE CODE: C

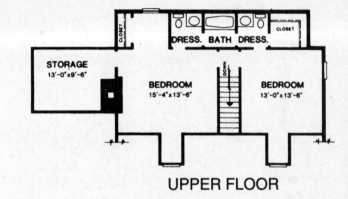

UPPER FLOOR

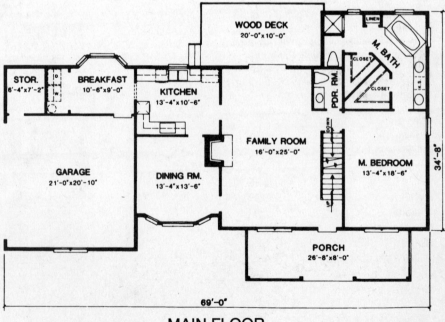

MAIN FLOOR

TO ORDER THIS BLUEPRINT, CALL TOLL-FREE 1-800-820-1283

Plan C-8645

PRICES AND DETAILS ON PAGES 12-15

Superb Views

- This superb multi-level home is designed to take full advantage of spectacular surrounding views.
- The two-story-high entry welcomes guests in from the covered front porch. An open-railed stairway and a 23-ft. domed ceiling are highlights here.
- The sunken living and dining rooms are defined by archways and face out to a large wraparound deck. The living room has a 13-ft. cathedral ceiling and a nice fireplace. The dining room offers a 9½-ft. domed ceiling and a wet bar.
- The octagonal island kitchen hosts a Jenn-Aire range, a sunny sink and a bayed breakfast nook. Nearby, the utility room reveals a walk-in pantry, laundry facilities and garage access.
- The quiet den boasts a second fireplace, a cozy window seat and deck access.
- The entire upper floor is occupied by the master bedroom suite, which has a spacious bayed sleeping room with a 12½-ft. cathedral ceiling. Other features include a huge walk-in closet, separate dressing areas and a private bath with a curved shower and a Jacuzzi tub.
- The exciting daylight basement has a recreation room, an exercise room and another bedroom, plus a sauna and a hot tub surrounded by windows!

Plan NW-229

Bedrooms: 2+	Baths: 2½
Living Area:	
Upper floor	815 sq. ft.
Main floor	1,446 sq. ft.
Daylight basement	1,330 sq. ft.
Total Living Area:	**3,591 sq. ft.**
Garage	720 sq. ft.
Exterior Wall Framing:	2x6

Foundation Options:

Daylight basement

(All plans can be built with your choice of foundation and framing. A generic conversion diagram is available. See order form.)

BLUEPRINT PRICE CODE: F

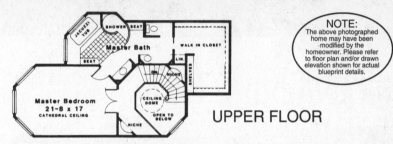

UPPER FLOOR

NOTE:
The above photographed home may have been modified by the homeowner. Please refer to floor plan and/or drawn elevation shown for actual blueprint details.

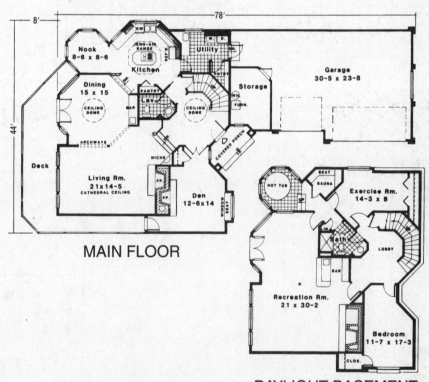

MAIN FLOOR

DAYLIGHT BASEMENT

Decked-Out Chalet

- This gorgeous chalet is partially surrounded by a large and roomy deck that is great for indoor/outdoor living.
- The living and dining area shows off a fireplace with a raised hearth, plus large windows to take in the outdoor views. The area is further expanded by a 17½-ft.-high vaulted ceiling in the dining room and sliding glass doors that lead to the deck.
- The kitchen offers a breakfast bar that separates it from the dining area. A convenient laundry room is nearby.
- The main-floor master bedroom is just steps away from a linen closet and a hall bath. Two upstairs bedrooms share a second full bath.
- The highlight of the upper floor is a balcony room with a 12½-ft.-high vaulted ceiling, exposed beams and tall windows. A decorative railing provides an overlook into the dining area below.

Plans H-919-1 & -1A

Bedrooms: 3	Baths: 2
Living Area:	
Upper floor	869 sq. ft.
Main floor	1,064 sq. ft.
Daylight basement	475 sq. ft.
Total Living Area:	**1,933/2,408 sq. ft.**
Tuck-under garage	501 sq. ft.
Exterior Wall Framing:	2x6
Foundation Options:	**Plan #**
Daylight basement	H-919-1
Crawlspace	H-919-1A

(All plans can be built with your choice of foundation and framing. A generic conversion diagram is available. See order form.)

BLUEPRINT PRICE CODE:	B/C

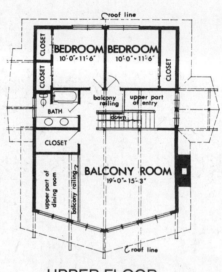

UPPER FLOOR

DAYLIGHT BASEMENT

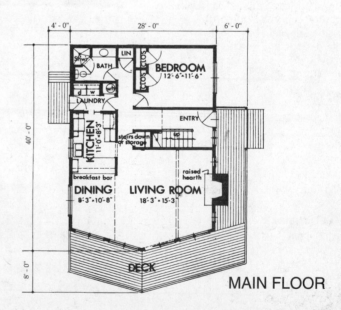

MAIN FLOOR

Plans H-919-1 & -1A

PRICES AND DETAILS ON PAGES 12-15